Radha Viswanath was born in Andhra Pradesh and spent most of her life in Delhi. Trained as a teacher, Radha entered journalism late in life. After a distinguished career as a political correspondent spanning three decades, she retired from active journalism. She has the honour of being the first woman journalist to be admitted in the long and distinguished category of Parliamentary journalists, in 2006.

An avid reader with a keen interest in Hindu mythology, she aims to bring the complexities of the Indian political discourse into intricate and rich mythological narratives.

RAVANA LEELA

THE ONE WHO FORCED
GOD TO BECOME HUMAN

RADHA VISWANATH

RUPA

Published by
Rupa Publications India Pvt. Ltd 2017
7/16, Ansari Road, Daryaganj
New Delhi 110002

Sales centres:
Allahabad Bengaluru Chennai
Hyderabad Jaipur Kathmandu
Kolkata Mumbai

Copyright © Radha Viswanath, 2017

This is a work of fiction. Names, characters, places and incidents are either the product
of the author's imagination or are used fictitiously and any resemblance to any actual
person, living or dead, events or locales is entirely coincidental.

ISBN: 978-81-291-4903-9

First impression 2017

10 9 8 7 6 5 4 3 2 1

The moral right of the author has been asserted.

Printed by Nutech Print Services, New Delhi

Acknowledgements

I have had an enduring love affair with books. Anything from pulp fiction to the Bhagvad Gita would do. As a journalist, writing has been my profession and writers of various genres my work companions. But I never thought I would write a book, leave alone venture into the infinitely layered minefield of Indian mythology.

I did it, thanks to my entire family. This book is the result of their conviction and encouragement. Do I have words enough to thank any of them adequately? I'll try.

Viswanath, my husband of forty-five years—for just being there. You are a pillar of strong and silent strength. Raghu and Rajiv, my adorable twins—for believing that 'Mom can do no wrong.' Supriya, my darling daughter, my best friend, my confidant—years and oceans failed to put distance between us. Lalit Bhushan, my nephew and critic—the only one who read *Ravanaleela* as it took shape, and gave valuable suggestions. And of course, Yelchuri Muralidhar Rao, a scholar of Hindu scriptures—your guidance in finding the right names and context was invaluable.

Thank you all!

chapter 1

*I*t was a dark, moonless night, the darkness accentuated by ominously thick and black clouds. Amidst the sounds of whistling winds and thunder came yet another sound. A sound that tore the earth apart. A form emerged from it—slowly and painfully, like a germinating seed emerging from the soil. The earth groaned in pain, its sound merging with the sound of thunder.

'Sorry Dhara, did I startle you?'

'Is that you, Sumali?'

The imperceptible nod was all she needed to confirm her guess.

'No, I wasn't startled, but bruised by your clumsy manner. But it's all right,' Dhara reassured him, happy to see an old friend. 'You know, I almost did not recognize you,' Dhara continued. 'It has been so long since I saw you last. You seem to have lost weight, which I suppose is a result of age catching up. But tell me, what work brings you here now?'

'Work!' Sumali's gaunt lips twisted in the semblance of a smile. 'What work do I have here? None. None at all! In fact, I have no work anywhere. Life, which was so full of laughter and happiness, has become dreary and depressing, Dhara. I came up just to feel a whiff of breeze, and breathe for a while.'

Sumali started to walk on, but paused for a moment to look at the slowly narrowing slit in the ground. 'Dhara, please do not fill up so fast. I'll need to return the same way soon, and I would hate to hurt you again,' he said before walking briskly away, feeling the torrential rain sting his face.

The darkness did not bother him, he could see well enough, thanks to his long spell in the Naga-loka. Sumali breathed deep, feeling the passage of air through his bronchial tubes, and remembering the time when he roamed the earth with such pride. Rare tears pricked his eyes as he pondered over his position as a refugee in the netherworld, after being a king who had ruled the earth with unquestioned authority. To be fair, the nagas treated him and his family well. They had been granted necessary powers to survive in that world. For, in the Naga-loka, earthly elements were absent. There was no air, no water, no light, no heat. No sun, no moon—so no day and night.

While Sumali and his family members had been granted the ability to survive in these environs, there was a taboo on marriage with the nagas. This was one desire that rose up in Sumali's mind each time he watched an icchadhari nagakanya take on a human form to cohabit with the human or deva that took her fancy. This taboo, in a way, ensured that the refugee rakshasa clan did not multiply. The naga leaders were also unwilling to help him recover his lost territory on earth. Sumali understood this unwillingness, but he could not come to terms with the ban on naga-rakshasa marriages. His numerous children were thus forced to live lonely lives. Sumali, however, conceded that his family, which included the wives of his two brothers and their children in addition to his own wife and children, were lucky to have found asylum in the Naga-loka.

Actually, even the earth's surface had lost its intended character, Sumali thought as he cast an eye around him. Prithvi was to have been home to humans, devas, rakshasas and yakshas. The manavas and devas had conspired to push the rakshasas out and took help from none other than Vishnu himself. The yakshas had distanced themselves from this attempt and, in the process, had created a home for themselves just above the earth's atmosphere. Then, humans, with their plundering and greedy habits, had pushed devas off the earth. Serves the devas right, mused Sumali as he settled on a huge rock to rest his aching legs. But thanks to the amrit they had received fraudulently, the devas did not have to seek refuge underground, but had moved on into the upper realms.

Besides a sense of righteous indignation at having been denied a fair share of the bounties that had emerged through the churning of the ocean of milk—the saagar manthan—Sumali also felt sorry for Dhara, who had gotten a raw deal. He loved and respected the ground that had been his home for the better part of his life. With humans not showing her the respect she richly deserved, her strength was ebbing fast. No wonder she had let out such a groan when he had broken ground a little while ago.

How he longed for his two brothers! If only they were with him now, life would not be so lonely. His younger brother Mali had been killed in the deva-danava war and their eldest brother Malyavant had taken the death of their darling little brother to heart. He had blamed himself for it, seeing it as his failure to protect his brother. He had lost interest in life and had gone to live in the forest to do penance. Sumali would have done the same, had his elder brother not stopped him. Malyavant had in fact put him in charge of their families. Sumali had obeyed, but he felt that he had not discharged this responsibility adequately as none of their children could find marital bliss on account of their circumstances in the Naga-loka.

'Sumali, snap out of it! Blaming yourself will get you nowhere. Nor is self-pity the mantra for change.'

'Dhara, I wish you would stop eavesdropping on my thoughts. But tell me, was it fair for Mali to have been killed at such a young age? His wife Vasudha was left with four young children. And what life do they now have under my protection?'

Dhara laughed derisively. 'Nice to hear you talk about fairness in life. Were you and your brothers "fair" to the rishi-munis when you made life so very difficult for them? What goes around comes around, Sumali, you know that.'

'What nonsense! We were young then and we did it all in fun.'

'What is fun and games for the cat is a life and death situation for the mouse, isn't it?'

Sumali did not reply. Perhaps there had been excesses in their exuberant actions. Sumali's thoughts moved to his brothers, which brought a happy, dreamy look to his eyes and a smile to his lips. Malyavant, the eldest of the three, was very protective towards his younger brothers and was ready to take on the world to ensure that his brothers enjoyed whatever they set out to enjoy. He was also the strongest of the three. Mali was the youngest and best loved for this reason. Their mother, Devavati, had always urged the boys to be careful so that her youngest child came to no harm because of the rough games the elder two insisted on playing.

Their father, Sukesha, on the other hand, had indulged his sons in the extreme. 'Boys will be boys' was his attitude. But it was not as if they had enjoyed unbridled freedom. Their father was very particular about their behaviour and attitude towards women. He did not want his sons to bother women and girls in any way. 'Women must be respected' was his credo and he himself practiced it zealously. Such was the love and respect the three brothers had for their father that this sentiment remained the sheet anchor of all their actions in life.

They had been such a team—he and his brothers—roaming and playing together! They would bother the rishis and laugh when they broke their tapasya, causing them to run helter-skelter to get out of the rampaging path of Sukesha's sons. They had derived special fun from uprooting fruit-bearing trees in the ashramas maintained by gurus and munis. The human children studying at the gurukulas had been their favourite playthings. They would throw dead animals or huge boulders into their midst and chase them all over the place. The children's petrified shrieks as they ran to safety had made the three brothers roll in mirth. The confusion they had created among ordinary humans was simply hilarious! They would run off with children and men alike, and hang them from trees, or fling them into the oceans and rivers.

Sumali did not tire of recalling a particular incident from his childhood, which had influenced and changed the lives of all three brothers. On that fateful day, as usual, they were playing and having heaps of fun. The students of one gurukul, with whom they had had several face-offs, had organized themselves into squads to ambush them. Their act was so juvenile that the three brothers had decided to humour them for some time before turning on them. The brothers ran as the young brahmcharis of the gurukul chased them and threw stones at them. The idea was to lead the boys to a desolate spot in the middle of the forest, scare the daylights out of them and then vanish. It would be dusk by then and the tired, hungry fellows would not be able to find their way back.

As it happened, their plan did not quite work, and Sumali, who knew the area like the back of his hand, somehow found himself in the middle of quicksand. He was being sucked in inexorably, and he called out to Malyavant for help. Malyavant quickly climbed a nearby tree and bent a branch so Sumali could hold on to it. Sumali managed to grab it, but unfortunately, the branch broke. Sumali panicked and started to cry, but Malyavant was quick to grab the end of the broken branch. He told Sumali to trust his elder brother and started pulling him up along with the branch. But Sumali noticed that the tree itself was in danger of being uprooted and toppling into the quicksand because of Malyavant's weight. Sumali no longer feared for his own life and began urging his elder brother to save himself and to go get help. Malyavant refused to leave Sumali.

While the two were thus engaged, two strong hands appeared out of nowhere and pulled the two boys to safety. It was Sukesha, who had been fetched by his youngest son Mali to rescue the brothers. Mali clung to his brothers and wept in relief, even as their father hugged them and thanked the good fortune that had saved his sons. Initially, Sumali and Malyavant lauded Mali's presence of mind and quick thinking, which had made him run for help.

But then, they realized that something was not quite right. There hadn't been enough time for Mali to go and fetch their father. And Sukesha had reached the spot after the two brothers had been deposited on firm ground. And then there was a telltale movement at his shoulders and they almost saw their father withdraw his elongated arms back into his body.

The fear of the near-death experience was immediately replaced by curiosity and they showered their father with questions. How had he managed to reach them so fast, almost immediately? Did he know magic? How could he elongate his arms like that? Could he stretch them to touch the sky? And what was the secret of his immense strength? Such strength that got him there in next to no time, even when Mali, not really a baby and quite hefty for his age, was perched on his shoulders?

Questions Sumali regretted having ever asked. For the answers had changed the lives of the three brothers.

chapter 2

Sumali was lost in thought. The ache in his legs and the burning in his lungs, which had made him pause for rest, were long gone. The torrential rain and thunder that had lashed the earth and the icy winds that had accompanied the downpour had also ceased. So lost was Sumali in thought that he did not even notice this change. What was playing on his mind were Dhara's words—words that he had tried desperately to prevent her from uttering; words that he had tried not to hear, when Dhara went on nonetheless; words he had blocked from his consciousness for so long; words that he was scared to hear because that would put the seal of reality on what he had spent a lifetime trying to deny and disbelieve.

It all began with that near death experience that he and Malyavant went through and the discovery of their father's supernatural powers. Despite persistent questioning by all three boys, Sukesha remained dismissive about his abilities. 'Oh! I've had them since I was a baby,' he had said casually, refusing to elaborate any further.

There was, however, a difference in the manner in which his three sons reacted to Sukesha's response. Mali, treated as a baby by everybody, remained child-like in his response. He possibly did not even hear it—so full was he of his heroic act in saving his two elder brothers. Malyavant felt a twinge of irritation that he was not being treated as an adult. He wanted to acquire similar powers so that his father would acknowledge his status as an adult. Caught between these two incongruent responses, Sumali was confused. He sensed an intense pain in his father's manner, but could not fathom the cause for it. He yearned to remove that pain but did not know how.

With their curiosity aroused and no information forthcoming from their father, the brothers, led by Malyavant, began ferreting out bits of gossip that abounded in their palace. The brothers came to hear that their father had been abandoned by his parents almost immediately after birth. And just now, Dhara had stated the same thing in unambiguous terms. Her words continued to echo in his mind.

'I'll begin at the very beginning, Sumali. I want you to hear this recounting completely and accept it as something that has happened—nothing can change it. Holding on to the hurt that your father nursed all his life will not change it. Letting go of this sense of guilt will not be a disservice to your father's memory. Once you experience this catharsis, you will be able to focus on the future.

'It was the time when Brahma just began this creation—the creation of prakriti and purush. He aimed at achieving a perfect balance between the two. As the first step of his magnificent scheme, he made water, which had the capacity to nurture life. He wanted someone to watch over the process of life taking shape and, towards that end, made some beings. They were rakshakas—the protectors. Soon, many of these beings were consumed by hunger and demanded to be fed. Brahma gave them a choice: "Remain true to the objective I created you for, or start eating and stop being rakshakas." All but two opted for the second course and Brahma called them yakshas, as opposed to rakshak. The two that decided to be protectors were Heti and Praheti. In due course, when the process of creation concluded and prakriti and purush were both enabled to be self-regenerating, Praheti decided that, since the task for which he had been created had been completed, he should end his own existence. So he opted to retire to the jungles for tapasya. Heti, on the other hand, thought that, with the successful conclusion of the primary task entrusted to him, he should move on to doing other things. He felt that he had earned his title as "rakshak" and had the right to eat and regenerate as did the rest of Brahma's creation. He thus chose to marry and become a householder. He asked Yama, the god of death, for his sister's hand in marriage. Her name was Bhaya, and the couple was soon lost in the bliss of physical intimacy. A child was born out of this union, but neither parent was ready to accept this new responsibility. They abandoned the newborn and moved on in search of new pleasures.

'This abandoned child was Sukesha, your father, whose hungry cries drew the attention of Parvati. The mother of the universe— Adi Parashakti—could not bear the thought that a mother could leave a young and helpless newborn baby. So moved was she by the child's plight that she prevailed on Parameshwar, her consort, to bless the baby with boons that would enable it to survive. She bemoaned the lack of maternal instincts in rakshas women and decreed that in future, rakshas babies would be capable of taking care of themselves immediately on birth.

'Sukesha thus roamed the worlds with great aplomb. He grew to be a handsome, strapping young man and was noticed by one and all for his good looks and obviously great physical strength. One such person who took more than a casual interest in Sukesha was a gandharva called Chagramani. There was a special reason for Chagramani's interest in the youthful Sukesha. He was very fond of his only daughter, Devavati, and was worried that she would leave him when she married. He did not want that to happen, as he would then lead a lonely life. But then, he could not prevent her from finding a suitable mate for herself. Chagramani thus saw Sukesha as the ideal groom for Devavati, as the rakshas had no attachments and thus could be persuaded to stay with his father-in-law. The arrangement worked well and Sukesha gave up his wild ways and settled for domestic bliss in Chagramani's household.

'When the first child of Sukesha and Devavati was born, Chagramani felt that his son-in-law needed to be cautioned against following in his father's footsteps. Thus he told Sukesha the story of his birth, how he had been abandoned by his parents and how he had survived because of the mercy shown by Parvati and Parameshwar. The story came as a great shock to Sukesha. For, after seeing how Devavati's father doted on her, Sukesha had often wondered about his own parents. Chagramani's disclosures about his parents were a humiliation. He felt betrayed and never forgave his parents for what they had done to him. But he ensured that his own children received the best parental care anyone could wish for. He was a model parent, and received full support in this from his wife.

'Sumali, it is true that your father nursed a grouse against his parents for what they did to him. But there is no reason why you should feel ashamed of it. Stop brooding over it and move on with life. You and your brothers did not have to go through a similar ordeal. You were well-loved and taken care of. You continued in your father's footsteps and took good care of your children. You and your brothers were also lucky with your wives. Your decision not to marry rakshasa kanyas but to choose wives from the gandharva clan—to which your mother belonged—was possibly among the best decisions that you took in life. That the three girls are sisters has also helped.'

Sumali went over Dhara's words several times. Dhara had confirmed several details of his father's childhood and youth that he had picked up through palace gossip. But hearing the story in its entirety had left Sumali stunned. He was now able to truly appreciate his father's feelings and feel his pain as a palpable reality.

Dhara's narrative, however, was wide off the mark in one aspect, Sumali thought. In a vicarious way, he was glad that Dhara, despite her propensity to know his deepest feelings and thoughts, was mistaken this once. She presumed that he, Sumali, nursed the same grouse as his father—the sense of betrayal by his parents—when in fact he was carrying the burden of a personal cross. Just as his parents had abandoned him when he was a baby, Sukesha's own sons had abandoned him when he had needed their emotional support the most. And he, Sumali, who had felt and instinctively understood his father's feelings, had turned his back on him. Instead of heeding his inner voice, he had blindly fallen in line with Malyavant's plans and had gone in search of personal glory.

Malyavant had been so taken up with the concept of special boons from the gods that he had insisted that the three brothers should do something to acquire similar powers. He had suggested tapasya as the way to achieve this objective. It was he who had decided that they should meditate on Brahma as he was their great-grandfather. Had he not created their grandfather Heti, who thus was Brahma's manasaputra? Sukesha was informed of this decision and the three brothers had gone off to the idyllic environs of Meru Parvat for tapasya.

Tapasya was not easy. Extending the hours of daily meditation was not good enough, even though a time came when the brothers chanted Brahma's name for more than twenty hours a day. They progressively gave up food and drink, then sleep and then stood on one foot for long years before Brahma revealed himself to them. What an experience that had been! So dreamlike and so stupefying. The luminous sight of Brahma had filled the brothers with such wonder that they had not known how to react, leave alone seek boons. Brahma, of course, knew what the brothers wanted and blessed them. 'All of you will have long lives. Your physical strength will put you in an unassailable position. This fraternal bond of love among the three of you will withstand all adversity,' he said.

Oh! What a heady feeling it was to be blessed by Brahma himself! Their parents would be so proud of them, they thought as they made their way back home. However, when they returned, they found that everything had changed. Sukesha had ended his life soon after his sons left and Devavati had followed suit. Even before they came to terms with the reality that they were orphaned, there came the realization that there was no place for the three rakshasas in Gandharva-loka. While Malyavant tried to deal with this issue, Sumali was consumed with remorse at the loss of his parents. He should have remained with his father and helped him overcome his sense of betrayal by his parents. He felt that he had failed his father when he had needed empathy and sympathy. What made it worse was the fact that he alone understood his father's angst and yet he had not been there to provide strength and support.

But there was no time to grieve over the loss of their parents. They needed to do something to prevent being thrown out of Gandharva-loka. With Mali looking up to his two elder brothers for direction and Sumali in no frame of mind to attend to any such issues, it was Malyavant who devised a plan to salvage the situation. He said that they should marry gandharva kanyas as that would help them regain their status in this elevated world. And, given their precarious position in what was once their homeland, Malyavant also decided that their brides would be sisters so that there would be no tension on the domestic front. As luck would have it, he was soon able to locate such a trio of gandharva kanyas. Sundari, Ketumali and Vasudha were three sisters whose parents had expired recently. They were ready to marry the three brothers as that would solve their own problems.

The marriages—Malyavant to Sundari, Sumali to Ketumali and Mali to Vasudha—helped to the extent that the brothers were able to stay on in Gandharva-loka. However, they were not allowed any share in the wielding of power and authority. Malyavant quickly grew tired of this situation where he and his brothers, despite their matchless physical strength, could not rule the land or wield power of any kind.

Being Malyavant, he came up with a solution soon enough. Sumali and Mali, as usual, fell in line with his plan, which was to move to a new place where they would be supreme. It should be so beautiful and rich that everyone would envy them and want to live there. 'I once heard father say that Kailash was the most beautiful place in the world. I am sure you know that Kailash is Shiva's abode, the same Shiva and Parvati who gave father such super powers,' Malyavant said and suggested that they should seek the help of Vishwakarma, the divine architect, who had designed Kailash and numerous other residences for devas.

Malyavant led his brothers to Vishwakarma and asked him to construct a city for them. While Vishwakarma did not refuse, there was stiffness in his manner indicating that the first architect of the universe was not happy to do their bidding. To secure the deal, Malyavant praised Vishwakarma's skills. 'The palaces you built for the devas are held as the ultimate in beauty, design and utility, not to mention splendour,' he said in conclusion of his eulogy of Vishwakarma's skills and added: 'I should like a complex close to either Mount Meru, Mount Mandara or Mount Himawat for us three brothers. The complex should compare adequately with Kailash.'

Vishwakarma was in a fix. He did not like the idea of being instrumental in enabling these rakshasas to live in a place like Kailash. It was clear to Vishwakarma that the rakshasa streak in Malyavant was straining at the leash to break free, and that he would wreak havoc on the world if he got the chance. He also knew that Malyavant's brothers would never oppose him. There were enough rakshasas in the world now to threaten peace on earth and he did not want to feel responsible for unleashing another set on the hapless humans and devas.

At the same time, Vishwakarma also knew that he had no

legitimate grounds to refuse the project. Also, refusal would only lead to trouble for himself. It was time for some quick thinking and Vishwakarma came up with an idea that would save him from working for Malyavant and also take the rakshasa brothers far away. That would ensure safety on earth, he reasoned, and made the offer. 'Indra once had a complex built for himself on earth, but later chose to reside in swarga along with the other devas. The architect for the project was Maya. I am sure you have heard of him, he was my guru. He trained me and taught me the nuances of architecture,' he said and explained that the complex was located along the southern coast on Mount Trikoot. 'The city is so exquisite that it is considered better than Kailash itself in certain aspects. Its security is unparalleled. No invader can even dream of breaching it. You and your brothers can live there happily in peace,' he said.

Vishwakarma, while making this offer, was proffering some good advice. He was telling the rakshasa brothers that their long-term interests would be better served if they gave up their wild ways and learnt to be content with a peaceful lifestyle.

The offer was accepted gladly and the brothers moved with their families to the city, which was their home for long years. That city was Lanka. The very thought of it filled Sumali with nostalgia. He trained his eyes in the general direction of Lanka and saw that it was as beautiful as ever, with the golden roofs of buildings glinting tantalizingly in the moonlight. He felt happy and content and his thoughts slowly began to shift.

chapter 3

Lanka! The magnificent city that was paradise on earth! Full of beautiful mountains, valleys and waterfalls! Full of sweet fragrances of a myriad variety of fruits and flowers! Breathtaking with all its spectacular buildings and gardens! The construction was superb and the embellishments of gems made the buildings—oh! So beautiful! The sun's rays reflecting off the gems and building surfaces gave the impression of thousands of suns in the sky. At night, these same structures reflected the moonlight in such a fantastic fashion as to drive the darkness away completely. There never was need for artificial lighting.

Such was their happiness at having Lanka as their home that Malyavant, Sumali and Mali were glad that Vishwakarma, instead of constructing a city in a half-hearted manner, had given them Lanka, which was built by his guru Maya for Indra himself. Life for the brothers was now an ocean of pleasures and their wives multiplied this feeling manifold by giving them lovely children.

The first to arrive was Suptaghna, born to Malyavant and Sundari. Close on his heels came his brother Viroopaksha. Sumali's wife Ketumali gave birth to Akampana almost simultaneously with Viroopaksha, and Kalakarmukha and Bhasakarna came soon thereafter. Mali's first son Aneela was also born before Sundari gave birth to a daughter. She was the first baby girl in the family and was named Anala on Mali's desire—to match his son's name. The three sets of parents doted on her.

There was nothing more anyone could ask for. But such is life that if you have everything that you ever coveted, you get restless.

You want change; something that will excite you, challenge you. This was exactly what happened with Malyavant, who always wanted his supremacy to be acknowledged and celebrated. What good was all the strength they possessed if the world did not know of it? Their strength was as good as nothing if it was not used to expand their area of influence, he fretted.

Sumali agreed with Malyavant, but Mali reasoned that they should be happy that they were so well provided for. As time passed, arguments over this among the brothers became more frequent and more heated. Malyavant wanted to wage wars with kings in other regions and annex their lands, peoples and assets. Sumali urged patience, saying their children were still young and needed their guidance to grow into strong independent warriors before they could undertake such expeditions. He, however, vetoed his elder brother's proposal that the next generation of Sukesha's lineage should endeavour to secure divine powers through tapasya. Thorough training in martial arts would suffice, he insisted. He knew Mali felt similarly.

Mali, however, had other concerns. He was the first one to awake to the growing danger to their idyllic existence. That the threat came from within the family ranks worried him all the more. He felt that the three of them should talk things over and evolve a strategy to foster unity and affection among all their children. But he stood in awe of Malyavant, who still treated him like an immature child. Sumali was more approachable and gave due consideration to any suggestion that came from the youngest brother. Besides, Mali thought he stood better chance of success if he enlisted the support of Sumali to influence Malyavant.

Mali found an opportune time and broached the subject with Sumali: 'Bhrata, life is not what it appears on the surface. There are numerous fights among our children on a daily basis. Vasudha and her sisters try to resolve these differences, but objectivity is lacking in these efforts. I notice that each mother takes the side of her own children and the result is that a chasm is developing among the women. As the eldest in the family, bhrata Malyavant should exercise his authority to establish harmony in the family.'

Sumali looked at his younger brother with a mixture of admiration and love. His baby brother, who, as a child, had needed so much looking after and care, had grown to be the most perceptive of them all. He had articulated what Sumali felt only vaguely at the back of his mind. Mali was right about the immense strain that their family bonds were being subjected to. His point that the bond shared by their wives as siblings was much weaker than their maternal love for their own children, needed to be kept in mind when dealing with rivalries among the cousins.

'I agree with you, Mali. But you know how it is with our elder bhrata. His sole focus these days is when and with whom he can wage war. I have to exert all my powers of persuasion to hold him back. It is useless to draw his attention to these things. He will only say that it is natural for children to fight and compete among themselves and that there is no need for us to intervene,' Sumali said, and promised to counsel the children and their mothers.

Mali then came up with a suggestion. 'Bhrata, I can see that the fights will only increase as time goes by, because more children will be born to us. So, in the interests of peace and family harmony, I think we should stop producing more children to contain the damage,' he said.

Sumali laughed. What a ridiculous prescription! 'Trust you to suggest the opposite of what elder bhrata wants. He wants us to have as many children as possible at the earliest so that we match the devas and manavas in numbers. Then, our superior strength will help us win our wars,' Sumali said, making it clear that the conversation was concluded and that he did not want to discuss the topic again.

But Mali was determined. He had four sons by then. He loved
the only girl child in the family so much that he had named his
second son, Anala, after Malyavant's daughter. His other two
sons were named Sampati and Haaru. And there Mali stopped—
he did not produce any more children. In contrast, Malyavant
and Sundari had five more sons, taking the total number of their
children to eight. Vajramushthi, Durmukha and Yagnakopa came
singly and the arrival of Matta and Unmatta together as twins
filled Malyavant with immense joy. Sumali was the proud father
of four daughters—Raaka, Pushpotkata, Kaikasi and Kumbhinasi.
His sons—Vikata, Dhoomraksha, Suparshva, Danda, Samhadri and
Praghana—completed the brothers' brood of twenty-six children,
including the five girls.

Malyavant, in his eagerness to build a battalion of warriors,
pushed all their children to be fiercely competitive. With Sundari
towing her husband's line in fixing priorities for the children,
Ketumali and Vasudha turned against her. They would oppose
whatever Sundari said or did, plainly out of spite. Sumali's attempts
to mollify the two younger sisters for the sake of peace in the
household came to naught. So, he turned his attention to the
children and tried to spend with them as much time as possible.
He set an example by treating them all as equals, praising everyone's
achievements and talents and resolving their tiffs.

Two benefits arose from this course of action. His rapport with
the children and consequently his influence among them, increased.
He used this to foster goodwill and brotherhood among the cousins,
in the process generating a consciousness and appreciation of
each one's special skills. He started this practice when he noticed
that Mali's children, who were as mild as their father, were being
ridiculed by the elder and more boisterous cousins. He learnt of
Sampati's considerable acoustic skills when the young lad was being
mocked by his cousins for the same and devised a game to test

these skills. Aneela and Hara vouched that Sampati could hear other people's thoughts also, if he tuned his ears to them. He could literally hear a pin drop in soft grass, or the faintest of chimes from the other side of the globe. Knowing that the usually reticent sons of Mali would not make tall claims just for fun, Sumali organized an elaborate procedure to verify these claims. He also declared that if Sampati did indeed possess such skills, then everyone should stop making fun of him and respect his abilities. Sumali commissioned an extremely skilful goldsmith to make gold anklets for a tiny red ant. The ant was secured inside a crystal ball. Sampati, who was not informed of the details of the arrangements, was asked to focus on finding the hidden crystal ball and to describe any sounds he heard. He surprised and impressed everyone when he said he heard the chiming of small gold bells.

Similarly, Dhoomraksha had extremely powerful eyes that could see through the thickest of barriers. He could look into the deepest layers of the earth, sighting happenings in the netherworlds. Then there was Praghana, Sumali's youngest son, who was so nimble on his feet that he could go round Mount Trikoota in the blink of an eye.

These and other happy memories of the days gone by increased Sumali's longing to be in Lanka and he took a step towards Mount Trikoota. He had to sit down immediately on account of a sharp pain in his foot. Sumali bent and pulled out the thorn that had pierced his foot and was about to throw it away when he noticed that it was part of a banyan tree that had snapped under his foot, with several of its branches getting entangled between his toes. 'Sorry Dhara,' he said and bent once again to push the tree back into the soil.

Dhara chuckled. 'I did it on purpose. You seem to have forgotten that you cannot step into Lanka. That prick was my way of reminding you,' she said and added, 'I owe you an apology. And thank you for caring enough to replant this precious tree. Enjoy your reverie, I won't disturb you again.'

Sumali's lips stretched into a smile as he let his mind slip into memories of those times. He recalled how, during a competition among their children, Vajramushti had discovered his special ability. Sumali had devised a war game to test the childrens' skills at strategizing. Vajramushthi's performance was below par. He was so upset that he banged his fist against a tree. The tree broke and fell to the ground and Vajramushthi marvelled that his hand did not hurt at all. He punched more trees, all of which met the same fate without causing him any discomfort. In the days that followed, this became a favourite sport for him and he was quickly joined by quite a few of his cousins.

The scale of destruction was phenomenal. Uprooted trees lay everywhere, jungles disappeared and animals lost their natural shelter. Water bodies dried up and rainfall became unpredictable and scarce. Prakriti was unable to keep up with the pace of destruction and Sumali began worrying. His efforts to inculcate moderation among the boys did not yield the desired results. Mali also noticed the degradation of nature and came to speak to Sumali about it.

After a thorough discussion on the subject, Mali came up with an idea. 'Bhrata, if we don't stop this wanton destruction of trees, Lanka will soon become a barren land. All its beauty and riches will disappear. I do not have to stress that urgent action is called for. I want to remind you that we still have considerable powers from our tapasya. Let us use the same to nurture nature back to health.'

A good idea, no doubt. But expending their powers on restoring Lanka and its environs would leave them vulnerable to attacks from enemies. Malyavant was waiting for the day when he could wage wars to expand his area of influence. And frankly, the thought of conquest and expansion had occurred to Sumali too, even though he claimed it was only their elder brother who desired it.

Mali was not deterred, though. He admitted that trying to convince Malyavant to follow any such suggestion would be a complete waste of time. He made Sumali promise that he would not tell their elder brother about what he was doing and went ahead with his austerities to donate the power of his tapasya to help earth recuperate. Mali's efforts paid rich dividends and very soon, Lanka glowed in her pristine beauty. What surprised Sumali was the fact that Mali, after losing his supernatural powers, attained a strange glow on his face and appeared to be at peace with himself.

But this very aspect spelt doom for the youngest son of Sukesha later on, when the brothers waged a war against the devas. Sumali felt personally responsible for Mali's death. Unlike Malyavant who had led them into the war, he—Sumali—knew that Mali had given up his divine blessing of long life to keep Lanka healthy and prosperous. He was sworn to secrecy and so could not disclose the fact to Malyavant.

A movement near Lanka broke Sumali's train of thought. He sat up straight and focused hard.

'That is Kuber, treasurer of the devas. He is the new occupant of Lanka,' Dhara answered Sumali's unspoken question.

Sumali hushed Dhara with a wave of his hand as thoughts raced through his head. A plan of action was taking shape in his mind. He turned quickly to return to his family. But this time, there was a spring in his step and a smile on his lips.

'See you soon, Dhara,' Sumali said as he silently and smoothly slipped into the ground.

chapter 4

*K*aikasi clutched her father's hand as she gasped for breath. This was her first foray onto prithvi since fleeing to Naga-loka so long ago. Her lungs felt bruised as air gushed into their shrunken recesses. Oh! How nice it was to breathe like this! And how sweet the pain felt! She felt alive again. Her skin tingled as a mild breeze caressed her. She felt her cheeks grow warm as blood coursed through her veins. It was a wonderful feeling and Kaikasi savoured it hungrily, marvelling at the things that her eyes were seeing after ages.

Kaikasi, the second daughter of Sumali, felt overwhelmed that her father had taken so much trouble to bring her to the earth's surface. She squeezed his hand to convey her gratitude and he patted her arm comfortingly. Kaikasi also felt honoured that she was the chosen one for undertaking a special task for her family. It meant a lot to her that her father reposed such faith in her abilities. Kaikasi looked at her father as he sat by her, her eyes full of love and admiration for the man who had been managing three families single-handedly under trying circumstances. Sumali had a faraway look on his face. He was thinking of the task ahead for her, Kaikasi assumed. Knowing her father, she did not want to rush him into speaking before he was ready. She turned her gaze towards the horizon to see the sky turning a bright orange—a sign that dawn was not far away. Kaikasi longed to feel the hot rays of the sun on her body, as she had during her golden childhood when she and her brothers and sisters had played till they were bathed in sweat. She could almost hear the sound of their laughter.

Alas, the laughter had not lasted. The atmosphere of gay abandonment in Lanka soon gave way to war. Kaikasi recalled the events that were still fresh in her mind. Her father Sumali, who maintained a network of informants across the globe, came to know that the devas and manavas were plotting against the rakshasa clans. Their specific target was the progeny of Sukesha. Kaikasi, who always hovered in her father's vicinity, was witness to the exchange. Sumali had responded with uproarious laughter: 'Oh, so those weaklings think they can kill us all!' he had said. 'No Prabhu! They plan to seek Shiva's help,' the informer had responded. Sumali had dismissed him with a wave of his hand, secure in the knowledge that Shiva had an abundant affection for Sukesha, whom he had saved from death and given a new lease of life. Confirmation of his assessment came a few days later alongside news that the delegation planned to meet Brahma with their tales of woe. Sumali remained unperturbed. After all, Brahma was the one who had granted powerful boons to Sukesha's three sons—long life and immense strength being part of those blessings.

Sumali's mood changed perceptibly when the news was brought to him that a much larger group, which included many rishi-munis, had called on Vishnu. Unlike Shiva and Brahma, Hari felt duty-bound to protect ascetics who performed yagnas and tapas for the welfare of all humanity. Thus, when this group complained of the excesses of Sukesha's clan, Vishnu promised to move with a huge army to remove the troublemakers from the face of the earth.

Given the seriousness of the situation and the looming danger to their very existence, Sumali told his two brothers about it. Kaikasi recalled that it was late in the day and the entire family was having dinner when her father told them about the impending war. Her uncle Malyavant went into a terrible rage. 'Why could Vishnu not tell those tale-carrying wimps to go fend for themselves, like Shiva did?' he fumed. A few of her brothers, particularly Suptaghna,

Durmukha, Samhadri and Unmatta, tried to impress Malyavant by suggesting that Vishnu should look out for his own safety as he planned to fight the strongest people in the world. Possibly swayed by these remarks, Malyavant announced his decision. 'Why should we sit here and wait for Vishnu to come to kill us? The boys are right and I am happy that they have spoken like brave and valiant men. We are strong. Our father was like Shiva's own son and all of us have the protection of boons from Brahma. We will launch the attack on them,' he declared. 'Nothing and no one can defeat us,' he thundered.

'This is our chance to defeat the devas and establish our rule in Swarga-loka,' Malyavant said while addressing his forces before setting out for the war.

Sumali too was thinking of the war against the devas that had changed their fortunes. They had fought ferociously. Thousands of rakshasas had perished, and the three brothers had managed to inflict heavy casualties on the enemy. It was an evenly matched fight and could have gone either way, if Mali had not been killed. Mali had fallen to Vishnu's discus right in front of Sumali's eyes. Indeed, it was he, Sumali who had been engaged with Vishnu at that time, both showering arrows on each other. Unexpectedly, Vishnu's mount Garuda had spread his wings to their maximum span and used them to inflict death and destruction on the forces around Sumali. Garuda had built up such a gale with his flapping wings that the rakshasa sena had been blown away like hay. This had enraged Mali. Using the power of his mount to scare the enemy was against the rules of war, according to Mali. Even though he had lost his chariot in the melee, he tried to assist Sumali, who was countering Vishnu single-handedly. Mali picked up a mace and targeted the eagle. His powerful blow on the eagle's beak made it spin around and lose its balance. Hari retaliated by throwing his discus, which severed Mali's head from his body.

It was a stunning blow that neither Malyavant nor Sumali could deal with in the moment. They needed time and calm to take stock. So they tried to retreat to Lanka. Sumali picked up Mali's head and torso, hoping against hope that he could be resurrected somehow.

Surprisingly, Vishnu came after the retreating rakshasa forces. A basic and sacred principle of warfare is that a retreating enemy is never attacked. Malyavant therefore stopped and questioned the leader of the deva force. 'You call yourself "God", so how can you indulge in such a blatant flouting of dharma?' he asked.

'Dharma for me is to protect those that are troubled and threatened and seek my help. You and your people have perpetrated innumerable acts of cruelty on hermits doing tapasya in the woods. Their tapasya is for the welfare of this universe. They harm none and will not harm anyone even to protect themselves. You harassed them for your vicarious pleasure. You did not spare devas, yakshas, kinneras or gandharvas, even though they did nothing to harm you. Since all of them sought my intervention to protect them from you rakshasas and I promised to free them of this menace, I shall eliminate all of you from the face of this earth,' he declared.

With Vishnu hot on their heels, Sumali and Malyavant somehow managed to reach the safety of Lanka. Mali was beyond any help. His life had ended. Malyavant blamed himself for Mali's death and also for the colossal loss of life in his army. He told Sumali to take charge of the family and retreated to the forest in search of peace. His wife Sundari, unable to bear the loss of her children in war, followed him, and Vasudha ended her life on her husband's funeral pyre.

Sumali shivered involuntarily at the memory of his journey into the Naga-loka along with Ketumali. All his sons had perished in the war. Anala and the twins—Matta and Unmatta—were the only survivors among Malyavant's children. The girls had also escaped death as they were prohibited from participating in war. Sumali had also stopped Mali's four sons from joining the troops on the grounds that they were needed at home to take care of the women and manage Lanka's affairs. The reality, however, was that these boys—Aneela, Anala, Sampati and Hara—did not have what it took to fight and win a war. Strategizing and counselling was their forte.

By now the sun had risen high in the sky and its hot rays beat down remorselessly. The birds had stopped chirping and stayed in the shade of the trees. Kaikasi closed her eyes and raised her face to receive the hot rays on her face. A thin layer of perspiration began to form on her skin. Sumali, who had remained impervious to the advance of the day and was completely still, now inclined his head. Kaikasi instinctively knew that her father was ready to speak. 'Pituhoo,' she addressed him softly, indicating that she was ready to receive instructions.

'Child, please hear me out before you ask any questions,' Sumali began and on seeing Kaikasi's enthusiastic nod, continued: 'Lanka is our home and none of us is happy with the kind of life we have in the Naga-loka. Finding a way to return to Lanka has been a constant thought for me. Our golden Lanka is currently under illegal occupation by Kuber, who is the treasurer of the devas. But I admire the fellow—he is capable and gets what he wants. He has given me an idea that might make it possible for us to reclaim Lanka.

'I feel that if only we have someone like Kuber on our side, we can take Lanka back. After considering all aspects, I think you are the right person to produce a child like him. For this you will have to marry Kuber's father, Maharshi Vishravasu. Can I depend upon you to achieve my objective, Kaikoo?' Sumali ended with the childhood endearment for his daughter.

'You know you can depend on me to do anything to please you, pituhoo,' Kaikasi responded readily. 'Just order me and you will not find me wanting in my efforts. But...,' she trailed off.

'But what, Kaikoo?' Sumali nudged her encouragingly.

'The success of this endeavour is dependent upon the maharshi agreeing to marrying me. How is he to be persuaded? What will I have to do to convice him?'

'Vishravasu is a Brahmin and a rishi. He will not refuse anything that is sought of him.'

'I see...but it will be difficult for me to stand in front of him and ask him to marry me,' Kaikasi said diffidently.

'I know child. But he is very powerful and will not need to be told what you desire. He will read your mind and accept you. I am sure of that.'

'Then consider the task done, pituhoo,' Kaikasi promised and seeing her father's hesitation, she asked: 'Is there something more that I need to know?'

'Yes, Kaikoo, there is. And this is the problem,' Sumali said and took a deep breath before continuing. 'The problem is...the moment you start talking to Vishravasu or any other being on prithvi, our link will be severed. It will not be possible for us to communicate in any manner. You will be completely on your own. Our contact will be re-established only when we both reach Lanka,' he said and looked closely at Kaikasi for signs of self-doubt and hesitation.

Kaikasi showed none. 'When and how do I reach Vishravasu,' she asked, determination coming through in every single word.

Sumali heaved a sigh of relief. The tension left his face. He hugged Kaikasi just for a moment before making certain mental calculations. 'I will send you to him at the appropriate time,' he said.

Both gazed at the dipping sun on the western horizon for a while. 'Now,' said Sumali and Kaikasi found herself standing in front of the maharshi, his eyes closed in deep meditation.

chapter 5

*K*aikasi plucked at a flower, pulling some leaves along with it. It was clear that her mind was far away and that the action was borne out of a preoccupied mind. It had been a few months since that fateful evening when she had been sent to Vishravasu's doorstep. Sumali's wish had been fulfilled and the muni's child was growing inside her.

Though happy on that count, Kaikasi hated the nausea and restlessness that accompanied the pregnancy. And more bothersome was the loneliness she suffered at the ashram. Vishravasu rarely spoke. He was always engrossed in his austerities. And during the little time he spent away from his tapasya-related activities, another woman at the ashram took care of all his needs. The lady was Devaparni—dharmapatni to Vishravasu and mother of Kuber. Devaparni too rarely spoke. This was depressing and often Kaikasi contemplated going away, even though she knew that this option was not open to her. She had to have her child and bring him up to achieve her father's cherished goal of reclaiming Lanka for the rakshasas.

Kaikasi tried to divert her mind with more pleasant thoughts. She recalled the events of that fateful day when her father had sent her to the the maharshi's ashram. Her heart had been aflutter with nervous anticipation and her hands had turned clammy with perspiration as she looked at the man who would be her husband. That is, if he agreed to father a child through her. Sumali had assured her that he would not let her down. What would happen if Vishravasu did not oblige her? With her contact with Sumali cut off, where would she go? How would she fend for herself?

Even as these questions had tormented her, the man she was gazing at sat immobile. His eyes were closed and not a muscle moved anywhere in his body. He was covered in a thin film of sweat, which made his body glisten like bronze. His chiselled features looked so perfect that Kaikasi had wanted to reach out and touch him, if only to assure herself that he was indeed a living person and not a statue sculpted by an expert shilpi. This picture of perfection had stirred strange emotions in Kaikasi's bosom. She had shifted her weight onto one foot and leant against a tree, ready to wait interminably for the rishi to open his eyes. After what seemed like a very long time, but was actually only a few moments, he had opened his eyes and seen the damsel in front of him. 'Who are you, beautiful young lady, and what can I do for you?' he had asked in a deep resonating voice.

'My name is Kaikasi and I am here as per my father's command,' Kaikasi had responded, her eyes lowered demurely and the toes of her right foot tracing patterns in the sand. Her father had been right. She did not have to utter a single word more. Vishravasu had known the purpose of her visit.

'I see!' A half smile had played at the corners of his lips as he had raised his head skyward. 'You want a child from me,' he had said thoughtfully. 'But the timing of your request makes for frightening-looking children, who will also be cruel in their thoughts and deeds.'

Kaikasi had dipped her chin further into the folds of her sari to gain a moment to think before she replied the muni. She realized that her father had chosen the timing using the very same calculations that had led Vishravasu to this conclusion. Choosing her words carefully, she had said in a low, halting voice intended to sound bashful: 'It is true that I am a rakshasa kanya. But I do not think it is possible for any child of a tapasvi like you to be cruel.'

Kaikasi smiled at the memory of the look on Vishravasu's face

as she had said those words. He had seemed completely taken in
by her.

Even as she was lost in reverie, Kaikasi's subconscious mind
registered a particularly sweet smell. The fragrance, which was a
mixture of floral and fruity aromas, was so overpowering that she
inadvertently started walking towards it. As she advanced, Kaikasi's
mind returned to the present, noticing the ethereal beauty of the
mangrove ahead. Even as she reached out to push open a makeshift
gate that separated this particular mangrove from the rest of the
grounds, Kaikasi was rudely jolted out of her reverie by a hand
that grabbed her. It was Devaparni trying to stop her from entering
the mangrove.

'This is a prohibited area. No one should wander about here,'
she said.

'But why...why...' Kaikasi stammered, trying to frame a cogent
question.

'There is a curse over this area. So do not ever come here
again. I am telling you this for your own good,' Devaparni said
and quickly turning on her heel, hurried off. She clearly did not
want to prolong her conversation with Kaikasi.

Kaikasi stood there, confused. She looked at the retreating figure
of Devaparni and tried to understand what had just transpired.
Was it genuine concern that had led her to prevent Kaikasi from
entering a haunted place? Or was it natural animosity towards her
husband's second wife that had impelled her to prevent Kaikasi
from going to a specific part of the hermitage? Kaikasi mulled
over the possibilities, but was unable to arrive at any conclusion.
She, however, heeded Devaparni's warning and walked slowly back
to her quarters.

Kaikasi gradually learnt the answer to her questions as the
days went by. With the ice broken between them, Devaparni began
spending considerable time with Kaikasi, sharing details of life at

the hermitage, and the responsibilities of the muni's wife or wives. Kaikasi now marvelled at the total lack of jealousy in Devaparni, and came to respect her. Her little gestures ensured that Kaikasi's pregnancy progressed smoothly. In fact, it was Devaparni who helped deliver the baby when the time came. The child proved Vishravasu's predictions to be correct. He was huge; he had ten heads and his voice, when he cried, scared all the animals in the hermitage. Vishravasu named the child 'Dashagreeva' meaning one with ten necks.

It was during an idle conversation between the two women on a lazy afternoon while the baby slept that Kaikasi broached the subject of the cursed mangrove. Devaparni laughed and said that the curse had been responsible for their husband's birth in the first place. Curious to know the details, Kaikasi begged the older woman to tell her the whole story. Devaparni was happy to oblige. She told Kaikasi that she had heard the story from her father, the sage Bharadwaja. She began her narrative with great enthusiasm: 'This hermitage actually belongs to a king called Trinabindu. He used to come here for quiet meditation on weighty matters of governance. This was in the Krita-yug, when Brahma the Creator was rather upset with the rakshasas. Intended as protectors of the universe and its assets, the rakshasas had grown arrogant on account of their superior physical strength and had begun abusing their power to the detriment of all other creatures. So Brahma gave birth to a child after his own heart. This manasaputra of Brahma was named Pulastya. Born with the same traits, attributes and abilities as Brahma himself, Pulastya applied himself to the task of achieving his father's objective like a true Brahmin.

'Pulastya decided to meditate and fine-tune his strategy and selected this hermitage for two reasons. One was its location— close to the Meru Parvat, renowned for its serenity and beauty; and two, the ashram remained unoccupied for long stretches of time, with its owner, Raja Trinabindu, using it only occasionally. Once Pulastya settled here for meditation, the ashram came to be called "Rishi-teertham".

'However, once he began his tapasya, Pulastya discovered that the ashram was a favourite place for those who sought out beauty and serenity for their enjoyment. The place was particularly favoured by young girls who used the brooks on the premises for swimming, sang songs, played games, plucked flowers to make garlands and climbed trees to pick the best fruit. Their constant chatter and laughter disturbed Pulastya. His requests that he not be disturbed had the opposite impact on the girls. They made it a point to run, play and sing right in front of him and derived great enjoyment from seeing his frustration. On one occasion, Pulastya was so irritated that he uttered a curse: if he so much as set eyes on a girl, she would become pregnant. The threat worked and young girls stopped going anywhere near him. In fact, they were so scared that they avoided Rishi-teertham altogether.

'Raja Trinabindu happened to visit the ashram around that time. He was accompanied by his daughter, Maanini. The Rajkumari, unaware of the presence of a muni in the ashram, leave alone being aware of his curse, went wandering around the ashram. She was drawn to the mangrove by the sound of the mellifluous rendering of the Vedas as also by its heavenly fragrance. She stood in front of Pulastya, lost in his music. Pulastya sensed the presence of another being near him and opened his eyes. Maanini introduced herself and complimented his singing before taking her leave.

'By the time she reached her own living quarters, Maanini felt changes in her body. Her father discovered the cause of her condition and took her back to Pulastya. He folded his hands in reverence and said: "I am Trinabindu, king of this region. I know that with such total control over your sperm, you have no use for a wife. But my daughter unknowingly became a victim of your curse.

Her life will be ruined if you do not marry her. She is a learned scholar and discharges her duties diligently. She will serve you by keeping your yagna fire going, and taking care of your hearth and your health. Please, accept her as your wife.'

'Pulastya realized that this unblemished virgin would suffer ignominy if he rejected her and agreed to marry her. Raja Trinabindu thanked the muni profusely, conducted the necessary rites and returned alone to his kingdom. Maanini soon impressed Pulastya with her behaviour and one day, as she was massaging him to relieve him of fatigue, he blessed her, saying that she would give birth to a highly virtuous son, whose mastery of the Vedas, sense of justice and depth of understanding would be recognized the world over.

'And that child is Vishravasu,' Devaparni concluded, with obvious pride that she was his dharmapatni.

Kaikasi had a lot of questions, but their conversation was interrupted by the raucous crying of the infant. It was quite some time later that Kaikasi found the opportunity to engage with Devaparni. By then Kaikasi had become adept at domestic chores like milking the cow, tending a fire without letting it go out or emitting too much smoke, taking care of flowering and fruit trees, keeping the house and surroundings clean, making floral patterns on the floor with rice flour and so on. She also learnt human anatomy while practicing the art of massaging. She learnt the differences between yagna, tapasya and jaap. And most importantly, she learnt to anticipate her husband's needs without being expressly told.

Her mastery over these aspects of ashram life, however, failed to give Kaikasi any joy. Two things were bothering her. One was the change in Devaparni's attitude. Gone was the friendly guide and philosopher. Instead, Devaparni had become unpredictable. At times the first wife of Vishravasu was friendly and helpful.

At others she was distant. The worst was when she chose to be sarcastic and disdainful. She would emphasize on Kaikasi's inferior rakshasa descent, and ill-treat Dashagreeva.

Kaikasi's second worry arose out of this situation. Kaikasi admitted that Devaparni's jibes had a grain of truth in them. Having seen the power of tapasya possessed by Vishravasu and his son Kuber, she worried that mere physical strength might not be enough to regain Lanka. Her father's strategy and her own efforts might not serve the intended purpose. Her doubts on this score multiplied as the days passed, since she could not consult anyone in this regard. Oh, how she longed for the wise counsel of her father! And Dashagreeva was still too young for her to know with any certainty if she could depend solely on his physical strength when he grew up. The child showed no inclination towards learning of any kind, and spent all his time playing rough games.

Kaikasi weighed her options and devised a plan that could improve the chances of achieving her objective. She would beget another child, one who could be either a rakshasa like Dashagreeva, or a tapasvi like his father Vishravasu. If the child was a rakshasa, then he would double Dashagreeva's strength when the time came. And if he turned out to be his father's son in mental attributes, he would still be an asset to his elder brother, she surmised.

Kaikasi was pleased with her brilliant thinking. It was a win-win proposition for her.

chapter 6

*K*aikasi sat feeling defeated, dejected and sad. She was only vaguely aware of the usual ashram sounds in the background. Her mood of detachment and despair was such that she did not even care what Dashagreeva was upto and whether he would achieve the task of reclaiming Lanka when he grew up. However, uppermost in her muddled thoughts was the fact that Devaparni had left Rishi-teertham and gone away—all because of her. Despite the occasional derogatory jibes from Devaparni, Kaikasi had come to respect her and always bit back the angry retorts that rose up to her lips when the older woman was particularly nasty. But one day Kaikasi had lost her cool, which had led to an angry exchange between them. Soon after this incident, Devaparni had left the ashram—ostensibly to look after her ailing father, Maharshi Bharadwaj.

But perhaps she was being unfair to Devaparni. Her decision to leave Vishravasu's ashram could have been triggered by Kaikasi's second pregnancy. It was during this turbulent period that Kaikasi had asked probing questions about Kuber. The questions were aimed at finding out if there were any special steps she could take to ensure the birth of an intelligent child. Kaikasi had wanted to know if she could enhance the chances of her next child being both physically and mentally strong. Devaparni had become angry and had shouted at Kaikasi, ridiculing her ignorance of basic facts. She had said that Kuber was not her son's name but the designation by which his position was known. The name given to him at birth by his two grandfathers was Vaishravana. He had inherited the tapas-shakti of two generations on both sides of his family. Her father was a maharshi, and he had taught her all the Vedas and rituals connected with yagnas. And Vishravasu was the son of Pulastya, Brahma's manasputra, whose tapasya was of legendary proportions. And Vaishravana had done his own tapasya to merit his appointment as a dikpalaka with charge over all the wealth of the devas. Kaikasi would have to undergo several births before she could even dream of giving birth to a son like Vaishravana, worthy of Vishravasu.

Devaparni's implied insult to her parents had upset Kaikasi and she had entered into an argument with Devaparni. So angry was she that she had almost disclosed the details of her parents—something she guarded zealously for fear of her real purpose in marrying Vishravasu becoming known. Such a development could jeopardize her very continuance at the hallowed Rishi-teertham ashram. She had told Devaparni that pride as an attribute was not very becoming in someone claiming such illustrious lineage and that she too had enough to be proud of about her own ancestors. She had then stormed out.

Kaikasi had regained control over her emotions soon enough and had gone to make peace with Devaparni, whom she had taken to addressing as 'vahni' or elder sister as a mark of her respect and affection. She had never shown similar respect for either Anala or Raaka, her own two elder sisters. Kaikasi had been crestfallen to learn that Devaparni had gone away. Kaikasi had surmised that Devaparni would return soon, definitely before her child arrived. Kaikasi knew that she would need her assistance then.

But Devaparni did not return for her confinement. Kaikasi's hope and expectation on this count and also that childbirth would be easier the second time was dashed to smithereens and it took all of Kaikasi's willpower to survive the ordeal this time. All through the long hours of labour pain, when it felt like she would breathe her last with the next bout of pain, Kaikasi kept reminding herself of the importance of having this child. When it finally came, the child was more frightening than Dashagreeva had been at birth. The boy had huge, unusually shaped ears. They looked like two huge pots attached on either side of his head. On account of this aspect, Vishravasu named him 'Kumbhakarna' meaning one with pot-like ears.

Years went by, but Devaparni did not return. Kaikasi's remorse on this score became particularly acute because of the way her two sons were growing up. While they were being brought up in the peaceful and serene environs of an ashram, Dashamukha—another name that Dashagreeva came to be called by—and Kumbhakarna exhibited only rakshasa traits. Strangely, this worried Kaikasi rather than pleasing her. She wondered why neither child showed even the slightest similarity to their father. Was it the strength of her father's desire to repossess Lanka that was responsible for this? It was possible, she thought, and waited for the day when this cherished goal would be achieved. At the same time, she also longed to have a child who would take after Vishravasu. So, Kaikasi had her third child. This was a girl, but her grotesque rakshasa features did nothing to lift Kaikasi's spirits. Vishravasu maintained his calm and named his daughter 'Surpanakha', which meant one with large and wide fingernails and aptly described the girl's special feature.

Regaining control over Lanka stopped being a priority for Kaikasi. She pined for Devaparni's company. Her return would mean that Devaparni had pardoned her. So lost was she in her thoughts that it took her a while to realize that there was a hand on her shoulder trying to shake her out of her inertia. She turned her eyes listlessly to the hand and then to the face of the person whose hand it was.

'What causes that deep frown on your beautiful brow, priye?'

The rarely used term of endearment and the concern in Vishravasu's voice brought a film of moisture to her eyes. But nothing could be done. It was a hopeless situation. She merely shook her head and turned her face away, lest the maharshi spied tears in her eyes.

'Come now, Kaikasi! Won't you share your cares with me?' he said, settling on the grass by her side. 'Have I hurt you in word or deed?' he persisted.

'Please don't even think like that, nath,' Kaikasi responded, still not trusting herself to look at him.

Vishravasu said nothing, but the way he gently kneaded her shoulder let her know that he was waiting for an explanation from her. There was so much compassion in his touch that it opened the floodgates of her emotions and Kaikasi bared her heart to him like never before.

'I have ruined your life. Your life, which was as serene as a pond of fresh water, I have muddied beyond redemption. Devaparni, who is the ideal partner for you, has left. It does not matter that she said she wanted to look after her ailing father; the truth is that she could not bear the turmoil I brought into your life. You were such a beautiful family—you, Devaparni and Kuber—I came and broke it up. And as if that was not enough, I burdened you with three children. You willingly gave me Dashagreeva because I desired that child. But Kumbhakarna and Surpanakha came because I insisted for my own selfish reasons. I even used feminine charm and subterfuge to beget these children. But believe me, nath, I had hoped that either or both of them would be like you—gentle, erudite and compassionate. But no, they are like me—rakshasas whose sole purpose is self-aggrandizement, wilfulness and cruelty. And there is nothing I can do to rectify things,' Kaikasi wept bitterly.

'You are too harsh on yourself, priye! Do not blame yourself for anything, least of all for the birth of our children. The timing of our first meeting was such that only rakshasa children could emerge from our union. I see now that you have a very strong desire for a child who will tread the path of dharma. You have been a dutiful and loyal wife to me and it is my responsibility that your genuine wishes and expectations of me are fulfilled. I shall expend a portion of my tapas-shakti and beget such a child for you,' Vishravasu promised.

'What about the ones we already have?' Kaikasi asked, a faint ray of hope kindling in her heart.

'They will reap the fruits of their actions. But remember, Kaikasi, we, as parents, can only sire children. We can neither decide their destiny, nor alter it. Each one charts a life as his or her mind commands,' so saying Vishravasu rose, ending the conversation. He paused a moment later and turning his head slightly, announced: 'Devaparni will return soon.'

Kaikasi's spirits lifted with these parting words. She too got up to return to her daily chores at the ashram. There was a spring in her step and a song on her lips. She felt happy—a feeling that had become almost alien to her in recent times.

Kaikasi's mood remained happy in the months that followed and when her fourth child arrived in due course, her joy was boundless. The child was a gentle and peaceful looking son, and his birth was accompanied by the chirping of birds. There were other auspicious signs—peacocks danced in the gentle breeze and trees bore fragrant flowers and mouth-watering fruits. Vishravasu welcomed the baby in exactly the same manner as he had welcomed his other children and named his son Vibheeshana. Kaikasi wondered what the name meant, particularly since the sage had named his other three children on the basis of their particular and special physical traits. She, however, refrained from asking, for fear of hearing some dark facet of the gentle-looking child. She was happy with things as they stood and did not wish to unsettle her cup of contentment.

However, there was just one thing that was lacking in Kaikasi's life. Devaparni had not yet returned.

Kaikasi was milking a cow one evening when her thoughts shifted yet again to Devaparni. She wondered if her husband had spoken of Devaparni's return only to cheer her up and whether there was any truth to his claim. Suddenly, a shadow fell across the pail of milk held tight between her knees as she crouched beside the cow. She looked up to find Devaparni standing there, a happy smile on her face. The yelp of surprise and happiness that escaped Kaikasi's lips startled the cow and the milk almost spilt out of the pail, even as Devaparni steadied Kaikasi with a hand on her shoulder.

Moments later, the two wives of Vishravasu were sitting under a tree and chatting happily. Devaparni cradled the newborn Vibheeshana as she spoke about what she had been doing at her father's place. Apologies were exchanged—from Devaparni for having gone away without informing Kaikasi and from Kaikasi for having enraged Devaparni with her intemperate utterances. By and by, however, the mood changed and Devaparni shared her reason for leaving Rishi-teertham in such a hurry.

'I am sorry that I was often curt with you, Kaikasi. Initially, I really believed that your behaviour occasioned my impatience, but on that day, when you shouted back at me, it dawned on me that the fault lay with me. I was becoming jealous. Jealous of you for your ability to be frank and open; for your zest for life and your purposeful approach to achieving your goals. I was ashamed of myself. My illustrious parents—sage Bharadwaj and Susheela—did not bring me up to be vicious and jealous. My father is an exalted soul, he is one of the Saptarshis, who are immortal. So I knew that I needed to cleanse my soul and that I could do it only with help from my parents. Our husband knew why I was going away and he agreed with me that the reason should not be disclosed to you. I am sorry if I worried you and made you blame yourself.'

'No, vahni!' Kaikasi put a hand on Devaparni's arm. 'There is nothing for you to be sorry about. I went through a process of catharsis myself and it did me good. I am no longer the scheming, uncouth person that I was when I came here. I am now at peace with myself,' Kaikasi said and was about to delve into the reasons that had made her entice Vishravasu when suddenly, out of nowhere, Vishravasu appeared in front of them, reminding them that the children were waiting to be fed and that the baby should be allowed to finish his nap in his cradle.

The trio walked back to the ashram, with Kaikasi trailing behind slightly. She wondered if Vishravasu's arrival at that particular juncture of their conversation was pure coincidence or a part of the all-knowing sage's larger strategy.

chapter 7

M atru shree!'
 Kaikasi turned her head towards the familiar voice that was calling. She pushed back a strand of hair from her sweaty forehead and used the same hand to shield her eyes from the sun, just as the familiar, wiry figure of Kuber turned the last bend in the path and came into view. Kaikasi's face broke into a happy smile and she waved in greeting. Kuber, who had quickened his pace to reach her fast, bent to touch her feet.

'Pranam, matru shree!' he greeted Kaikasi.

'Chiranjeevi bhava,' Kaikasi responded. 'What brings you to Rishi-teertham today, Vaishravana?' she asked, adding in the same breath, 'Today is not the day of your usual visit.'

'I was just passing by and thought I would see you all for a while before getting along with my work. After meeting pita shree and matru shree, I came looking for you,' Kuber said and added with a smile, 'I looked for you in the "Kaikasi corner".'

Kaikasi chuckled at the mention of the 'Kaikasi corner'. The reference was to a spot just outside the gate leading to the cursed and abandoned part of the ashram, which, because of her preference for it when seeking solitude, had acquired this name. It was there that Devaparni had first spoken to her, so many years ago when she was new to life amidst ascetics, and that was the place to which Kaikasi retreated whenever faced with a difficult situation. It never failed to provide solace to her, whatever her problem was.

'I do not have to seek out that corner today,' Kaikasi smiled. 'I was gathering wood for fuel,' she waved a hand at the pile of dry twigs she had been bundling when Kuber's voice had interrupted her.

'Let us go and sit there, please! I love sharing your bench with you. I too find peace there,' Kuber urged.

As the duo started walking towards 'Kaikasi corner', Kaikasi thought of the immense change that had come about in her relationship with her stepson since her arrival at the ashram so many years ago. His initial nods of bare acknowledgement had soon given way to a mutual feeling of respect and empathy between them. This had happened despite her determination to hold him as the 'enemy' and keep him at arm's length. Kuber was a presentable young man with impeccable manners and great solicitude for all beings. He treated her on par with his own mother, showing Kaikasi the same degree of respect that he showed Devaparni. Kaikasi's apprehensions that he would blame her for Devaparni's departure from Rishi-teertham proved baseless, and their bonds of affection had only grown stronger since the birth of Kumbhakarna. Kuber had not once mentioned his mother's absence to Kaikasi and had continued to treat her with the same consideration as he always did. Kaikasi, who had come to address Kuber as 'Vaishravana', just as Devaparni did, despite his title 'Kuber', was also overwhelmed by the affection he showered on his half-brothers and sister. Seeing them together filled Kaikasi with immense satisfaction and she secretly hoped that their association with Vaishravana would inculcate the higher values of life in her own children.

Kaikasi and Kuber reached the 'Kaikasi corner' and sat on the bench under a huge banyan tree in companionable silence. Kaikasi's thoughts revolved around a comparison of her own children with her stepson. Physically also, the differences between them could not have been starker. Vishravasu's firstborn son was a picture of perfection. He had chiselled features that radiated his inner beauty. His body glistened and his muscles rippled with good health at his every movement and there was a smile playing around his lips at all times. Much more than the way he looked and carried himself, Kaikasi was drawn by the manner in which he dealt with Dashagreeva, Kumbhakarna and Surpanakha—whose rakshasa lineage was underlined through their features. All three were huge, with wrestler-like physiques, as against the wiriness of Vaishravana. Dashamukha, despite his good looks, had an odd demeanour because of his ten heads. And his eyes reflected a determination that bordered on adamant. Worse, he showed an instinctive hatred towards his elder brother—an attitude that Kaikasi tried very hard to change. As for Kumbhakarna, his head was disproportionately small for the rest of his body on account of his unusually large and misshapen ears. But it gratified Kaikasi that he remained civil in his dealings with Vaishravana. He showed due respect and courtesy to him as an elder and appeared amenable to reason when his elder half-brother tried to resolve disputes among his younger siblings.

Kaikasi turned and looked at Kuber's profile, his eyes half-closed as he drank in the serenity in the atmosphere. Placing an affectionate hand on Kuber's knee, she asked: 'Were you born so mature, Vaishravana?'

Kuber laughed off the compliment, saying that he had been through his own set of follies. 'Oh, maate! You make me sound perfect. But that is not true. At one time, after being appointed Kuber by Indra, I became very proud and thought no end of my achievements.'

With a little prodding by Kaikasi, Vaishravana recounted an incident to illustrate this. 'After being appointed dikpalaka for the north direction, I went to Kailash to pay my respects to Shiva. I saw the happy couple with their two children—Ganesha and Shanmukha. Mount Kailash was barren and snow-clad. I, in my ignorance, thought that Shiva and Parvati could not adequately feed their elephant-headed and pot-bellied son Ganesha. Exalting in my new-found riches, I invited him for a meal at my place. I had an elaborate and rich meal prepared for Ganesha and expected that he would not only be pleased with my hospitality but would be grateful for the sumptuous meal. I personally supervised the serving of the meal, telling Ganesha to eat to his heart's content and pressing more food onto his plate. I was amazed that there was no end to Ganesha's appetite. He kept asking for more and soon there was nothing left in my stores, and then I also ran out of the wherewithal to procure more supplies. But he again said "more, please". I realized my folly and sought his pardon.

'Ganesha then gave me a lesson that I will never forget. He told me that food does not quench the appetite, particularly of the mind. It only fuels the appetite, and a greater search for food. He said, "You have tried creating more food to assuage my hunger; in other words, you tried to feed hunger. My father, on the other hand, deals with the issue by eliminating hunger itself. That is why I sit at his feet in Kailash rather than in your well-stocked kitchen."'

As Kaikasi and Vaishravana sat laughing over Kuber's travails in procuring more and more food for Ganesha, Surpanakha trudged up the path screaming for her mother. 'Look at you sitting here in this stupid little corner, laughing with this fellow! And there, near the pond, your two sons are trying to drown each other,' she said, accusation and disapproval dripping from her words.

Even before Kaikasi grasped the import of Surpanakha's words, Vaishravana was on his feet. 'Surpa kanye,' he said, reproach sounding in his voice. Placing a restraining hand on the girl's shoulder, he continued, 'That is not how you talk to mother. And anyway, there is no need to disturb her for this small matter. Come, we will both knock some sense into them.' With these words, he led Surpanakha away, taking leave of Kaikasi with a nod.

Kaikasi watched after them wistfully, her joy of a moment ago evaporating into nothingness. Surpanakha always had this effect on her. She was very different from all her brothers. Despite being a girl, she had no empathy for her mother. Dashagreeva and Kumbhakarna were more amenable to discipline than this girl. Surpanakha's wild looks were perfectly matched with her wild ways, mused Kaikasi. Another reason why her daughter's presence pushed Kaikasi into despondency was her uncanny resemblance to Sumali. The similarity was not just in looks and features, but in her gestures and habits also. Every time Surpanakha looked at her, Kaikasi felt that her father was questioning her about her mission to repossess Lanka.

Kaikasi's heart lurched at the memory of her father. She had promised him that she would beget a son who would replace Kuber as the ruler of Lanka, so they could all make it their home once again. It had seemed a simple enough task for her at that time. What she had not reckoned with then was the change that would occur in her own way of thinking. Dashagreeva was now a fully grown young man, physically and mentally fit to undertake and achieve specified tasks. She knew that he would do her bidding without asking any questions.

But it was not easy for her to send him on any such adventure. In the years that she had lived at Rishi-teertham, she had developed bonds, affections and attachments not only with the people at the ashram but also with specific places within the sprawling ashram premises. Like this stone on which she was now sitting. The very sight of the gate that closed off the mangrove that lay beyond filled her with a sense of peace and tranquillity. To sit on this stone was like sitting in her own mother's lap. It was witness to so many of her personal travails. It was no small matter that she never left this spot without finding an answer to whatever her problem was. Then there was Shabala, the cow, which was a direct descendent of Kamadhenu. She loved Shabala as if it was her own child and not a cow.

More importantly, there was Vishravasu and Devaparni. She loved and respected the rishi for his unquestioning acceptance of her and whatever she asked for. Such was his mental power and acumen that he probably knew the real purpose of her coming to him. Although she could not tell for sure, but it was possible that he hoped that she would not try to complete her task. It was no mean matter tha the always conducted himself as a perfect husband—he never made her feel insecure about her inadequacies as compared to his learned dharmapatni, Devaparni. And Devaparni! What an angel she was! She had accepted Kaikasi's entry into the household as a second wife to her husband, and became her guide and friend. But for Devaparni, Kaikasi would have found it impossible to adjust in her new home and cope with her responsibilities.

Home! That was what Rishi-teertham had become to her. She no longer pined for Lanka. She was happy here. She had a family and everything else she could ever ask for. Would she want to break up this home to secure Lanka for her father? Should she? She loved her father and wanted to see him happy and would do whatever was within her capacity to make him happy. But there was a conflict. Happiness for her father and siblings would mean not mere unhappiness but complete destruction for this family of hers. Did this family deserve it—for all the kindness, love and affection it had showered on a complete stranger like her? And, was she not 'mother' to Vaishravana, just like Devaparni? Should she, could she, destroy his life and make him homeless to fulfil her father's desire? If Sumali claimed Lanka as his home because he had lived there once upon a time, was Lanka not Kuber's home, as he had been living there even before she had arrived at Rishi-teertham?

Kaikasi recalled Vaishravana's experience with Ganesha. Just like hunger breeds more hunger, enmity breeds more enmity. If

Dashagreeva overthrew Kuber in Lanka, it might not be long before Kuber did the same to reclaim Lanka. So, if she initiated this process, even if it was to fulfil her promise to her father, it could be the beginning of a war between brothers. A war, that would bring happiness to no one.

Oh! What was she to do? What would be the correct course of action for her? Questions tormented Kaikasi and she lost track of time. She did not realize that night had fallen and nature had gone to sleep. She too slipped into a disturbed sleep, too tired to think any further. Voices calling out her name and people approaching her with torches in their hands were but a vague realization for her.

chapter 8

'You are a cheat, a scheming villain; you tricked me, you abused my trust...' Kaikasi had been raving and ranting in this vein for quite some time, her loud and high-pitched voice echoing in the still dark night.

Vishravasu, the target of her ire, sat quietly in front of her, hands folded across his chest; not a muscle in his body moved and his face was as calm as ever. Devaparni was exerting all her strength to keep Kaikasi pinned down so that she did not become physically violent towards their husband.

Kaikasi paused for breath. The total absence of reaction from Vishravasu was only enraging her further. 'See, you have nothing to say in your defence! You have no defence! You hate me. You hate my children also. You only pretend to be this wise muni, when you are actually conspiring with your first wife to keep my children from developing to the best of their abilities. That is why you never let them come near you while you are doing your puja and meditation. You do not want their wisdom to be developed. You are worried that Dashagreeva and Kumbhakarna will surpass Kuber if their mental faculties are nurtured. That is why you have kept them like ignorant fools so that their physical strength will also not be of any real use to them...' Kaikasi paused for breath again. She felt parched and ran a dry tongue over her dry lips in a bid to moisten them.

Vishravasu's eyes flickered towards Devaparni before returning to Kaikasi. As if on command, Devaparni reached behind her and held a glass of water to Kaikasi's lips. She gulped down huge quantities, almost choking on the water. But she felt refreshed. Devaparni dabbed the younger woman's face with the end of her saree, wiping the sweat from her brow. This act of solicitude deflated Kaikasi. Her eyes filled with tears of helplessness and she gazed dejectedly at her husband. 'You tricked me…fooled me into believing that you cared for me…cared just as much as you do for vahni…but no, that was only to deceive me. I was made to believe that I was discharging sacred responsibilities at Rishi-teertham when, in reality, I was being turned into a slave. A slave that cleans the stables, tends the cows, collects fodder and fuel. Oh god! What a fool I have been! What a wasted life mine has been…' Kaikasi was now only muttering, tears streaming down her cheeks. Tears that Devaparni wiped periodically with the edge of her saree.

Vishravasu and Devaparni had gone looking for her when Kaikasi had not returned for the night. When they found her, Kaikasi was in a stupor, mumbling incoherently and sobbing intermittently. Devaparni had tried to rouse Kaikasi without effect. Vishravasu and Devaparni had then carried her back to her sleeping quarters.

As she lay on her own bed, Kaikasi had continued in her delirious state, muttering to herself and laughing and crying intermittently. Devaparni had rubbed turmeric and hot oil on the soles of Kaikasi's feet and Vishravasu had sprinkled water on her face to wake her. It was when these ministrations had taken effect and Kaikasi had come round that a torrent of anger had erupted from her. The tirade took Vishravasu and his wife by surprise. So overcome was she with multiple emotions that Vishravasu and Devaparni waited patiently for Kaikasi's anger to expend itself.

Vishravasu now started to speak in a soft, soothing voice. 'Kaikasi dear, you are a wonderful person. You have sacrificed your life for a cause that you hold dear. You have endured a lot of hardship in the process. That you went through it with such grace and patience, in the face of such tough challenges, speaks volumes for your strength of character. You are also a great mother,' Vishravasu tipped his head a fraction—an indication that he was organizing his thoughts. Kaikasi looked from Vishravasu to Devaparni and back again, wondering if she was imagining the sincerity in her husband's voice and if she was hearing right. Devaparni squeezed her shoulder, her arm slipping around her, conveying friendship and affection. The slight nod of her head confirming the veracity of Vishravasu's words was also reassuring, though slightly confusing.

'It is not easy to keep a secret for so long. It sears the keeper's heart, and fatigues the mind. It is all that fatigue that is coming out now.'

Kaikasi's eyes opened wide and her mouth gaped as the import of Vishravasu's words sank in. 'Secret…what…what secret are you talking about?' she spluttered. 'What do you know? And…and… how do you know?' she demanded.

'Little innocent Kaikasi! Did I not know why you had come, when you first came to Rishi-teertham? So, if I knew that you wanted a child from me, would I not have also known why you wanted the child? The purpose for the child to be born was that he should take over Lanka for your father.'

Kaikasi felt completely lost. Words failed her. She sat there, staring at the impassive face of her husband. But for the comfort of Devaparni's proximity and her hand running reassuringly across her back, Kaikasi would have fainted in disbelief. 'Vahni…' she looked at Devaparni, unable to even form a question, and the imperceptible nod from the older woman confirmed what she feared. Devaparni too had known…right from the beginning.

Kaikasi leant away from Devaparni, feeling exposed, guilty and betrayed. Devaparni felt the movement and stretched out her hand to keep a reassuring grip on Kaikasi's arm. 'Then why…why…' words failed Kaikasi and she just looked from one to the other.

Vishravasu bent forward a little, keeping his gaze fixed on Kaikasi's face and holding her eyes. 'Why did I not confront you? Why did I oblige you?' he asked in the same soft voice. Kaikasi could barely nod. 'Because you are a blessed person, chosen to play an important role in a larger cosmic sequence of events,' he said and added: 'I will tell you some parts of this cosmic pattern that I can decipher. Listen carefully.

'Once upon a time, long long ago, Brahma became bored of his solitary existence in a lotus arising out of Vishnu's nabhi. He looked down, hoping to strike up a conversation with Vishnu. But Vishnu, and also Aadi Sesha, whose coils form Vishnu's bed in the ocean of milk, were both in deep slumber. The deafening silence and stillness ate at Brahma and to overcome them, he created four manasaputras. He named them Sanaka, Sanandana, Sanatana and Sanat kumaras.'

'That is not how creation happened,' interjected Kaikasi. 'My great-grandfather Heti was among the first beings Brahma created,' she said authoritatively, regaining some of her composure and dignity.

'You are right, Kaikasi,' Vishravasu explained patiently. 'My grandfather Pulastya was also created by Brahma as a first being. In fact, my grandfather is called "Pulastya Brahma" and even I am recognized as "Vishravasu Brahma". The point is, even though none of us can vouch for it, Brahma appears to have completed his task of creation in phases. He created a different line each time, possibly because he was not completely satisfied with the results of his previous attempt. Creation, as we know it today, is a synthesis of these various attempts and the individual manner in which each line progressed with time.

'Right now I am referring to one particular line that concerns us. In fact, this line joins the two lineages that you and I are products of. I was telling you of the time when Brahma created four children from his imagination; he then asked them to procreate. The four boys refused, thus angering Brahma, who decreed that they would remain the same as they were just then—prepubescent brahmcharis—eternally. Thus they retained the physical appearance of five-year-old boys, even though they were able to develop their mental capabilities exponentially.

'Since the four boys refused to procreate, Brahma, recalling the Ardhanareeshwara incarnation of Shiva, created a luminous female, using the flesh of his left thigh. This was Saraswati, and Brahma invited her to have children with him. Saraswati, however, argued that Brahma, as her creator, was like a father to her and so she would not take him as her husband. Brahma would not listen and tried to catch her forcibly. Saraswati ran from him. But with no place to go, she kept running around him. Brahma was so besotted with her that he kept turning his head to keep her within sight. It was so painful a process that Brahma sprouted four heads, each one facing a different direction, becoming the chaturmukha-Brahma that we know now. The controversy was resolved later by Shiva and Vishnu, following which Saraswati agreed to be Brahma's consort.

'But let us not digress,' Vishravasu said and returned to the main subject of Brahma's four manasaputras. 'These boys soon became highly erudite and learned. They roamed the worlds, exploring and enlightening, and one day, they reached Vaikuntha, the abode of Vishnu. They were stopped outside Vishnu's chambers by his two gatekeepers—Jaya and Vijaya—who told them that none could disturb the Lord just then, and least of all, children like them.

'Being treated casually like children by the gatekeepers annoyed the kumaras. They accused Jaya and Vijaya of misleading Vishnubhaktas, pointing out that Vishnu was available to his bhaktas at all times. And for the sin of having denied them access to their Prabhu, Jaya and Vijaya would lose their divinity and be born in Bhoo-loka as mortals. Just then Vishnu emerged from his chamber to see what the commotion was about and learnt the details of the altercation. Jaya and Vijaya beseeched Vishnu to pardon their ignorance of the kumaras and lift the curse on them. The curse could not be reversed, Vishnu explained, but he offered them a choice. He said that the two gatekeepers could either serve seven births as his bhakts or three janmas as Vishnu-haters. Jaya and Vijaya, unable to bear the prospect of separation from Vishnu, chose the second option of three births as Vishnu-dweshis. Dashagreeva and Kumbhakarna are Jaya and Vijaya, and they chose your womb to be born as Vishnu-haters,' Vishravasu said.

Stunned by the explanation, Kaikasi sat there, staring at Vishravasu in complete disbelief.

Vishravasu continued: 'I hope you now understand, Kaikasi, why I could not involve Dashagreeva and Kumbhakarna in any of my daily rituals, focused as they are on Vishnu. As of now, they know neither Vishnu nor Shiva and so are able to lead normal lives. I wanted them to be like this for as long as possible; to grow up physically and mature mentally before they came into the Vishnu-dwesha-mode. We cannot prevent this from happening and it will lead to their final, painful exit from this world.'

Vishravasu's words sank into Kaikasi's consciousness inexorably, hurting every fibre in her being. She could hardly hold herself up and appeared in danger of total collapse. Devaparni sprang into quick action, sprinkling liberal quantites of water on Kaikasi's face. Vishravasu came over to help and the two of them slowly eased Kaikasi into a supine position and watched over her to ensure that she slipped into deep slumber before they left.

Vishravasu, however, returned to Kaikasi's bedside. He put the forefinger of his right hand on the central point between her brows and pressed lightly, with a silent chant on his lips. He then placed his palm on Kaikasi's head and stroked her hair affectionately.

Devaparni, who had stopped at the door to watch her husband, gave him a quizzical look and asked: 'Why did you do that?'

'To make things easier for Kaikasi. She cannot handle this information on her own and will not want to be guided by us. So, I pressed our conversation into her subconscious. When she wakes—and it may be two or three days before she does—she will not be able to recall it, even though she will know that she received some vital information. Much depends upon what she does recall and what she does with that. All our lives, particularly those of Dashagreeva and Kumbhakarna, are bound to change drastically,' he said, before slipping out, placing a guiding hand under Devaparni's elbow.

Devaparni shook off her husband's hand. 'Unfair,' she said emphatically. 'That is unfair to a mother. You cannot burden a mother with the details of her children's past and future and not provide her with the wherewithal to guard and protect her children or give her some way in which to find solace.' Devaparni's eyes bored into Vishravasu's, holding him accountable and beseeching him to take action.

Vishravasu looked long and thoughtfully into his wife's eyes. 'I salute the mother in you. I will do what you want me to do,' he finally said and re-entered the room.

He placed the palm of his right hand on Kaikasi's chest, feeling the steady beat of her heart. He bent over her and spoke softly into the sleeping woman's ear. 'Here is a mantra that will help you protect your sons from harm. Turn to Shiva and seek his grace. Chant his pancha-akshari mantra. "Om Namah Shivayah! Om Namah Shivayah! Om Namah Shivaya!"' he chanted into her ear.

'Seek his blessings and ensure that your children take the prasad after your puja,' he said before straightening and turning to Devaparni. A silent question in his eyes earned him a nod and a smile. The couple then left the room, closing the door behind them.

chapter 9

The past ten days had been amongst the most taxing of his life, torn as he was with worry for his mother, who had been found in a stupor by his father and stepmother on a night when he and his siblings were out at a rowing competition. But thanks largely to the ministrations of Devaparni, the situation had improved remarkably and now it was just a matter of waiting for his mother to recover fully. After the first couple of worrisome days, Devaparni had told them that Kaikasi had possibly sustained some kind of mental trauma and that it could take a full moon cycle for her to recover. Dashagreeva had hardly left his mother's side during all this while. In fact, he had insisted on watching over Kaikasi at night, a time when his two brothers, he felt, might doze off. Even during the day, when Kumbhakarna and Vibheeshana were to take turns at the bedside, he would be there. Devaparni prevailed on him to get some rest.

However, Dashagreeva felt no fatigue, and he watched his mother's every restless movement and listened to every murmur that emerged from her throat like a hawk. For some reason, he felt responsible for Kaikasi's sickness. Once she got well, he promised her silently, he would be there for her, always. 'I will make you happy, janani!' he promised her, smoothing the furrow that had formed on her brow. Keeping his senses extra sharpened to deal with any emergency that might arise helped Dashagreeva glean some insight into the matters that were bothering her. In her stupefied and semi-conscious state, Kaikasi would often mumble and mutter. While no words could be deciphered from these sounds, the emotions that prompted them came through clearly to the watchful son.

One of the first words he identified in his mother's mumbled ramblings was 'Shamuloo', which was the pet name by which she had called him since childhood. It was a secret code between them as she never called him that when anyone else was in the vicinity. This was enough for him to understand that he was somehow centric to whatever was ailing her. Or perhaps she sought some action from him to alleviate her condition. He went over various incidents and conversations with his mother in a bid to discover the root of her troubles. What did she want him to do, Dashamuka pondered while attending to Kaikasi through the long and silent nights.

Janani wanted him to be 'great'; in fact, she wanted him to be the greatest and best, Dashamukha recalled fondly. And one measure of this greatness was his achievement in whatever he was being taught by his father. He was good, Dashamuka thought to himself, reviewing his academic performance objectively. He loved sangeet, found ganit challenging and vyakaran extremely engaging. He was excellent at martial arts also, which pleased his mother immensely. Even Vishravasu was happy with his pace of learning. The one thing he found impossible to cope with was ritualistic procedures and scriptural messages. For some reason, these irritated and agitated him. Kumbhakarna, who was not so good at academics, also found the training in rituals distasteful. Only Vibheeshana was comfortable during these sessions. And janani was always goading him to excel in that also, saying it was very important to master the rituals and scriptures. 'I will really try to make you happy on this score, janani,' he said, placing his hand in her palm by way of making a promise.

His time by his mother's bedside was a great learning experience for Dashagreeva as he came to see the deep bonds of affection that existed between his mother and stepmother. Devaparni took on the additional responsibility of caring for Kaikasi as an integral part of her daily routine, paying great attention to Kaikasi's personal hygiene, medication and nutrition. She involved Surpanakha in these activities, giving her stepdaughter a sense of contribution to caring for her mother and also teaching her the nuances of patient care. It required all of Surpanakha's willpower to keep her cool and do as told by Devaparni, as such discipline and dedication did not come naturally to her. The stepmother's strict supervision and the stepdaughter's awe of her helped.

Dashagreeva's initial suspicion was that his stepmother was somehow responsible for Kaikasi's problems. He vaguely remembered the time when Devaparni had gone away and how unhappy his mother had been after that. He, therefore, could not believe his ears when he heard his mother make positive references to Devaparni in her unconscious state. It was not so much her words, which were quite unclear, but the tone of her voice and the softening of her facial features whenever she referred to 'vahni' that convinced him that the two wives of Vishravasu had a very strong and affectionate bond. Kaikasi's references to 'vahni' were second only to 'Shamuloo', and made Dashamukha wonder if the two of them were either somehow responsible for her present sickness or held the key to her return to normalcy.

In the quiet of the night, Dashamukha concentrated on deciphering his mother's mutterings. He not only heard every sound that emanated from his mother's lips with a keen ear but he also spent a lot of time analysing whatever words he picked up. As the days passed he felt he understood what was being said. References to his sister were also frequent. These gave Dashagreeva the impression that his mother worried for his sister. It was true that she was wilful and sometimes at odds with herself. But she was amenable to discipline. She obeyed Devaparni without question, because she held her in such awe. She also loved her mother dearly in her own way. Surpanakha had implicit faith in Dashagreeva and his sense of fairness. The brother would go to great lengths to make his sister happy.

On certain nights, Dashagreeva thought he discerned a chant in his mother's ramblings. All he could make out was the 'Om' part of the chant. Dashagreeva was surprised that this chant soothed him, unlike the agitation that his father's chants generated in him. This new feeling turned his earlier belief that he was completely anti-god in his head, and left him wondering about his religious leanings. It also turned another of his firm beliefs in his head—his belief about his mother's religiosity. While he knew that janani was in awe of her husband and admired his spiritual prowess, he had never thought that she herself was religiously inclined. And given the fact that women were not considered eligible for any kind of austerities, it was taken as a matter of course and nothing to comment about. So it came as a great surprise to him that his mother was muttering chants in her present condition.

One day, when the three brothers stepped out of Kaikasi's room while Devaparni and Surpanakha bathed their mother, Dashamukha asked if they too had heard janani muttering chants. 'How would I know? She just mumbles; makes incoherent sounds. And that is because she is unwell. We must not pay much heed to any of it,' Kumbhakarna said. Vibheeshana, on the other hand, said that he had noticed some repetitiveness in janani's mutterings and added: 'It will do her soul a lot of good and all her sins could be absolved because of this.' Dashamukha let the pompousness of the remark pass and suggested that they should all be more alert when watching over their mother, because her condition had improved significantly in the past few days. 'And if matru shree's prognosis is anything to go by, janani could be coming round any time now,' he said, pointing out that the moon cycle would conclude in a couple of days.

The conversation among the brothers ended as Devaparni and Surpanakha emerged from Kaikasi's room. Seeing the brothers standing outside, Devaparni came over to talk to them. 'Our worries will soon be over, putra. Kaikasi is recovering well and she may regain consciousness in just a day or two. However, she will have to take ample rest in the coming weeks to regain her lost strength,' Devaparni announced the good news and with a word of caution not to slacken their watch over the patient, she left to tend to her various other chores. Dashagreeva, who had decided to remain with his mother at all times, returned to her room.

It was well past midnight the next day when Kaikasi awoke, as if from a normal night's sleep. Moonlight was streaming into the room and cast shadows on the floor. It also illuminated the room pleasantly and somewhat surrealistically. It was an unusually still night, with not a leaf stirring. Dashamuka was fanning his mother with a palm leaf fan when his ever alert eyes noticed her eyes flicker open. He reached for the jar of water kept handy, half expecting her to motion for a sip of water to wet her parched lips.

'Shamuloo,' her voice was low, but clear. Dashagreeva, who had bent to pick up the water pitcher, jumped in joyous surprise. He could not really believe that she had actually called out to him and that he had not imagined it. But the wave of her hand, motioning him to come close, confirmed that his happiness was not misplaced, and he rushed round the bed with an ecstatic 'janani' escaping his lips. He crouched on the floor and held Kaikasi's extended hand in both of his. Tears rolled down his cheeks, releasing the unrelenting tension he had been living with for over a fortnight now. Kaikasi stroked his hair affectionately and wiped his tears.

'Is it morning yet?' Kaikasi asked, clearly under the misconception that she had retired to bed just the night before.

'No, janani. Dawn is still sometime away. I think you should try and sleep a little more.'

A perplexed look came into her eyes. 'Why are you not sleeping then? And what are you doing here at this hour?'

Dashagreeva took a moment to come up with an appropriate response that would be true but not alarming. 'You have been slightly unwell and sleeping for a while now. Matru shree thought it best that we kept watch over you so you would not be alarmed if you woke at an odd time.'

The answer seemed to satisfy Kaikasi and she remained silent for a while. Her son continued to look at her intently, noting with some satisfaction that his mother's eyes remained open and wakeful.

'I see...' Kaikasi spoke after some time, before falling silent again. Dashagreeva noticed that she was thinking and gathering her strength to speak again. Then she made an attempt to rise but found herself unequal to the task. A look of surprise came into her eyes as she realized that she must have been in bed for quite some time. 'How long have I been like this, putra?' she asked.

Kaikasi continued to speak without waiting for a reply. 'It did seem long, Shamuloo...very long. I lived my life many times over in my thoughts, you know. And I think I should tell you all about it,' Kaikasi said, signalling to her son to help her sit up. She brushed aside his suggestion that she was too weak to talk, and tried to prop herself up. Her immense willpower was in evidence and Dashagreeva had no option but to help her by piling a couple of pillows behind her.

'Thank you, Shamuloo,' she said, her voice betraying her fatigue. She breathed deeply to steady the quiver in her body and resumed. 'I must first tell you why I call you "Shamuloo". It comes from my father's name. His name is Sumali and I love him dearly. But I cannot not let anyone know about it, so I call you Shamuloo only when the two of us are alone.'

His curiosity was aroused. He had never seen his grandfather and he had never heard him being mentioned by anyone at the ashram. Words failed him and he came to sit by his mother on the bed, stroking her hand comfortingly. His mother had fallen silent; the sickness of the last fortnight had obviously taken a toll on her.

However, it was not fatigue that silenced Kaikasi. She was confused and unable to decide how to go on. And amidst the million thoughts and images that crowded into her mind, there was a chant that kept resonating in her mind, but she was unable to understand what it was. She saw her husband saying something earnestly to her, but his words were lost to her. She felt, rather than saw, Devaparni. She had played an important role in whatever it was that Kaikasi was trying so hard to recall. She remembered that she had to do something very important, but could not recall what it was. There was a feeling that she was forgetting something very important; something that was vital to her.

The effort to remember was exhausting. Dashagreeva felt his mother slumping and was concerned that she was overexerting herself. 'Would you like to lie down and sleep a little, janani?' he asked.

'No,' Kaikasi's retort was sharp. She was worried that her memory would fail her completely if she slept now, and then she would never be able to pass on vital information to her dear son. 'I must talk...talk to you...right now,' she said and straightened herself. The movement made her head spin and her eyes blur. With characteristic determination, Kaikasi decided that she would start talking and let that act channel her thoughts and words. Jumping into deep waters is the best way to learn how to swim, she thought.

A torrent of words poured out, sweeping Dashagreeva along with its intensity. Time stood still as Kaikasi talked earnestly to her son, jumping from subject to subject, intermingling events and issues with her aspirations and compulsions. Such was the impact of what she said that Dashagreeva did not realize when his mother stopped speaking. He sat there like a statue, trying to understand the implications of this conversation for him.

That is how Devaparni found him when she entered the room sometime later, bearing fresh water for the patient. Her entry jolted Dashagreeva back to the here and now, and he got up and left the room, without showing her the normal courtesy. Devaparni looked at the door through which he had left and back to the prone figure on the bed and wondered…

chapter 1 0

'Thank god we found you!' exclaimed Kumbhakarna as he dropped down heavily beside Dashagreeva. Vibheeshana, who was just a couple of paces behind him, came round and sat on the other side of his eldest brother. 'You have been missing the entire day and matru shree has been very worried,' he said accusingly.

Dashagreeva looked from one concerned face to the other and responded contritely: 'Sorry, I wandered and lost track of time,' he said.

'Well said, bhrata, well said indeed! "Lost track of time", is it? You have been missing since dawn and now, dusk is falling. And we have been searching the entire ashram since lunch,' Kumbhakarna said, the complaint apparent in his voice. He had obviously not enjoyed foregoing his afternoon siesta to comb the grounds for his brother; his keen eye was scanning his brother's face for a clue about the disappearance.

'Luckily for us, janani is a lot better today. She is talking to everyone normally, and even ate her meal herself, instead of being force-fed by matru shree,' Vibheeshana heaved a sigh of relief as he stretched his legs.

'Vibheeshana, will you please go and inform matru shree that we have found bhrata and he is fine? You know that she has been very worried for him,' Kumbhakarna urged his younger brother.

Vibheeshana, whose legs were aching after all the walking they had done, would have liked to rest a while, but he rose nonetheless, proud to be the one to tell matru shree about their success.

Kumbhakarna watched their younger brother for a while before turning to his elder brother. 'Bhrata, I can see that something is bothering you. Please share it with me. Together, we can overcome any hurdle, you know that,' he said, placing his arm around his brother's shoulders.

Dashagreeva was more than willing to unburden his heart, secure in the knowledge that Kumbhakarna would respect the confidentiality of the information and also come up with constructive and helpful suggestions.

'You know, janani woke up long before dawn and spoke to me at length about various things. She was not rambling, mind you. She was fully in control of her senses. She knew what she was saying and what she wanted. She shared with me the central issue that was at the core of her recent sickness. I have been mulling over her words all day. I appreciate the gravity of her words, but am at a loss as to how we can achieve her goal.'

'Go on, tell me all the details and I am sure we will find a way of doing whatever it is that needs to be done.'

'It is rather complicated and confusing. So listen carefully, Kumbha,' Dashagreeva said and then took a deep breath before continuing. 'Do you not find it rather odd that we never thought about who janani was, where she came from, or who her family was? We just took our family for granted and believed that everyone— pitru shree, matru shree, janani, and all of us—had lived here all our lives,' he paused again, gathering his thoughts before continuing.

'But that is not true. Janani came here to marry pitru shree. Before that, she lived in Naga-loka with her father and brothers and sisters.' Dashagreeva had to pause again, this time on account of a surprised interjection from his brother. 'Is that so?' he said in a voice filled with disbelief and asked: 'Is she a naga kanya?'

'No, she is not a naga kanya. She is in fact a rakshasa kanya. Her father was a king on earth before he was forced underground by the devas. There was a war between the devas and rakshasas in which that double-dealing Vishnu led the devas and vowed to finish the rakshasa race. It was an unfair war that the scheming Vishnu waged, flouting all rules of fairplay. Our grandfather, a brave and noble person, was forced to retreat to the Naga-loka to save the women of the family.

'Then how did janani come to Rishi-teertham?' Kumbhakarna's face reflected his confusion.

'Be patient, Kumbha. I will tell you all what I know. Janani's father did not give up on his dream to return to his old home. He had the power to come up to the earth's surface, and used to make occasional trips there, just to gaze at his lost home. It hurt him badly when that home was illegally occupied,' Dashagreeva paused and looked at his brother to gauge the impact of what he had said.

As Kumbhakarna nodded sympathetically, his elder brother disclosed dramatically: 'That home is Lanka and the illegal occupant is our half-brother, Kuber.'

'What!' Kumbhakarna jumped up in complete disbelief. 'Then...is that why...how....janani...' he spluttered, a million thoughts racing through his mind.

'Yes. Janani came here to restore Lanka to her father...somehow. That is a secret that no one here—including pitru shree and matru shree—knows. She has harboured it like a volcano in her breast and raised us in the hope that we would be able to achieve this task for her.'

'I see,' Kumbhakarna said thoughtfully, trying to digest the information. Both brothers remained silent for some time, each grappling with his own thoughts. 'What about the rest of her family?' he asked after a while.

'Janani's father is the second of three brothers,' Dashageeva's tone indicated that he was launching into a long explanation. 'In fact, the three of us remind janani of her father and his two brothers, in terms of temperament. I, according to her, am like her eldest uncle—in holding that the end justifies the means, and going head on at it without caring for consequences. You resemble her father, being more balanced and with an eye for justice above everything else, and Vibheeshana is like her youngest uncle, with his excessive emphasis on what is theoretically correct and in accordance with the dharma shastras,' he paused reflectively.

'And what about our sister?' Kumbhakarna was curious.

'Surpanakha reminds janani of her eldest cousin sister...her name she said was "Anala"... Wilful and always wanting to have everything her way,' Dashagreeva said with a short laugh. His brother joined him at this apt description of their sister's basic character.

Kumbhakarna returned to the question at hand. 'I still do not know how janani came to Rishi-teertham and how we can capture Lanka for her. And, if we do, how it will belong to her father?'

'It was her father's idea that janani should come here. He knew that given Vishnu's protection of the devas and his avowed objective of eliminating all rakshasas from earth, Lanka could not be won through a physical war alone. For any rakshasa to regain a foothold anywhere near Lanka, he would need higher mental and strategic abilities than rakshasas are generally endowed with. So our grandfather decided that a child born to a rakshasa and Brahmin couple would be best suited to undertake this task. Janani was the kanya he selected and he sent her here to have children with pitru shree,' Dashamukha concluded with a significant look at his brother.

Kumbhakarna nodded. There was another long silence between the brothers, each reassessing their position. 'Do you think this can actually work? Do we really have the right or ideal combination of the requisite mental and physical attributes?' he said, more to himself than as a question to his brother.

'I said the same thing to janani. Her answer was that while we are not equipped for the task right now, we have the potential. What we lack is the mental discipline, which we can master through the kind of austerities that pitru shree observes. Remember how she used to push us to learn the processes?'

'Yes...but I hated it. His lessons were boring enough, even though you quite excelled in most subjects. But there was something extremely distasteful about meditation and things like that. You hated them more than I,' Kumbhakarna paused as memories of their learning years with their father made a comeback.

'True, but that is something that I cannot explain even now—this distaste for the practice of meditative and concentration skills. At the same time, we have to accept that they do generate a power from within,' Dashagreeva turned to look his brother in the eye. There was a new enthusiasm in his voice as he spoke urgently: 'Kumbha, do you remember the time when the two of us used to be ridiculed by all the boys who came here to learn from pitru shree? I was laughed at for having so many heads and hands and you for your large ears. We went crying to pitru shree and complained about it. He fixed it immediately, remember?'

'Yes, I remember...he just held my head between his two hands and chanted silently for a while and I felt my ears shrinking. At the end of it, he told me that my acute sense of hearing would not be affected by my ears becoming a normal size.'

'And what he did with me was even more amazing. He held me tight by my shoulders and told me to concentrate with him. I sat in front of him with my eyes fixed on his tilak. Slowly, one by one, nine of my ten heads dissolved, and the same happened with nine pairs of my arms. But I did not lose them. They are all there, inside me somewhere and they will come out when I want them or need them. Meanwhile, my ability to think with ten different minds, examining each issue from ten different aspects at the same time, has remained with me.'

Both brothers fell into a reflective silence, their main dilemma being whether they could approach their father now to teach them the same techniques that they had rejected on many earlier occasions. Moreover, would it be proper for them to seek such skills so that they would be able to defeat his eldest and dearest son—the one who had brought renown and glory to his name?

They knew the answer and so were looking for a way around the problem. Dashagreeva came up with an idea. 'Listen, Kumbha, while the two of us ran away from pitru shree's practical training, Vibheeshana was a diligent pupil and learnt all those skills. I have heard pitru shree speak highly of Vibhee's achievements on this score. We can ask him to train us, without telling him why we want to learn them now...'

His younger brother cut him short. 'We will have to give some reason, which, if not the whole truth, will still not be a lie. Let us tell Vibhee we want to learn the science and art of meditation because we want to do tapasya. We will tell him that we want to do tapasya to please god and secure boons, as did Kuber and our grandfathers. Then he can also be with us and be a guide, if we encounter a problem or hitch.'

'Kumbha, don't tell me that we have to do tapasya to please that double-crossing devil, Vishnu. I will not be able to endure it.'

'Bhrata, when did I say we have to please Vishnu? We want our tapasya to yield us boons that will make us invincible against Vishnu. Did you not tell me that our grandfathers meditated for Brahma, who is our prapitamaha, our great-grandfather, on our mother's side and our pitamaha, our grandfather, on our father's side? So we will do tapasya to please Brahma.' Dashagreeva agreed that this was a brilliant proposal and the two brothers fell into an easy conversation. There was, however, one point on which the brothers differed. Kumbhakarna felt that it would be unethical to go to war against their half-brother Kuber. After all, he had always been a good and caring elder brother to them. He wanted them to use their boons to secure a position like Kuber, thus making their mother proud. They could then have a grand palace built specially for them and invite their grandfather and the rest of their family to come and live with them. Dashagreeva argued that the task expected of them was to repossess Lanka so that janani's family could return to what was their home. This alone would make them happy and this alone would constitute the brothers delivering on their mother's desire.

The difference of perception persisted despite arguments back and forth and they were still at it when they heard their youngest brother calling out to them. Vibheeshana was suspicious about what his two elder brothers were up to. His curiosity had to be satisfied before he would let them off the hook. It pleased him immensely to be asked to be teacher to his two elder brothers. 'Only if you will not tell pitru shree,' he insisted, thinking their father would consider him presumptuous to take on such a task. He also said asking their father was an option they should consider. 'Pitru shree is a kind and generous person and will not mind teaching you what you had earlier abandoned because of your lack of interest.'

Dashagreeva came up with a fine little deception to coax Vibheeshana into doing the needful and also ensuring that this fact was not brought to the notice of pitru shree and matru shree. The deal was struck, including the secrecy clause, and the three brothers returned to the ashram.

chapter 11

Frustration was writ large on the faces of all three brothers. Dashagreeva was pacing up and down, his irritation showing in every muscle and sinew of his body. Once in a while he would glare at his two brothers, silently accusing them for the situation on hand. Kumbhakarna ignored his elder brother and his angry glares, but Vibheeshana cringed every time he felt his brother's eyes on him.

With Kumbhakarna not showing any reaction to his anger, Dashagreeva shifted his focus to his youngest brother, whose discomfiture increased manifold with every accusing look thrown at him. Kumbhakarna felt sorry for Vibheeshana and decided to take matters into hand. He sat up straight and looked directly at his elder brother. 'Bhrata, that is enough. Getting angry is not going to solve anything. And why subject this young one to your pointless and irrational rage? What has he done?'

'What has he done?' Dashagreeva mimicked Kumbhakarna's tone with an exaggerated shrug of his shoulders and with eyebrows raised. 'Wasn't he supposed to be the master at tapasya and expected to guide us in this endeavour?'

'No!' Kumbhakarna cut him short. 'Vibhee was not supposed to be the "master" at tapasya. He is only better at it than the two of us. We all know that he has neither done tapasya on his own nor ever watched anyone do it. So, with advice from him, we have to devise our own methods to achieve our objective. Stop making him miserable and sit down. Once all of us become calmer in mind, we can think of a strategy.'

Dashamukha stopped mid-step on hearing his brother's chastising words. He looked from one to the other brother, thought a moment before finally sitting down at some distance from the other two. 'So you accept that we have wasted all this time? And do you know how much time?' he articulated his frustration through his questions. Once again, he looked at his two brothers, and his irritation found another reason to burst through when he noticed Vibheeshana go into a mental calculation of the time they had spent on meditation. 'I know the answer, you idiot! It has been ten full years since we came here,' he snapped.

Vibheeshana, whose spirits were already low, felt even worse. He was battling his tears, but his voice said it all. 'I wish we had never come here. We were all so happy at home with pitru shree, matru shree and janani,' he said wistfully.

'And Surpanakha!'

Kumbhakarna's jaw dropped. This was unexpected. Here he was trying to stop his younger brother from uttering words that would be construed as 'weak' by bhrata, and yet Dashagreeva himself was indulging in nostalgia. He looked unbelievingly at his elder brother, wondering if he had misheard.

No. He was not mistaken. Dashagreeva was no longer there with them. He was far away, back home, with their pretty little sister, Surpanakha. He exchanged a look with Vibheeshana and both sat there, waiting for their bhrata to snap out of his dreamy world.

'Her name should have been "Chandramukhi". She has such a lovely face...beautiful like the moon. But she is called "Surpanakha" because her nails are broad. Well, what is in a name, after all! Whatever her name, she is pretty, sweet, and above all, our loving little sister,' Dashagreeva continued in his dreamy voice. 'You know, she deserves a much better life...the life of a queen. That is what I will give her, once we return home...find her a nice husband... it would be such a treat to see her happily married, possibly with children of her own.'

He paused for a moment. 'She has a free spirit…a spirit that refuses to submit to rules and codes. Earlier, I used to wonder about this peculiar aspect in her. But now that I know the secret of our birth, it fits…I understand.'

Kumbhakarna and Vibheeshana both started—the elder one with concern that bhrata was disclosing information that was to be kept secret from the younger one and the youngest brother wondering if he had heard right, and that there was something that he did not know.

'Bhrata…' Kumbhakarna's voice rang an alarm bell, even as he placed a warning hand on Dashagreeva's arm.

Placing his other hand reassuringly on Kumbhakarna's, Dashagreeva smiled. 'Do not worry, Kumbha. Vibhee should also know what we know.'

'Then, why…why…' Kumbhakarna trailed off, unable to articulate his question.

Dashagreeva smiled again. 'Why did I insist on keeping it a secret from Vibhee?' he completed the question, and acknowledging his brother's half nod, proceeded to answer. 'Vibhee believes in complete truthfulness. So, had he known our secret when we were still at home, he would have informed everyone about the purpose of our tapasya.'

'Yes, I understand…I agree…' Kumbhakarna said and watched the confusion on his younger brother's face with some amusement. In a way, he was relieved that bhrata had decided to tell Vibhee their secret, and waited for him to tell the story in his own way.

'Actually, I think it was presumptuous of us to even think that pitru shree would not have known everything—janani's antecedents, her mission in approaching him…and…' he paused before adding: 'what we are trying to do now.'

Kumbhakarna's eyes widened and his jaw dropped as he tried

to digest what bhrata had said. Of course! Bhrata was right! Pitru shree would have known all these aspects.

Vibheeshana's patience, however, was at its breaking point. 'Will both of you stop talking in riddles and tell me exactly what it is that you have kept from me,' he demanded in an aggrieved tone.

Dashamukha laughed again, this time indulgently. 'My little epitome of patience, it amuses me to see you getting so very curious. I like it…it shows that you do have feelings,' he laughed uproariously at the sight of Vibheeshana's cheeks, which were blazing pink with a combination of emotions.

'Jokes apart, Vibhee, listen carefully. For, what I am about to tell you is a serious matter. I hope you have the mental equanimity to accept the truth,' he said and waited a moment till Vibheeshana nodded his head.

'As putras of sage Vishravasu and grandsons of the venerated Pulastya, we are Brahmins. At the same time, from our maternal side, we have rakshasa blood flowing in our veins. Janani's forefathers were of an illustrious line of rakshasas, descending directly from Brahma. However, they fell on bad times on account of excesses committed by some rakshasas against humans and devas. Vishnu responded to the appeals of the humans and devas and set out to destroy all rakshasas. This forced our grandfather to take refuge in the Naga-loka. He vowed to avenge this injustice and towards this end sent janani to pitru shree to beget children—Brahmin rakshasas—who would be physically strong enough to stand up to the devas and mentally equipped to foresee and counter the deceitful ways of the devas in war,' Dashagreeva concluded and watched closely for his brother's reaction. He deliberately omitted to mention that winning control over Lanka from Kuber was the mission. He was glad he could depend upon Kumbhakarna completely and thus faced no danger of this detail being disclosed to his youngest brother.

He could see that Vibheeshana was deliberating on what he had been told, and waited in silence. Kumbhakarna moved closer to his younger brother and placed a hand on his shoulder, indicating oneness of purpose and, at the same time, appealing for the continuation of this unity of purpose. Vibheeshana straightened himself and looked from one to the other brother before he spoke. 'So, this is it...the big secret that you kept from me. From the moment we left home with permission from pitru shree to do tapasya, I could feel that there was some ulterior motive that had led to your decision. I imagine that even you two learnt of these details about our past only recently. It could only be janani who told you,' he shifted slightly away from the affectionate hand on his shoulder even as he placed his own hand over it.

It was a while before he spoke again. He weighed his words carefully before uttering them: 'Since janani is the source of this information, I feel that the story is from her point of view. While I love janani dearly and have no reason to doubt anything she says, I do feel that there is a second side to the story—this side, we have no means of learning. But I will say this—I am your brother and will be with you through thick and thin. My only condition is that whatever we do, we must not transgress the boundaries of dharma. For, dharma is sacred and must prevail,' he said.

'Pompous little brat,' thought Dashagreeva even as he nodded to show his agreement.

'Well spoken, like a mature and balanced person,' thought Kumbhakarna as he looked at his younger brother with eyes full of affection and admiration. 'See bhrata, we tend to think of Vibhee as a child. But he has grown up into such a wise person,' he said aloud.

Dashamukha found it difficult to hide his impatience with his two brothers who spoke so highly of empty words like 'dharma'. What good are these values if they deny you your rights, he thought to himself, even as he made an attempt to return to the issue at hand. 'But these issues will arise only if we successfully complete our tapasya and attain the boons that we seek,' he reminded them. 'By the looks of it, we are a long way off from achieving our objective,' he added.

Vibheeshana's face, which was glowing under the praise he had received from his brother, crumpled again. He looked at Kumbhakarna for support, which came forth readily enough. 'Bhrata, our tapasya till now has been very preliminary. We have been performing our austerities for only a few hours every morning. Clearly this is not sufficient. We should put in longer hours and also incorporate stricter rules of conduct for ourselves.' Vibheeshana nodded vigorously to second this view.

Dashagreeva looked at them, his mind busy with an idea that had come to him. 'Very well. Let us give up rest completely, except for sleep at night. We will eat only once a day, after we complete the day's austerities. We will review the situation once again after another decade.'

Even as his two younger brothers agreed to this plan, the eldest brother said: 'Before we start again, let us perform one yagna for the ten years of tapasya we did. Can I request both of you to collect the wood necessary to invoke agni?' he said.

Vibheeshana was flummoxed. 'But bhrata, a yagna cannot be completed without an adequate offering to agni. What do we have to offer?'

'I know that we need to make an offering to agni at a yagna, Vibheeshana. Do not think you are the only one who knows these things,' the curtness in Dashamukha's voice did not break further argument.

The yagna began early the next morning, with hardly any conversation among the brothers. Vibheeshana led the chanting of the Vedas. Kumbhakarna, even as he joined in the incantations, focused on trying to read his elder brother's mind. He knew instinctively that Dashagreeva had something in mind. His manner indicated that it could be something extreme in nature, and knowing Dashagreeva's determination when he made up his mind, he worried. He was also worried at the coldness that had crept in between his two brothers, the elder one taking offence at what he considered the youngest brother's pretentious attitude and the young one not really equipped to deal with the situation, but adamant in his own way about not being party to any wrongdoing.

Dusk was falling when the yagna reached its final stage, when the yagniks have to make an offering for poorna-ahuti, or complete consumption. The two younger brothers were painfully aware that they had nothing ready for the poorna-ahuti, but, knowing that their eldest brother had something in mind for this purpose yet not having the courage to interrupt the proceedings, they waited for a signal from bhrata. It was difficult to see clearly in the creeping shadows of dusk, which were compounded by the smoke that arose from the yagna-kund. He would have missed it completely had he not been watching Dashagreeva so closely. The eldest brother drew his sword out of its sheath and moved it to his throat in a smooth movement of the arm. Kumbhakarna was on his feet and next to his brother before anyone could even blink, and put a restraining grip on the hand with the sword. 'What are you doing?' he shouted. Vibheeshana sat where he was, looking as if he had lost the power of movement, shocked to the core.

Dashagreeva alone was in complete control of the situation. 'Do not stop me, Kumbha. I have nine more heads. Pitru shree said they would come out when I needed them. I believe him. Even if that does not come true and I lose my life in the process, I would consider my life well-spent. The two of you can continue on the journey we have embarked upon. I pray that you succeed and bring joy to janani.'

With these words, in one clean stroke, Dashagreeva chopped off his own head, ensuring that the severed head fell directly into the fire. The flames leapt up as if in welcome and the shadows thrown up by the raging flames made for an eerie sight.

*T*here was nothing to disturb the peace that prevailed all around. A gentle breeze rustled the leaves of a myriad trees and flowering shrubs, and carried an intoxicating combination of all their fragrances. A brook flowed silently by and the dying embers of agni from a yagna-kund competed with the orange-red rays of the setting sun. Three men sat in front of the yagna-kund, gazing intently into the remains of the yoga-agni. The fading sunlight and the last flickering flames from the yagna-kund formed psychedelic patterns on their well-bronzed faces and naked torsos. The expression on each of their faces was one of serenity and contentment, giving all three countenances an ethereal glow.

At long last, one of them spoke. 'Bhrata, you have sacrificed your ninth head today,' he said with a wave of his hand that encompassed eight other yagna-kunds that had gone cold a long time ago. 'Do you think there is anything to be gained by continuing with our tapasya?'

'It will not be long before our prayers are answered, Kumbha. I can feel the presence of the object of our tapasya around us,' Dashagreeva said and looked at Vibheeshana also before adding: 'You know, somehow, it does not seem to matter which way the result of our tapasya goes. What does matter to me is that we continue our efforts earnestly for another ten years, at the end of which I will sacrifice my tenth and last head. If Brahma chooses not to be pleased with our austerities, so be it. What is important to me is that I have given this endeavour my unstinted best. My life on this earth will end then. But there is bound to be a next birth where I will carry the fruits of all this tapasya with me and fulfil my objective then.'

Kumbhakarna's eyes showed a flicker of movement. 'I did not think Brahma, who was so kind to our ancestors, would be so hard to please. The sacrifice of nine heads has not moved him...I wonder...maybe we should have chosen to concentrate on Shiva... or even Vishnu.'

A sudden violent and impatient movement of his elder brother's hand silenced him. 'Do not even mention their names in front of me, Kumbha. They do not deserve respect from anyone. One is a wimp and the other is a cheat,' he said.

Dashakantha continued in response to the quizzical look on his brother's face. 'Shiva cannot do anything on his own. He is always running to Vishnu to get him out of problems that he creates for himself through his mindless deeds. Even so he is conceited and thinks no end of himself and his powers.

'Oh! I see that you do not believe my words and think I speak with a prejudiced mind. But no, I speak from personal experience. I had once gone to call on him, as urged by Kuber. When I reached his abode, Nandi—that monkey-faced bull, who is his gatekeeper and mount, would not let me in. He quarrelled with me. He thought he was so powerful that he could curse me...he said that a monkey would be the end of me, or some such thing. Even as he was screaming at me and I was countering him, Shiva the great did not even come out,' he said and looked at his two brothers for endorsement of his view.

Kumbhakarna's curiosity was aroused. 'And Vishnu...' he said suggestively.

'He is the real culprit. But for his machinations, rakshasas would have been immortal, not devas. You know what happened when the ocean of milk was churned. The devas and rakshasas churned it together, using Mount Mandara as the churning stick and the serpent Vasuki as the churning rope. Actually, Vishnu had instigated the devas to perform the task, promising them amrit that would make them immortal. But weaklings that they were, and also because their declining strength and vitality was the main reason for their seeking amrit, the devas sought help from the rakshasas to undertake the task. They promised the rakshasas that the fruits of the churning process would be shared equally between them. But when the time came, Vishnu played a dirty trick and gave the amrit to the devas, leaving the rakshasas with nothing. The double-dealing cheat!' Dashagreeva spoke spiritedly.

'Yes. If the rakshasas had received their fair share of amrit, they would not have been hounded to the netherworlds. They would have been on par with the devas and then justice could have prevailed. But as things stand now, the rakshasas must secure divine grace in order to gain the same immortality that devas have by virtue of consuming amrit,' Kumbhakarna spoke dreamily.

'We cannot ignore the fact that there were certain preconditions that both sides had to adhere to,' Vibheeshana's voice was calm and firm. 'It was Vishnu who proposed that the devas and rakshasas should pool their strengths to churn the ocean and laid down that whatever emerged through the churning, should be shared equally by the two sides. The only condition he set out was that both sides should perform the task with unstinting effort and complete dedication. The devas followed this rule honestly and even though they were physically inferior to the rakshasas, they put their heart and soul into the churning. The rakshasas, on the other hand, were so confident of their physical ability to complete the task that they busied themselves with thinking up ways of how they could steal the amrit when it emerged.

'As it happened, it was haalahal vish—poison—that emerged first. The rakshasas refused to accept it and it was Shiva, on behalf of the devas, who consumed the deadly poison.

'And when amrit finally emerged in the hands of Dhanvantari, the rakshasas snatched it and ran away with it, intending to deny the devas their share. Vishnu intervened only when there were squabbles in the rakshasa ranks over who should get the first sip of amrit. Reason would not have worked with them, so Vishnu took on the guise of a pretty damsel, Mohini, and had the pot of nectar given into his hands.

'Also, do not forget that Vishnu played an important role in the churning process itself. He did not participate just to favour the devas. He became a turtle and held Mount Mandara up to ensure the successful completion of the churning process. Before he intervened, Mandara was unable to take the pressure of the churning and was therefore sinking,' Vibheeshana concluded like a man resting his argument in a legal battle.

Kumbhakarna was impressed by his younger brother's poise and wisdom. The ninety years of austerities had honed his mind and had made him lose his sense of awe for his two elder brothers. Now he spoke and behaved like an equal, which he truly was, he thought. Kumbhakarna shot a sidelong glance at Dashamukha to glean his reaction to Vibheeshana's arguments in support of Vishnu and was disappointed to see the stony look on his brother's face. He decided to further probe their younger brother's thoughts in the hope that bhrata would appreciate Vibheeshana's mental maturity, even if he did not agree with his views. 'Does that mean that you do not agree that rakshasas were wronged when they were denied amrit?'

'Right and wrong are relative terms and are subjective perceptions rather than objective standards, bhrata. Look at the impact of this development. Amrit ensued from the ocean of milk and the devas, who received it have become immortal. What next? What do they have to strive for? For, it is fear of death that drives the world. Once that fear is removed, there is no purpose to life itself. Rakshasas, on the other hand, have found a cause to fight for—do you have a count of the rakshasas who have undertaken intense tapasya to overcome this perceived injustice?

'In this context, I must admit that there is one aspect about us that perplexes me. We identify ourselves as "rakshasas", particularly since janani disclosed our ancestry. How do we qualify as rakshasas? What part of us is "rakshasa"? Our great-grandfather Sukesha was born to a rakshasa couple. He married a gandharva kanya and had three sons—our grandfather and his two brothers. Thus, they were half rakshasa and half gandharva. All three brothers once again chose gandharva kanyas as wives. The rakshasa blood in their children was thus further diluted. Our own mother has married a manava—a Brahmin. So do we, children born out of this marriage, qualify as rakshasas at all? What percentage of our blood is rakshasa blood?

'But we carry this hatred towards Vishnu as the one responsible for denying rakshasas their due. And, what is the objective we seek to achieve through tapasya? It is the same as has driven scores of other rakshasas: secure immortality with blessings from the same gods that we say have tricked us,' Vibheeshana shrugged his incomprehension and fell silent.

Kumbhakarna's admiration for his younger brother grew by leaps and bounds. He had never credited his meek-looking and soft-mannered brother with such profundity. Once again he glanced at Dashagreeva to gauge his reaction. He sat like a stone, showing no sign that he had even heard what was being said.

Kumbhakarna decided to pose another question to Vibheeshana, but this time he sought to clear his own thinking rather than influence Dashamukha's thinking. 'You obviously think that our tapasya is wrong. Is that the reason why we are unable to achieve our objective despite such rigorous practice of austerities?'

Vibheeshana turned to face Kumbhakarna. 'No bhrata, tapasya in itself is not wrong. What we seek to do with that power decides its merits and demerits. Have you not observed our pitru shree conduct austerities on a daily basis? That is also tapasya. He has powers that we have no idea about. He neither flaunts them nor uses them to achieve worldly objectives. His tapasya makes him wise; helps him achieve enlightenment on life itself; therefore that power goes to improve the world and make it a better place to live in. Tapasya that is used to the detriment of any other being or nature is destructive, and so can only have negative fallouts.'

'Tell me just one more thing, Vibhee. How would you rate Brahma, Vishnu and Shiva? Who is partial to whom and whom does each of them consider his enemies?' Kumbhakarna asked.

'We will fall into a trap and tie ourselves up in knots if we hold these three as three different entities. They are one and the same. Their distinction lies in the different aspects they signify. Consider this, bhrata—we see Brahma sitting in a lotus that arises out of Vishnu's navel. So, logically, Brahma is Vishnu's son. Or, you could say that Vishnu is Brahma's father. But who is it that gives birth—mother or father? That is, Vishnu is not Brahma's father, but mother. So what would you say is Vishnu's gender—male or female? See! There is not even a gender distinction. It is the same god that creates, nurtures and demolishes. Depending upon the function being performed, god is known by a different name.'

'Will you both stop talking nonsense and get some sleep? We have to rise early and begin the last stage of our tapasya. The outcome will depend solely on our commitment and concentration. So I suggest that you calm your minds for easy repose,' the eldest brother's curt words put a stop to the conversation, which Kumbhakarna had enjoyed immensely. He marvelled at this hidden aspect of his younger brother and appreciated the deep wisdom in his words. His single thought as he stretched out flat on his back on the hard rock was that he should never be called upon to choose between dharma and filial loyalty. He knew that family loyalty would always rank first in his consideration, whatever the situation may be.

chapter 13

Brahma yawned. He yawned with his four mouths in his four heads. He did not try to stifle it. He did not even put a hand across his mouth to cover it—a mark of politeness when in company. And, he was in company—extremely august company, in fact. Seated in front of him was an array of maharshis, the who's who of erudite personalities. Each of these maharshis was accompanied by the best of his disciples.

Saraswati, seated next to Brahma, gave him a reproachful look. She clearly did not approve of his rudeness and impropriety when serious matters were being discussed in this great hall of learning. Brahma responded, but not with any sign of contrition. He let her know that, without prejudice to what was being presented at the sabha, he had other work to do and these deliberations could be continued at another meeting on another day. Saraswati could appreciate her husband's situation. The sabha had indeed dragged. Brahma had been leaving for an important undertaking on earth when all the rishis had arrived together, seeking to present their individual findings on various subjects. That had been quite some time ago and a variety of subjects had been discussed—from vyakaran, or grammer, to paak-shastra, the science of cooking. Just as one rishi concluded his presentation, another would rise and launch into his own pet subject, without even waiting for the customary permission from the chair.

It had been quite some time since Brahma had paid attention to the proceedings before him. His mind had been travelling increasingly to the three brothers who had been conducting a ghoretapasya on earth for a very long time. They were his own grandsons, being the offspring of his manasaputras. However, since the boys had a rakshasa lineage, and more importantly a rakshasa mindset, he had tested their patience and commitment for a long time. He was satisfied with their conduct and had decided to grant them boons. That had been about ten years ago in terms of time on earth, and the eldest brother had just made an offering of his ninth head. It was just as Brahma was getting ready to make the descent to earth that this large gathering of rishis had come calling. As behoves a gracious host, Brahma had remained to attend to his guests.

Had it been just one visitor, Brahma would have attended to the basics of hospitality like offering arghyam—water to drink—and padyam—water to wash one's feet—and then sought permission to attend to urgent work that required his presence. But standing at his doorstep were luminaries such as Panini, who had developed Sanskrit grammar; Varahamihira, the master at khagola shastra, or astronomy; Bhaskara Acharya, the mastermind of ganit, or mathematics; Bharata, the pioneer of natya shastra, ordance; Patanjali, who had given knowledge of yoga; and Dhanvantari, renowned for his work on health and healing. As if they were not enough, scores of each rishi's disciples stood reverentially behind their gurus. Exchanging basic pleasantries itself would take quite some time and clearly there was some matter that concerned them all equally. If he left without dealing with their concerns, he would earn the ire of these worthies and upset many others, including his consort, Saraswati.

However, once the rishis were comfortably seated and Brahma occupied his aasan, the congregation began singing praises of Brahma. Brahma endured it impatiently, hoping that they would disclose the purpose of their visit quickly. He was, nevertheless, happy to note that Saraswati seemed duly impressed by the superlatives being heaped on him and encouraged the rishis to speak without constraints.

That did it. Each rishi launched into a detailed presentation on the different aspects of his recent work and urged his disciples to demonstrate the points made by him. All of which was extremely time consuming.

It was while Brahma was thus occupied that Dashagreeva had severed his ninth head—his hand showing the practice at this task gained from the eight earlier occasions. Even as he was physically with the rishis, Brahma mentally noted the equanimity that prevailed at Meru shikhar. There was no rancour, no regret and no disappointment that their tapasya had thus far failed to produce the desired result. Brahma's mental eye also gleaned that the three brothers had commenced their next, and final, phase of austerities.

Brahma looked around. While he had been preoccupied with his thoughts of the three mortals seeking his blessings, the subject under discussion had changed. Brahma could not believe his ears. The man at the podium—he had missed his name—was pontificating on the nuances of the culinary art. He was arguing that cooking should be elevated to the status of a science, as it would be an injustice to treat it as just an art.

This was the limit. Did they have nothing else to talk about? And since all this oratory was keeping him from what he considered his bounden duty towards his bhaktas, Brahma wondered how he could put an end to the deliberations without ruffling too many feathers. He looked around and caught the eye of his favourite manasaputra, Narada. Narada quickly turned his gaze away, and in that instant it became clear to Brahma that the rishis were acting on a gameplan. The aim of the plan was, of course, to prevent him from appearing before Vishravasu's sons and granting them any boons.

He would not let them succeed, Brahma decided. For, the tapasya by the brothers had been at its most intense during this past decade. They had not broken their tapasya for food, rest or even air. They had been standing on one foot with their hands raised over their heads in complete supplication, their breath held within in a 'kumbhak'. It would not be long before the eldest brother sacrificed his tenth head. Since this was his last head, sacrificing it would mean certain death for him. He could not let that happen. He must intervene and intervene now, before it was too late.

Brahma stood up and cleared his throat, seeking and securing the attention of the congregation. 'Revered scholars, as much as I am enjoying this exchange of ideas—and I compliment you all for the progress you have achieved in promoting knowledge—I suggest that we continue with these enlightening and enjoyable interactions on another day.' Brahma was prevented from speaking further by the clamour of numerous voices. Several maharshis had leapt to their feet, all talking at the same time.

Naarada, who was also on his feet, held up his hand and gradually, order was restored. The triloka-sanchari folded his hands and said: 'Prabhu, we all know that you wish to reveal yourself to the Vishravasukumaras and reward them for their tapasya by granting them boons. We seek your indulgence in listening to our submissions in this regard. We agree that the three brothers richly deserve their due for their austerities over all these years and we cannot urge you to ignore their claims. However, there is a strong streak of cruelty in them. Their rakshasa pravrutti will receive a great boost with any boons from you and we fear that they will unleash a reign of terror and violence against peace-loving citizens. Life for mortals would become unbearable under such circumstances.'

'Naarada.' Brahma's tone was dangerously soft. 'Are you telling me what I should and should not do with my own bhaktas?' Without waiting for a response from the sage, Brahma turned and left.

Pandemonium broke the moment Brahma stormed out of the hall. Caught by surprise by the unexpected turn of events, Saraswati quickly took control of the situation. She cast her gaze around the room and all chatter died down as if a magic wand had been waved. 'Please share your concerns and also frankly state what you wish done,' her gentle voice, which was like a thousand veenas making music at the same time, laid the ground for a cogent presentation of what the maharshis wanted.

'Devi, these are rakshasas whose aim in undertaking this tapasya is to gain immortality and take over the three worlds. They want to dethrone Indra, humiliate Vishnu and install rakshasarajya in the Deva-loka. Should this happen, there will be no room left for hermits like us to live. Pralay would be a better option than having these brothers running amok in the world,' the sages said in unison and pleaded for her intervention to prevent the Lord of Satya-loka from granting these boons.

'I understand and appreciate your fears and apprehensions. I also agree that your fears are not unfounded. At the same time, you are all learned persons, and know that no one can stand between a deva and his bhaktas. Therefore, intervention from anyone, including me, is out of the question,' Saraswati's lilting voice failed to blunt the import of her words.

'This means that we have no option but to prepare ourselves for early deliverance through death. Since atmahatya—suicide—is a sin, we have to pray for early death through starvation,' said a muni as he urged those around him to follow him on this mission to seek death.

'Maate, we agree that Brahma cannot be prevented from granting the boons sought of him by his bhaktas. But maate, you underestimate your own powers. If you so desire, is it not possible that what is sought of the deva is something mild and less dangerous?'

Naarada's appeal to the devi's maternal instincts had the desired effect. It touched a chord in Saraswati and she promised to exert herself to influence the tapasvis.

chapter 14

*T*he three men were sitting in stony silence. They looked gaunt. Long years of severe austerities had converted these once-robust men into mere skeletons. Besides the tattered loincloths they wore, the men's bodies were covered with mud caked with sweat. Yet, their faces radiated a glow, which came from a power that was beyond the physical. However, the expression on each of the faces of the three men was at variance with the glow of tapasya. There were unmistakable shadows of defeat on their faces. Their shoulders drooped with a sense of resignation. Their tapasya had been in vain. No god had appeared to fulfil their desires.

This failure had serious implications for the three brothers. For, this was the final phase of their tapasya. The option of continuing with their austerities—till their chosen god, Brahma, revealed himself to them—had been foreclosed by the fact that Dashagreeva would have no further heads to sacrifice in the manner he had done for nine decades. They had completed the tenth decade of tapasya, and, as per the ritual they had established at the end of the first decade of tapasya, Dashamukha would make an offering of his head in the yagna-kund. This time, the customary sacrifice would claim his tenth head. Since he would then have no more heads, the act would end his life. It was this frightening prospect that occupied their thoughts. Dashamukha's two younger brothers knew that it was futile to try and talk him out of his pledge of honour.

Dashagreeva, the object of this worrisome situation, seemed impervious to the agitation raging in his brothers' minds. His gaze was fixed on the horizon as he contemplated his options and tried to come to terms with his failure. He had never failed. In fact, he had earned much praise from his father and other gurus for his quick comprehension and powers of concentration and recall. No; he had not failed; his tapasya had not failed. He knew that instinctively. In fact, he had felt a presence around him on more than one occasion during these last few years of tapasya. The presence—it could only be Brahma, the object of his veneration—melted away each time, as if snatched away by a stronger force. Could it be that there was someone somewhere who did not want his tapasya to reach its logical conclusion?

A sudden movement broke his chain of thought and Dashagreeva darted a glance towards his brothers. Kumbhakarna had risen and had begun pacing furiously, his agitation evident in every muscle of his body. Dashagreeva refused to take the bait and begin the discussion that his dear younger brother wanted. What was there to discuss? He would go ahead and fulfil the commitment he had made to himself. Death did not daunt him. He knew that he would take birth once again, if only to deliver on the promise he had made to his mother to place Lanka at her command. Even so, a twinge of sadness plucked at his heart as he looked at Kumbhakarna, a truly devoted brother. What would he do after his death, Dashamukha mused. Would he continue with the tapasya they had initiated together? Would more time enable him to achieve what they had set out to achieve? A wry smile twisted his features as he recalled his childhood days when he had been mocked for his ten heads and how he had wished that he were like the others, with just one head. Now he wished he had more heads so that he could continue chopping off one head after the other till Brahma appeared and granted him boons.

Kumbhakarna stamped his foot hard in frustration as he noticed the smile on his brother's face. His rage broke new ground when Dashagreeva refused to acknowledge his presence, leave alone his feelings. He was a fool. He should have persuaded his brother not to undertake this tapasya. What had they achieved in these hundred years? Nothing! And now he was faced with the prospect of losing his elder brother; a brother who was his leader, his inspiration and alterego. What would he do without him? Life was unthinkable without Dashagreeva by his side. Maybe he should follow in his brother's footsteps and give up his life as well. But atmahatya was a sin and he—Dashagreeva's brother and son of Vishravasu—could not commit this cowardly act. Nor could he return home with nothing to show for this century of intense tapasya. Even if he was ready to deal with the resultant humiliation and loss of face, how could he justify the loss of the towering personality of his elder brother? Would he have words enough to console janani or answer pita shree?

Kumbhakarna stopped mid-step and gaped at his younger brother who had begun preparing the yagna-kund. What was the matter with him? Instead of pleading with their eldest brother to give up his intended sacrifice, he was setting the stage for exactly that! Then his expression softened and he patted Vibheeshana on the shoulder before sitting down by his side. He realized that Vibhee was as concerned as he was at the prospect of what bhrata was going to do and that he was merely trying to distract himself from his agonizing thoughts.

The two brothers exchanged a look and the same thought flashed through their minds. They were remembering the numerous jokes they had shared on similar occasions in the past. After the first time Dashagreeva had severed his head and pledged to do the same once every ten years till the objective of their tapasya was achieved, they had prepared for each yagna in a very matter-of-fact manner, secure in the knowledge that another head would appear on their bhrata's shoulders. Each time there was an air of anticipation—anticipation that Brahma would come and stop them with kind words and grant them boons and soon they would start their journey home. They would wonder if pita shree would modify bhrata's name, now that he did not have ten heads, and how names like 'Ashtagreeva', 'Saptagreeva' and so on would sound. On one occasion, they had even debated the legality of name-change during a person's lifetime. Another interesting discussion they had had was when Dashagreeva, after severing his penultimate head, had declared that he was now 'Ekagreeva', as he had just one head like everyone else. Ekagreeva could not be a name since everyone was similarly endowed, they had said and laughed. Oh! How they had laughed with not a care about what was in store for them. Dashagreeva had always been part of these fun-filled conversations, deriving great pleasure in suggesting alternate names for his younger brothers. He specially targeted Kumbhakarna, saying he too should change his name since his pot-like ears had been modified. He had once examined Kumbhakarna's ears closely to come up with apt names and they had all roared with laughter when he proposed 'Pipeelikarna'—an allusion to the pointed tips of Kumbhakarna's ears, which resembled the leaves of the peepal tree.

The two brothers were jolted back to reality when Dashagreeva rose to his feet and walked purposefully in their direction. 'Come on, boys! We have wasted enough time. Let us perform the yagna,' he said, holding out his two hands to help them up. Dashagreeva had to use all his strength to pull up his two unwilling and resisting brothers. He smiled affectionately at them and put an arm around each brother's shoulders and drew them close. 'I am a very lucky man, you know, to have such loving brothers. I want you to promise me that you will not give up this tapasya after me. Can you not feel that we are very very close to achieving our goal? Do not forget that janani is waiting for us to return with success firmly in our grip. We cannot disappoint her. She should have the satisfaction of having achieved her life's ambition,' Dashakantha spoke encouragingly as he guided his brothers towards the yagna-kund. 'Kumbha, invite agni in all its glory, and Vibhee, let your voice not falter as you chant the mantras today,' he directed as he busied himself with arranging twigs in the yagna-kund.

Then it happened. Sparks were flying from the yoga-agni as Vibheeshana chanted vedic mantras and Kumbhakarna supplied the necessary offerings. Dashagreeva rose, sword in hand and positioned himself such as to ensure that his severed head would fall directly into the middle of the yagna-kund. Suddenly there was an electrifying spark that was brighter than the mid-afternoon sun in the sky and hotter than the agni blazing in the yagna-kund. But the voice that emanated from that haze was as soft and soothing as the sea breeze. An icy cold wind passed right through their bodies and the three brothers felt dizzy and blinded. They could feel only the blazing being in front of them. Instinct and reflexes took over and immediately the two elder brothers flanked the youngest brother protectively.

'Do not be frightened, vatsa!' The sound was like a lullaby, reassuring, and a wakeful sleep weighed heavily on their eyelids. 'I am pleased with your tapasya. What desire made you embark on such severe austerities? Just say it, and it shall be yours,' the apparition spoke in the same lilting, murmuring voice.

Dashagreeva was the first one to regain his composure. He prostrated himself before the ethereal being, fingers interlocked and hands outstretched, almost touching the feet of his saviour. 'I am truly blessed, pitamaha, now that you are pleased with my austerities and have come to grant me boons. I seek amaratva, immortality,' he said.

'That is not possible, vatsa! Every being born on this earth has to perish. So, I suggest that you choose the specific way and means of your end. Or, you can stipulate how you do not want to die,' Brahma said, his tone brimming with compassion.

Dashagreeva felt defeated. But it was momentary. For a fraction of a second, he also lamented the loss of his nine other heads, which would have enabled him to find a way out without any loss of time. He shook his head, made an elaborate event of rising to his feet, using the time to focus on the matter at hand. By the time he stood up and shook the dust off his body, he knew what to say. 'In that event, Prabhu I appeal to you to make me invincible against devas, danavas, yakshas, kinneras, kimpurushas, gandharvas, nagas and wild beasts. Men and other animals are so weak that I do not have to seek a boon from you for protection against them.'

'Tathastu!' decreed Brahma and added: 'I commend your dedication and devotion to duty. You shall have your nine severed heads back. Go and live in peace and without fear.'

Dashagreeva stepped back with profuse words of thanks and Brahma turned to Vibheeshana, who seemed to be lost in a trance. 'What do you desire, little one?' Brahma asked kindly.

'Oh! Great one! That you made yourself visible to me is boon enough for me.'

Brahma smiled. 'What did you seek to achieve through your tapasya? Speak your mind without fear. I am pleased with your sincere prayers and want to grant you a boon.'

'If it would please you, I beseech that I be given the strength of character to stand for dharma at all times and under all circumstances, irrespective of consequences,' Vibheeshana said with folded hands. He bent his head in reverence.

'Tathastu!' said Brahma and turned to the last brother in the line. 'What do you seek, bhakta?'

Kumbhakarna was suddenly confused. Vibheeshana's words, seeking adherence to dharma when he should have been asking for something to help realize their mother's ambition, had irritated him. He also failed to fully appreciate his elder brother's wish for invincibility. Though helpful in wars, strength alone might not be adequate to retrieve Lanka for janani. They would need position and power in addition, and that would please janani even more. He knew that their mother liked their half-brother Kuber largely because of the power he wielded over devas on account of his position. If the treasurer of the devas had so much power, then the king of the devas—Indra—would have even more power and that is what he would secure for himself. 'Please grant me "Indratva",' he set out to say only to get unaccountably tongue-tied even as he began to speak. So much so that he faltered a little on the last word, and it came out as 'nindratva'.

Even before Brahma's bemused 'tathastu' was completely out, Kumbhakarna slapped a hand to his mouth, looked wildly at Dashagreeva's shell-shocked face and Vibheeshana's stony look of incomprehension and, waving his hands in denial, shouted 'NO!'

Complete silence ensued. Only Brahma shook his head—a movement that was lost on all but Kumbhakarna. 'Prabhu, nindra is definitely not what I wanted to seek from you. In fact, why would anyone seek sleep as reward for a hundred years of tapasya? Please, give me another chance to articulate my desire.'

'There is no second chance, putra. What you asked for is what you got. You will spend your life sleeping. Even I cannot rescind that,' Brahma shook his head once more. He looked at the forlorn face before him and then added: 'I appreciate your predicament, vatsa. I will modify this boon to provide you with some respite. You will awaken once every six months, and stay awake for the whole day. What you eat and drink on that one single day will keep you well-nourished for the next six months of your sleep cycle. Your body and muscles will not wither away during the time you sleep. More importantly, every waking will be like arising from normal sleep; you will know all developments as if you were there. On the day that you are awake, you will be invincible. Nothing and no one will be able to harm you. Conversely, if you are awakened forcefully during your sleep phase, you will meet your end. And lastly, the boon will remain in abeyance till you reach home,' Brahma said and before anyone could react, he was gone, as if he were never there.

chapter 15

*T*he three brothers had hardly exchanged a word since their encounter with Brahma. It had been almost a month since that fateful day. Their tapasya had borne fruit; Brahma had appeared and granted them boons. But it had brought neither joy nor a sense of achievement to Vishravasu's sons who had invested a hundred years in pursuing this objective. Their brush with divinity had proved to be an anticlimax, where the successful completion of their austerities had yielded results, but these results did not pave the way for the furtherance of their ultimate goal. They felt cheated out of their just desserts. They sat around the yagna-kund feeling numb and paralysed. The leaping flames seemed to mock them.

Dashagreeva roused himself from this inertia long after the fire in the yagna-kund had died down. His brothers looked at him with glassy eyes but took his extended hands to pull themselves up. While none spoke, they fell in line behind the eldest one and began their silent trek back home. Only Kumbhakarna, who was the rearguard, looked back at the row of ten stone-cold yagna-kunds they had set up during the years of their tapasya. Anger and frustration returned and he stamped his foot hard before following his brothers. One step followed the other mechanically and Kumbhakarna was painfully aware that every step was taking him closer to six months of non-stop sleep. He was determined to delay that moment for as long as possible and swore that he would not close his eyes till the inevitable happened.

It was as if Dashagreeva had read his thoughts. He did not break his step even once and the trio walked on without pausing for rest. It did not occur to them to wonder why they did not feel tired, even though they walked for several weeks. And such was their preoccupation with their individual worlds of contemplation that none of them noticed that their gaunt bodies had miraculously reverted to their pre-tapasya forms, even though they had neither eaten nor rested since the beginning of this journey.

Early one morning, Dashagreeva suddenly stepped off the main path and led his brothers into a shady clearing. He sat down on the thick carpet of grass under a banyan tree and motioned the others to sit as well. 'We will reach Rishi-teertham by nightfall. We all know that we have to fulfil the promise we made to janani before setting out, and for that we need to plan our course of action,' he said and looked at the others, who merely nodded.

'We have to consider how best to utilize the boons we have received from Brahma,' Dashagreeva said, omitting any honorary prefix to the Creator's name. The mention of 'boons' sent Kumbhakarna into a rage. He jumped up, his face contorted by a mixture of quickly changing emotions. He waved his hands in agitation and paced up and down and shouted: 'It was a trick—a trick played by this same fellow who pretended to give us boons. He knew what I was going to ask for. He did not want to give me that. So the wily old man confused me...and now my life is over. Completely over. I am as good as dead,' he was close to tears.

'Sit down!' Dashagreeva commanded him, but there was compassion in his voice. Kumbhakarna obeyed, but remained sullen. 'It was a trick, but I do not think Brahma played it on us. He seemed as surprised as any of us when you asked for nindra. It was somebody else, who was possibly acting on orders from quite another quarter,' Dashagreeva said, indicating that he had spent considerable time pondering over this issue.

'What difference does that make? Is that any consolation? Nothing changes the fact that I will fall asleep the moment we enter Rishi-teertham,' Kumbhakarna buried his head between his knees in desolation.

'No, Kumbha! Do not despair,' Dashagreeva wrapped a comforting arm around his younger brother. 'When Brahma was laying down the conditions for his boon to take effect, I mentally stressed the point that our "home" is Lanka—not Rishi-teertham. Brahma conceded this point, I could see it from the look in his eyes. So you will remain awake till we secure Lanka for ourselves. And look at the bright side—you have defeated death. For, you are invincible on the day you are awake and no harm can come to you while you sleep. I promise to take care of this aspect,' he patted the younger one's shoulder, lifted his chin up and smiled reassuringly.

Vibheeshana gestured as if he wanted to say something, but thought the better of it and remained silent.

'This means that the onus of establishing our supremacy over this world lies largely on my shoulders,' Dashagreeva continued. It was clear that he had been thinking on this aspect also and that he was not wholly unhappy with the prospect. 'I am glad that I was able to secure invincibility for myself. I will need to groom an army that will lead us to victory after victory. Our conscientious dharma-keeper can join in whenever he thinks our cause is justified,' he threw a disparaging glance at Vibheeshana, who, once again, kept his counsel and did not respond.

'And now, the immediate task on our hands. I am sure you will agree that we do not have to disclose the details of our interaction with Brahma to anyone at Rishi-teertham. Anyway, we do not have to stay there for long. Ah! The very thought is exhilarating! We are adults who can do what we please, without having to seek parental consent,' Dashagreeva's thoughts focused on the future with great anticipation.

Vibheeshana looked sceptical and Kumbhakarna was clearly unconvinced. Life held no promise or charm for him.

Once again, it was the eldest brother who pulled the younger ones to their feet so they could begin the last leg of their journey. This time, however, there was a spring in Dashagreeva's step and a song on his lips.

He was ahead of his brothers by a significant distance and as he took the final turn in the path near the gates of Rishi-teertham, he came face-to-face with Kuber, who was leaving the ashram, obviously after meeting his parents.

'Ah! Kuber! The very person I wanted to see!' The effusive greeting came as a pleasant surprise to Kuber, who was used to curtness bordering on insolence from Dashagreeva. 'Henceforth, I want to live in Lanka,' Kaikasi's son declared.

'You are most welcome, my brother,' Kuber responded and added that he would enjoy having his family members sharing his home.

'You misunderstand me. I said I want to live in Lanka, but it would not be in the capacity of your guest. I want it as my home,' Dashagreeva said, stressing the 'my'.

Kuber was left in no doubt about his half-brother's intentions. 'You have only just returned home. We will talk this over tomorrow,' he said and hurried away, without giving a chance for further conversation.

'You pot-bellied bull!' Dashagreeva shouted after the retreating figure. 'Watch out, your monetary power has gone to your tummy,' he guffawed, elated by Kuber's discomfiture.

His two younger brothers had caught up with him by then and they caught a glimpse of the retreating figure in the gathering dusk. Even before they could quiz Dashagreeva about the cause of his mirth, they heard a voice call out: 'Who is there?' The person who had made the enquiry appeared soon thereafter and the three brothers rushed towards her. 'Janani!' they called out in unison.

Kaikasi was overjoyed to see her three sons, and it pleased her to note that they all looked just the same as they had when they set out for tapasya. It was a happy reunion and they all walked back into the ashram, talking excitedly. In fact, most of the conversation took place between Kaikasi and Dashagreeva, with the other two following them at a little distance. So happy was the mother to see her three sons after so long that she did not notice the near silence from the younger ones. 'I have great news for you, janani,' declared Dashagreeva before announcing dramatically: 'Prepare to undertake a journey to our homeland! I have secured the powers needed to make this possible.'

Kaikasi slumped and would have fallen had her son not caught her arm. He led her to the nearest stone bench and made her sit down and waited for her to speak. He could see that this was momentous news for her and that she needed a little time to digest it. On her part, Kaikasi could not believe her ears. She had waited so long for this day. It was the fulfilment of a promise she had made to her father and it was the reason why she was here at Rishi-teertham. But it was not unalloyed joy for her, because this was as much her home as Lanka had once been. She felt she belonged here; she had associations and memories here; she had genuine affection for Vishravasu, Devaparni and Vaishravana, which was amply reciprocated. She had even come to look upon Lanka as the abode of her stepson Vaishravana, her own days there having become a blurred memory.

Concern was mounting in the three brothers as their mother remained silent. Kumbhakarna had positioned himself on one side of her and Vibheeshana sat at her feet, looking earnestly into her face. Upon hearing the sound of approaching footsteps, they turned their attention up the path and stood up to greet their father. That he was accompanied by Kuber surprised Dashagreeva particularly, as he had seen his half-brother leave the ashram. Obviously, he had returned through a side gate to apprise his father about his meeting with Dashagreeva.

Dashagreeva's suspicion proved right. For, soon after the customary enquiries and pleasantries from both sides, Vishravasu addressed his wife. 'Kaikasi, I have made certain decisions, and I want to state them in the presence of all our sons. Please listen carefully and trust that I have taken these decisions for the best. Now that Dashagreeva has come of age, I want him to take care of you—his mother—and his siblings. Lanka will be your new home. Kuber will move to a new home, for which purpose he will consult Indra and Viswakarma. Devaparni, my dharmapatni, will choose where she wants to live—here or with her son in his new abode.'

Having said what he wanted to, the maharshi turned and walked away. Kuber bent and touched Kaikasi's feet in salutation. Turning to Dashagreeva, he said: 'I shall make just one last visit to Lanka tomorrow. I need to inform my subjects that Lanka will henceforth be ruled by you. They can then decide for themselves whether they want to continue to live in Lanka or make their home elsewhere.' Then, he too turned and walked away, without a backward glance.

Kaikasi sat like a rock. The fast-paced developments of the last few minutes had stunned her. Vishravasu and Vaishravana had seemed as strangers and not the loving husband and son that they had been all these years. In fact, during the past so many years, when her own sons had been away from home, she had come to love Vaishravana like her own son. He had reciprocated the affection and every time he came to Rishi-teertham, he would spend several hours with her. Now, all of a sudden, that bond had broken, dashing her hopes of similar bonds developing between him and his three half-brothers.

Kumbhakarna had begun to doze. He was not sure whether it was the fatigue of the past few weeks of continuous walking or if it was his boon, which was actually a curse, taking effect.

He felt muddled and could not understand what was happening around him. He had barely recognized his father and for the life of him, he could not identify the person who had accompanied him. And it hurt in the deepest parts of his heart that his dear bhrata had changed. He felt the difference acutely and wanted to tell him not to lose his sense of balance while dealing with his new self. The power of his boon had made him imperious and the only person who understood him inside out and could forewarn him or prevent wrong actions was now going to spend his life sleeping. Kumbhakarna wished that the righteous Vibheeshana would respect filial bonds and guide their elder brother on the path of virtue. Oh, it was becoming increasingly difficult to even think cogently. What could he do to stay awake and have one heart-to-heart conversation with bhrata? He tried to focus, and pulling all his senses together, he called: 'Bhrata!'

The single word sounded as if it was the mewing of a kitten that had fallen into the dark depths of a well. Kumbhakarna despaired that none could have possibly heard him and he had no energy left to call again. But no, he was wrong. His elder brother was already by his side, cradling his drooping body in his arms and exhorting him to stand up and focus on reaching home. 'We are not home yet, Kumbha. Just take a few steps and stand outside the gates of Rishi-teertham. Come, I will help you. Sitting down here is having this effect on you,' he said and carefully led him out. Their mother watched helplessly.

Dashagreeva was seething with rage. He did not relish the manner in which he had come into charge of Lanka. He wanted a fight between himself and Kuber—a war between true warriors. But that wimp had to go and give his sob story to their father and get him to intervene. While he had no expectations of Vibheeshana on account of his misplaced regard for 'values', he had lost Kumbha to sleep. Kumbha was the ideal younger brother, who always obeyed him unquestioningly. But things had turned out this way for a reason. He would make a reputation for himself as the most powerful person in the world. No, not this world alone, but in all three worlds!

By now he had reached the threshold of Rishi-teertham and Kumbha was in better control of himself. Clarity regarding two things came to Dashamukha. One, despite what he thought Brahma had conceded about their 'real home', Rishi-teertham was their home till their father decreed otherwise. Two, the effect of Kumbha's boon, once it came into play—which it did when they entered Rishi-teertham—would endure irrespective of where Kumbha was. Thus, he knew that he could not risk spending the night at the ashram because of its effect on Kumbha. He would have to make his way to Lanka at the earliest. He said as much to Kumbha, and returned to fetch his mother and younger brother.

Dashagreeva's journey continued.

chapter 16

A gentle breeze was blowing, taking Dashagreeva into blissful self-contentment. He looked down and what he saw gave him such pleasure that a smile spread across his face and he preened his luxurious and upturned moustache. He was jolted back to reality by a soft thud—the craft in which he was making an aerial survey had stalled; it needed specific instructions as to its destination. This was irritating, as he liked to ride in it aimlessly once in a while, just to enjoy the feeling of power it gave him. It was sheer providence that had enabled him to retain the 'Pushpak'. Kuber was taking off in this magical craft, claiming it as his own. But Dashagreeva's intervention had prevented that. Once again he touched his moustache with considerable pride. He gave strict mental instructions that Pushpak should keep circling Lanka at an easy pace till further instructions and looked at his city with a keen and roving eye.

He remembered going over the craftsmanship and powers of Pushpak with Vibhee and pitamaha Sumali. Brahma had given the sky-craft Pushpak to Kuber when he had appointed the latter as the dikpala of the north and had given him control over the devas' assets. It was intended to give Kuber the power of movement to equal the speed of the sun. It was completely mind-controlled and took orders from only those whom it considered its 'masters'. It could carry any number of people at a time and had the capacity to expand adequately to accommodate all its passengers. Even its speed could be set by mental instruction.

While appreciating the power of Pushpak and the power it in turn provided him with, Dashagreeva also mentally complimented the architectural skills of Vishwakarma, which had provided the high level of security in Lanka. While Kuber, Lanka's last resident ruler, had somewhat neglected its security aspects, Dashagreeva had set things right on this score soon after moving to Lanka. In fact, he had increased its protection manifold, he thought as he reviewed Lanka's security arrangements. The city-state had four protective rings. The outermost was the sea. The second ring was constituted by the Mount Trikoota range. The third ring comprised of dense forests inhabited by wild beasts. The last ring was a wall that circled the city and was made of gold, and had embellishments of precious gems. The wall and the stones upon it glinted in the sun in such a manner as to make it impossible for an intruder to even look at it for any length of time. In addition to these rings, there was a deep moat along the inner border of the golden wall. Alligators, sharks and killer fish abounded in the cold waters of the moat. So ferocious were these aquatic animals that even ships could not enter these waters. The only way anyone could gain entry was via drop bridges. These drop bridges were manned round the clock and records kept of the traffic that crossed them.

There were four drop bridges, one in each of the four cardinal directions. The main entry was from the north, where, behind the drop bridge was a door that was several feet thick, secured by huge logs. Atop the boundary wall near the four gates were catapults ready to repel any attempted intrusion. Security was a very high priority with Dashagreeva, given the fact that he had gone to war with every ruling clan on Jambudweepa. And it had taken him a lot of time and energy to put these arrangements in place.

Dashamukha recalled that he had inherited a deserted city, nearly all of its citizens having left with Kuber. It had taken considerable effort to attract people to come make their homes in Lanka. After each of his conquests, he would offer comfortable living to anyone willing to make Lanka their home. It had worked, with able help from his pitamaha, Sumali, who had arrived in Lanka shortly after Dashagreeva himself had reached it with his immediate family. In fact, Surpanakha had almost been forgotten in the high drama that had launched their journey to Lanka. Dashagreeva had been helping Kumbhakarna along and Vibheeshana had been with Kaikasi. It had taken him a while to realize that Kumbha was trying to say something. His speech was slurred, but Dashagreeva had made out 'Surpi' in his brother's mumblings. He had been amazed at Kumbha's presence of mind despite his sleepy physical state and had immediately sent Vibhee to bring their only sister along.

And, once they set foot in Lanka, Sumali had arrived. His joy at returning to Lanka was beyond words and had given him the strength to make repeated trips to Naga-loka to bring back the rest of his family. The only ones who chose to remain in Naga-loka were Malyavant's daughter Anala and Sumali's eldest daughter Pushpokta. Kaikasi's sister Kumbhinasi and the twin brothers Matta and Unmatta, as also Mali's four sons—Anila, Anala, Sampati and Haaru—had all come to Lanka and were now happily settled in their new homes.

Another valuable addition that had accrued to him, courtesy of Sumali, was Prahasta. Prahasta had been the chief adviser to Malyavant, who, as the eldest of three brothers, was King of Lanka back then. Prahasta's long years in Lanka in such a key position had given him an intimate knowledge of all aspects of Lanka. So much so that he had easily slipped back into the role of being chief adviser, this time to the new king, Dashagreeva. Sumali and Prahasta had together tutored Dashagreeva on the nuances of good governance, state policy and real politics. These aspects had been rather neglected in his own education under his father, Vishravasu. Sumali and Prahasta had found their student to be a keen and quick learner and were particularly pleased that he shared their views on expanding his territorial authority. Vibheeshana, who was among

Dashagreeva's dozen other advisers, gave him frequent headaches, citing various smritis and shastras to shoot down proposals on grounds of 'dharma'.

By now Dashagreeva was circling Lanka's shores and he made out the figure of his mother sculpting a Shiva linga with the wet sand, in preparation for her pooja. Dashagreeva smiled indulgently, thinking how janani had changed during the years he and his brothers had spent in tapasya. Her looks had also changed, and she looked more a combination of Vishravasu and Devaparni. Even her manner of speech reminded him of them. The irritable and garrulous janani of his childhood, forever shouting at them for one thing or another, was now only a memory. She spent considerable time each day in pooja and meditation and insisted that he partake of the prasad. This would provide him with divine protection, she maintained. Dashagreeva laughed derisively—did he need gods to protect him? He, who faced no threat of death from the devas, thanks to the boon granted by Brahma?

Dashamukha directed Pushpak to fly over the interiors of his golden Lanka. It was morning and there was much activity on the streets. Merchants were setting up their shops, displaying their wares and dusting them with fly-whisks. Early shoppers were out, hoping to get a good bargain as a shop's first customer of the day. Children were heading to school, sparkling clean in their freshly laundered clothes, slates under their arms. The king's heart welled with pride at his initiative. He had decreed that there would be no gurukuls, where children were handed over to gurus at the age of five. These children were expected to spend sixteen years as students at the gurukul. Dashagreeva had decided that there would only be day schools, with children returning to their parents in the evening after classes.

Oh! How luxuriant was the green of the gardens, mangroves, vineyards and various other crops! The soil of golden Lanka was so fertile that it yielded abundant crops, even without a lot of effort being put into farming. The fruit from the numerous vineyards kept the equally numerous breweries busy round the clock. Dashamukha wanted his people to enjoy life to the fullest. Madira flowed freely and madhushalas remained open round the clock, catering to men and women of all ages. The king imposed restrictions on the consumption of alcohol by schoolgoing children and men preparing to go to war.

Now he was passing over the secluded palace of Kumbhakarna, who was in his sleep cycle. The palace had been specially designed to make his brother's months of sleep comfortable. The architecture was such that enough sunlight illuminated Kumbha's sleeping chamber so that he was not deprived of this life-giving and life-sustaining component. However, the sunrays never touched the face of the supine figure. This ensured that his sleep was not disturbed. While he knew that Kumbhakarna's sleep was indeed very deep, Dashagreeva took the precaution of ensuring that the loud city noises were shut out of the palace. He also appointed trained masseurs to rub medicated herbal oils on the sleeping Kumbha so that his limbs were exercised properly.

The living quarters of his two other siblings and various cousins were also located in this part of the city. As he leant out over the rim of Pushpak, Dashagreeva caught a glimpse of Surpanakha coiled around her husband, Vidyutjihva. The king once again smiled contentedly. He had fulfilled what he had promised himself so long ago. She was happily married and enjoying life with her husband. As she often stayed till very late at night at the city's various madhushalas, she slept till late in the day. Vidyutjihva was a danava chieftain, whom Dashagreeva had encountered during one of his conquering expeditions. Dashagreeva had been so impressed with his valour that he had made an immediate offer of a high rank in his own army and the hand of his sister in marriage. Vidyutjihva's special trait was his tongue—it could shower thunderbolts merely by being stuck out of his mouth. In fact, the name 'Vidyutjihva' suited him excellently, as it meant 'electric tongue'. This quality helped Dashagreeva immensely when dealing with powerful foes that put up a spirited fight against his forces. At such times, Vidyutjihva would use his special power and shock opponents by brushing them with a sweep of his elongated tongue.

Dashagreeva's thoughts shifted to another woman in the family, who too was leading a happily married life now. This was his mother's younger sister, Kumbhinasi. A danava chieftain named Madhu had abducted Kumbhinasi in retaliation for Dashagreeva's abduction of several danava women during war. Outraged, Dashagreeva had marshalled his forces to vanquish Madhu. Vibheeshana had refused to join the expedition, arguing that abducting women and forcing attentions on them against their wishes was wrong. Having committed such a crime on numerous occasions, Dashagreeva had no moral authority to object to Madhu's actions, despicable as they were. Dashagreeva had scoffed at his younger brother's puritanical approach and had marched in search of Madhu along with an army. He had located the danava king easily, but the prevailing situation there had come as a surprise. Madhu was sleeping at that time and Kumbhinasi had pleaded for mercy. 'We are now married and I am very happy,' she had said, recalling the barren life she had led in Naga-loka. She had also informed Dashagreeva that she was carrying Madhu's child. This development had led to another lasting friendship being forged between Lankadheesh and Madhu.

Memories of his conversation with Kumbhinasi and the sight of several other couples in various postures of intimacy set Dashagreeva yearning for a similar lasting relationship. There were enough women in his life, but not one of them wished him well or was happy with his attentions. He too should marry and have a devoted wife, he thought. It then occurred to him that Vibheeshana also might desire a wife. But could they both enter wedlock and leave Kumbhakarna out? How could he consult his sleeping brother on this issue? There were still a couple of months to go before Kumbha would awaken for a day. He would discuss the matter with Vibheeshana before taking any action, he decided and commanded Pushpak to touch base.

chapter 17

*A*gentle breeze was blowing, caressing the abundant and curly locks on Dashgreeva's head. Coming as it was from the southern shores and thus wafting over his favourite Ashoka vana, the breeze carried with it the fragrance of myriad flowers. However, even the scenic beauty of the Ashoka vana, over which Pushpak was now hovering, failed to bring cheer to its regal occupant. His irritation increased further when Pushpak started bouncing, a reminder to the occupant that instructions about a destination were awaited.

Dashagreeva stamped his foot and waved his hands wildly around him. 'Oh! Just keep going, will you?' he screamed angrily at Pushpak, and then added in a slightly more reasonable tone: 'Go far away from Lanka. Go north. I need time to calm myself.'

Pushpak hummed and coursed through the skies at an easy pace, leaving the king to deal with his frustrations.

Dashagreeva's thoughts turned to the source of his irritation— his brother Vibheeshana. If only he had sought sleep instead of Kumbhakarna, the elder brother thought wistfully. It was not as if Kumbhakarna followed him blindly, or agreed with everything he suggested. They had their fair share of disagreements and differences, which they resolved through discussions. While he had the last word as the elder brother, decisions were taken after all differences had been thrashed out. With Vibheeshana, that was not the case. He was adamant and his sense of 'dharma' was rigid. If he objected to something that Dashagreeva said, he would stick to his stand and not budge an inch.

He could understand Vibheeshana's adherence to what he considered his 'principles', but could not tolerate his brother's attitude that anything and everything the king said or did was not dharma. What nonsense! Vibhee had been unhappy when Dashagreeva had vanquished all the kings and rulers in Jamboodweepa. He had said that the war was an unfair one as manavas, danavas, yakshas and nagas were all physically unequal to rakshasas. What was more, Vibhee found Dashagreeva's trophies from these conquests—the queens and princesses of the vanquished rulers—distasteful. He argued that the king's excesses towards these women had driven them to curse him, as a result of which a woman would be the reason for his downfall. Dashagreeva could almost hear his words even now: 'Bhrata, please do not make women suffer or shed tears.' Nonsense! He was giving them pleasure!

Even so, he had backed down. He had agreed to set all the rulers on earth free to administer their lands as they pleased. He had done that to please his little brother, and also because there was merit in his argument that wars should be between equals. He only drew the line at returning the women whom he had captured as souvenirs. But no. Nothing seemed to make Vibhee happy. He went around with a serious face, behaving as if the sun and moon were in their orbits only because he followed 'dharma'.

Then there was the issue of their marriages. Dashagreeva had suggested that they find three suitable girls and fix the wedding for Kumbhakarna's next wakeful day. Ah! What a sermon Vibhee had delivered on this innocuous subject! He had said that it was unfair to any girl to tie her to a man who slept for six months at a stretch. That would leave her to lead a lonely life. But why should life become lonely if the husband slept? There were a thousand things his wife could do. Dashagreeva stamped his foot, which set Pushpak wobbling and stalling.

Dashagreeva's irritation burst forth. 'Come on, Pushpak! I did ɪot tell you to stop midair like this,' he said and ordered it to move on. Surprisingly, nothing happened. Pushpak stayed where it was and the king once again instructed the craft to continue on its course. Words came from the innards of Pushpak, surprising Dashagreeva, who had never heard Pushpak speak before.

'Pushpak cannot obey. We are over Mount Kailash, abode of my Supreme Lord. Lord Shiva and Mata Parvati are out together. Their privacy is sacred,' Pushpak said in clipped, metallic tones.

This was too much! He, Dashagreeva, was the lord and master of this craft. How could it even suggest that somebody else was its master! And who was this Shiva that Pushpak should defy orders? Shiva, after all, was a weakling of a god, who, at the slightest whiff of danger, ran to Vishnu for protection. 'I do not care. Just move on,' he thundered. But Pushpak stayed adamantly immobile.

Dashagreeva's anger burst out in a flood. 'If you will not fly over this mountain, then set me down. I will uproot it and throw it down into Paatala. Then, I hope you will have no objection to continuing with our journey,' he said, every word dripping sarcasm.

Pushpak landed and Dashagreeva disembarked. Given his mood, the king wanted to kick the mountain out of his way. However, he realized that it was larger than it had appeared to him from up above. He decided to assess the mountain's size before deciding how he would move it out of his way. It might need a little more than two hands and feet, if the mountain's base was of a largish circumference. The Lord of Lanka walked around and was surprised to note that it took him a while to return to his starting point. He would require three or four pairs of hands to get a good hold on the mountain, he thought, but decided to use all his ten pairs to distribute the effort.

He willed all his ten heads to take position and his twenty arms to come to his aid. That done, he encircled the snow-capped mountain with all his hands. Next, he pried up the base of the mountain using all his hundred fingers, then pushed all his twenty arms underneath and exerted pressure to lift it up. However, just as it seemed that he was succeeding, all his hands got trapped under the mountain and an unexpected and rarely experienced sense of pain ran through his arms.

Caught a little off guard with this development, Dashamukha inhaled deeply to marshal his strength and attempted to lift the mountain again. Nothing happened. If anything, little droplets of sweat appeared on his brow. Dashamukha readied himself for another attempt. He flared his nostrils to inhale a huge quantity of air into his lungs, flexed the muscles of all his arms, gritted his teeth and pulled. Once again, not only did nothing happen, but Dashamukha felt his arms being crushed under the weight of the mountain.

Had the mountain's weight increased suddenly? What could be causing this abnormal pressure on his arms? Dashagreeva felt he needed to free his hands to restore proper blood circulation before making another attempt. But try as he might, he could not move a single arm. In fact, he felt the pressure on them increase significantly and his pain rise correspondingly. Such was the pain that he howled involuntarily.

Something was happening atop the mountain that it was pressing down like this, Dashagreeva was sure. Since he could not straighten himself from his crouching position, he willed the power of all his necks into the central one and elongated it as much as he could so as to be able to see what was happening at the top of the mountain. This increased the pain in his arms manifold, and he could not help but scream. It helped. The pain seemed bearable when he screamed. He continued to do so till his head was just level with the peak of the mountain.

All his screaming and all his concentration on elongating his neck were, however, not good enough. He could hardly see anything on the snow-covered mountain peak. Then he saw it—the nail of a toe, its pink standing out in the sea of white snow. Even before he could confirm that it indeed was a toe that he saw, Dashagreeva collapsed, hurting his neck in the process. And the pain in his arms! It kept growing in intensity, becoming more unbearable by the second. Just as there was no let up in the white pain in his arms, his screams too came without pause, becoming one continuous howl. Dashagreeva had no control over his vocal chords. In fact, he had no control over anything, imprisoned as he was under this mountain.

He lost track of time, aware only of pain. Now the pain was not limited to his arms. It was all over. In fact, so all encompassing was the feeling of intense, burning pain that he was unaware of his own screaming.

Oh, maa! What was this new pain on his ear lobe? Was his quota of pain still not complete? Realization dawned. Somebody was trying to say something to him. Dashagreeva paid attention, vaguely recognizing the sound as the voice of Prahasta. Such was his state that it did not occur to Dashagreeva to even wonder how Prahasta had come there.

'Pray to Shiva. Only he can save you now. Beseech him to release you,' Prahasta was shouting at the top of his voice to make himself heard over Dashagreeva's screams.

Something in Prahasta's voice made Dashagreeva obey him. He recognized superior power and might when he encountered it, and spent what seemed an eternity singing praises of Shiva.

'Om Namah Shivayah,' chanted Dashagreeva. His soul felt soothed. 'Om Namah Shivayah,' he repeated. His pain-tortured body calmed as if a cooling balm had been applied. 'Om Namah Shivayah,' he continued without his own volition and felt at peace with the world. Time stood still. Dashagreeva was lost to the world. His chant made way to hymns and stotras.

He did not realize when or how his hands were released. He did not know what prompted him to wring off one head and one arm and join them to form a crude veena, using his intestines to string this novel musical instrument. Tears of pure bliss flowed unchecked from his eyes. As he was lost in a world of his own, an ethereal, bright light glinted through his tears and made Dashagreeva aware of the ash-covered visage of Shiva next to him.

'You sing well, and I also like the way you compose your hymns,' Shiva said. 'But what a horrible voice you have! Not a bit of melody. Your reverberating screams terrified and shook the entire world. I had to come and stop you.

'I am pleased, Dashagreeva. But I cannot let your terrifying roar be forgotten by the world. So I will give you a new name. You will henceforth be known as "ravana"—the one who has no "rava", no melody, in his voice.'

The title given by Shiva pleased Dashagreeva. He prostrated himself before the Lord, extolled Shiva's virtues and powers through more chants and pledged that he would remain a lifelong devotee of Shiva. The three-eyed Shiva decreed that the veena crafted by Ravana would be called 'rudraveena', thus called after the Lord himself. At the same time, Rudra replaced Ravana's head, arm and intestines with a gourd and proper strings, restoring his devotee's organs to him. He also gifted him a sword called 'chandra-haasa'. Its crescent shape gave it the likeness of a smiling moon. 'I must give you a word of caution before you touch this sword. It should be used only for a just cause. If raised unjustly, it will vanish from your hand and return to my custody. From that day, your days on earth will be numbered,' he said, and was gone, as if he was never there.

Dashagreeva looked around and noticed pitamaha Sumali and Prahasta. He recalled that it was Prahasta who had told him to surrender to Shiva through devotion; he asked if either of them had seen where Shiva went. They looked at him with blank expressions and he understood that he alone had experienced Shiva. He quizzed them further on what had happened and was told that they had watched, mesmerized, as the mountain had slid off his arms. Dashagreeva then recounted his own experience, and they complimented him for securing such a powerful weapon. They also accepted his decree when he declared that he would henceforth be called Ravana, Dashagreeva being consigned to the pages of history.

Ravana then turned Pushpak around and returned to Lanka with both Sumali and Prahasta. On arriving there, however, he did not feel like calling it a day yet—such was his excitement over his interaction with the Trinetri—the one with three eyes. So he took off for another romp in the skies atop Pushpak after dropping his two companions in Lanka.

This time round, the ride felt different. He whistled softly, reliving the surreal experience of the day and enjoying every moment of it. He charted the same course all over again and soon reached the salubrious environs of the Himalayas. As he was enjoying its sights and scents, he caught sight of a young woman standing on one foot with both her hands extended above her head. The woman was obviously in tapasya. Ravana could not understand why such a young person would venture into the forest for austerities. He alighted closeby, dismissed Pushpak and approached the young lady.

She was beautiful! How her face shone! And how her long tresses rippled to the touch of a soft breeze! Such beauty could not belong in the manava realm, he felt, and decided that she must be either an apsara from Deva-loka or a magical illusion created by nature itself. What radiance! It was as if the rays of the rising sun had fused to create the glow on her skin. Her waist was so slim as to appear non-existent. Her body curved in three places as she balanced her weight on one foot. Her arms, raised and joined over her head, were like willows, gently swaying to accommodate the direction of the wafting wind. Her hair was unbound and unembellished. But flowers had chosen to settle among her flowing tresses. It was impossible to decide whether the flowers added to the beauty of her locks or the other way round.

Ravana could not take his eyes off her. He was convinced that this lady was made for him—to marry and live with for all times. If only she would open her eyes and see him! He was sure his love would be immediately reciprocated. He walked around her, admiring her beauty from all sides and broke into a small ditty to attract her attention. The song had the desired effect and the lass opened her eyes and looked enquiringly at him.

Ravana proceeded to articulate his romantic thoughts in lyrics, uttered to the accompaniment of a springy step. He also enquired who she was and why she was putting herself through the rigours of tapasya.

'My name is Vedavati. My father is Maharshi Kushadhwaja, son of Brihaspati, guru to the devas. Several devas, yakshas, rakshasas and gandharvas approached my father seeking my hand in marriage. But he wanted to give me in marriage only to Vishnu and so rejected all these offers. One rakshasa, who goes by the name Shambhu, did not take the rejection kindly and killed my father. My mother entered his funeral pyre as Sati. Since then, I have been meditating on Narayana, hoping that he will one day appear and take me as his wife,' she said.

Vedavati looked straight at Ravana, who was staring at her and made no movement to leave. 'I have told you that I have already taken Narayana as my husband. I wait for him to come and take me. You stand no chance and so please go away from here. Do not disturb my tapasya,' she added, curtness evident in every word.

Not one accustomed to taking 'no' for an answer, Ravana tried reasoning with Vedavati. Tapasya, he told her, was for old people and not for young and beautiful girls like her. 'I am Ravana, king of Lanka. I compare favourably with Vishnu in all aspects. What can he have that I do not possess? Marry me and I promise to keep you happy,' he said.

'Do not compare yourself with the Lord of the three worlds, rakshasa raja,' she warned and moved past him to signify the end of their interaction. 'Only fools can dream thus,' she said derisively as she turned her back on him.

Anger flared in Ravana. How dare this weakling of a manava kanya denigrate him? Ravana threw a hand out to grab her and caught the ends of her long and flowing hair.

Vedavati turned, her eyes flashing. She looked at her hair locked in Ravana's hand, raised her own hand and in one swing cut off that part of her hair. 'I cannot offer this sullied body to my Lord. It must be rejected,' she said and proceeded to set up a pyre. Even as Ravana watched, she stepped into the leaping flames.

Vedavati spoke even as her body caught fire. 'I could easily have killed you, Ravana. But that goes against my dharma as a woman. I could have cursed you. But that would have diluted my tapas-shakti. Remember, I will get my revenge. I will be born as an ayonija, one who is not born of a womb, and become the cause of your death.'

Ravana watched as if mesmerized. The fire soon expended itself and in its place rose a lotus. Ravana took the lotus and looked at it, still in a daze. The sight of an infant girl within it shocked him.

He did not know what do. He could not leave the baby in the midst of a forest. So he returned to Lanka in Pushpak with the lotus in his hand.

He sent for Prahasta for consultations. Ravana's account of what had happened upset his chief adviser. 'We must not speak about this to anyone,' Prahasta said.

'But what do we do with this?' Ravana asked, pointing to the lotus he had laid on a table. 'A baby will not go unnoticed for long,' he pointed out.

'True. If she stays here, she will be your ruin,' Prahasta said thoughtfully. He came up with a plan. He brought a casket, placed the lotus and the child in it and directed Ravana to throw it into the ocean.

The task accomplished, Ravana returned home to fall into a disturbed sleep.

chapter 18

*R*avana looked around. He was relieved that finally, after a very long time, a decision that pleased his heart had been taken by his royal court of advisors. Or rather, he had succeeded in getting the royal court's stamp of approval for what he wanted. Having returned all the kingdoms he had conquered to the original manava rulers—to satisfy Vibheeshana—he had been itching to establish his supremacy over the deva domains. The grandiose plan had to be implemented in phases, and this was what was happening now.

The court had broken into smaller groups, each of which was engaged in working out the specific details of the implementation of the decision just taken. Ravana tingled all over in anticipation of an invigorating war. Giving up this favourite sport in deference to Vibheeshana's wishes had not helped anyone, least of all his considerable army. His million-strong force along with all its paraphernalia had gone into deep inertia. He was glad that he had chosen Prahasta as his prime minister over Vibheeshana. Prahasta at least was a vociferous champion of waging wars to prove one's supremacy.

He looked around and smiled at the composition of the groups. He had noticed the bond developing between Vibheeshana and the four sons of his youngest uncle—Mali. They kept their distance from Prahasta, even though they had known him since the reign of Malyavant, but were quite comfortable with Vibheeshana. The feelings were mutual and Prahasta tended to treat them with an air of disdain. Matta and Unmatta stayed away from both groups and specialized in dealing with the logistics of any operation. Ravana admitted that they were very competent.

The prospect of war with the devas filled the king of Lanka with excitement. This war would be a lot more interesting than his past wars, most of which had been against manavas, who usually surrendered without any resistance. Ravana reached under his angavastra and, with the forefinger of his right hand, traced the scar on the left side of his chest. The scar was his trophy from his duel with Anaranya, the king of Ayodhya. He was a brave fellow, and had challenged Ravana to a duel, saying he wanted to avoid needless bloodshed. As was only to be expected, Anaranya's valour came to naught against Ravana's apparently limitless physical strength and stamina.

Ravana was playful when their sword fight had commenced, watched by the armies of both sides. That was why Anaranya had managed to draw blood first. That was a signal for the rakshasa king to turn aggressive and he was soon able to disarm and pin Anaranya down. Even so, Ravana had enjoyed the fight, as it was after a very long time that someone had decided to face him in battle. Having broken Anaranya's sword, Ravana had tossed his own sword aside and had used his fists to overpower his opponent. It was an unexpected punch on his forehead that had felled Anaranya. Another blow and the life would have left his body.

Ravana could have ended the fight thus, but he had indulged in a war of words with the prone figure of the king of Ayodhya, deriving vicarious pleasure in prolonging the moment before finally claiming victory. He had ridiculed Anaranya for even daring to challenge him. He could have surrendered at the very outset and lived to reach a ripe old age, instead of suffering this mid-life exit through an ignominious defeat—so unbefitting a king of his stature. Anaranya was lying flat on the ground, his arms pinned to his sides by Ravana, who sat astride him with a foot on the king's chest. Difficult though it was even to breathe in that position, Anaranya had given a spirited reply: 'There is more to life than being merely alive. I would rather give up life than compromise my self-respect. As king of Ayodhya, it is my bounden duty to protect its citizens, even if I have to lay down my life in the process.'

'Oh! Is that so? And if that is so, what would you call all those kings who surrendered to me?' Ravana had asked.

'I will not pass judgement on the actions of other kings. I can only say one thing with certainty. You may have brought huge tracts of land under your control through your conquests, but not even one hand has been raised in blessing for you. Now I ask you, Mighty King of Lanka, what drives you to capture lands without any thought to winning hearts?'

Ravana had been amused by the stupidity of this fellow who posed as 'king'. 'Win hearts? Why should I win hearts? My people fear me for my strength and valour.'

'No, Lankeshwara! The basis of your rule should not be fear of physical violence,' Anaranya had insisted through lips clenched in pain.

It had irritated Ravana that this man, awaiting death and suffering immense pain, should still think he could preach to him. 'Empty talk of the weak,' he had waved a hand dismissively, easing his grip on his opponent's arms. 'And who are you to advocate non-violence? I know that you are a renowned hunter. Obviously you think killing unsuspecting animals is a sign of strength,' he had laughed derisively.

Anaranya had made a Herculean effort to gather his strength to respond to this charge. His voice, when he began speaking, had shown no signs of weakness: 'I cannot believe that you are so naïve as to even suggest that hunting down wild animals is not raja-dharma. A ruler is expected to maintain a balance between predator and prey in the wild. Surely, I do not have to remind you that my name is "Anaranya", which means the absence of jungle-rule.' Noticing the look of incomprehension on his adversary's face, the king had elaborated: 'It means that I ensure that a proper balance prevails even in the wild.

'Besides, I am dying in the battlefield like a true kshatriya ruler. My dynasty will remember me for this, and somewhere down the line will come a scion of my Ikshwaku vansha to balance the scales with you. Ravana, you may have all kinds of blessings from the gods, but do not even think that you can defy death. Yama will surely claim you at the right time,' Anaranya had said, drawing each word out with great difficulty, before his life had finally ebbed away.

Ravana liked to recall these words once in a while, either to scoff at the temerity of a manava to threaten him or to admire Anaranya's courage and gloat over his victory over such a brave man.

Ravana's reverie was broken by the entry of a dwarapalaka, who came bearing news that there was a messenger at the door, seeking an audience with the king. Ravana permitted himself a half-smile at the look on the dwarapalaka's face and the tremor in his voice as he took in the sight of Ravana, resplendent on his golden throne, specially crafted to accommodate his ten-headed and twenty-armed body. He liked to attend court with all his ten heads on display as it enabled him to keep track of what all his senior ministers were doing and hear different conversations without losing track of any. He preened his moustache at the thought of the impact the very sight of him would have on this visitor from a foreign land. He used his extreme left hand to signal that the messenger be ushered in.

'I come here from Alanka as doota of His Excellency King Kuber, bearing a message for his younger brother, Dashagreeva,' announced the visitor in a pompous voice, instantly sending Ravana into a rage. For one, the very name Kuber had selected for his new abode—A-Lanka—irritated him. He had informed that pot-bellied fellow several times that he should refer to his city as Alakapuri, and not Alanka—as if it was all that Lanka was not, or had everything that Lanka did not have. Secondly, his half-brother refused to acknowledge him by his new name, Ravana, despite being informed that this was now his official name.

The contents of the missive that the messenger read out in the same pompous tone did not improve Ravana's temper. 'Ever since my return from tapasya, I have heard extremely disturbing reports regarding your conduct. Wanton killing of innocent people in the name of war, destruction of natural resources and animals and troubling of kings and tapasvis have been regular activities for you. Note that such acts do not augur well for any ruler. They also bring a stigma to the fair name of our father, the great sage Vishravasu. I hope that you will heed my advice and conduct the affairs of your state in accordance with the high principles of governance, bringing peace and prosperity to one and all...'

Ravana could take no more of these patronizing and sermonizing platitudes. He stamped a foot, breaking his exquisitely carved and cushioned footstool into smithereens. 'Enough!' he shouted. 'Behead this self-righteous fool. Who does he think he is, to be teaching us how to conduct our affairs?'

Vibheeshana was on his feet even before two guards stepped forward to grab Kuber's doota. 'Bhrata, shanti, shanti! He is not teaching us anything. He is only reading a message. He has only brought a message from our eldest bhrata. A messenger is to be treated with respect and dignity; I know I do not have to tell you the basics of raajneeti. You may reply to the message as you see fit, but it is not right to punish the bearer of any message.'

'Do not exceed your limits, Vibheeshana! Remember that you are one of my council of ministers, not even the principal minister. I do not tolerate personal relationships being injected into matters of state,' Ravana thundered. 'I will not repeat my order. The court knows the consequences of insubordination,' he added with dangerous calm.

The courtiers dispersed even as the messenger was hustled out by man-eating rakshasas. Ravana and Vibheeshana locked looks—a sign that neither approved of the other. This attitude of his younger brother, irritating as it was at all times, had a particularly violent effect on Ravana now. He called out to him. 'Vibheeshana, you were right. The messenger is not to be faulted for bringing the message. The fellow who sent the missive must be taught a lesson. I shall leave immediately on this urgent task.'

Some courtiers, who were in the process of leaving the sabha, stopped and turned—Prahasta among them. He hurried towards Ravana, clearly intent on dissuading him from any hasty action, since the army was still undergoing training. 'You do not have to tell me anything, Prahasta! I do not need the help of an army to finish off this upstart. I can do it single-handedly with my bare hands,' Ravana said in the same impatient tone. With a swish of his angavastra and his characteristic stamp-the-foot routine, Ravana left.

The next moment he was airborne, heading towards Alakapuri. Ravana was ready to kill his half-brother. That heat of his temper, however, dissipated soon, thanks to the soothing and satisfying sights of Lanka from his vantage point on Pushpak. While the magical craft had instructions to fly to Alakapuri in the northern hills of the Himalayas, it had followed standard instructions to circle over Lanka before moving to any destination. Ravana felt a sense of calm as he inhaled deeply the refreshing scents of various gardens, crops and mangroves. A soft, mellifluous voice singing praises of Lord Shiva wafted with the breeze, multiplying his sense of contentment. Ravana wondered who the singer could be. He was not aware that there was any woman in Lanka who could sing so melodiously; he decided he would investigate when he returned.

The song continued to haunt Ravana even as he touched down in Alakapuri. Like Lanka, Alakapuri was breathtakingly beautiful. Ravana smiled to himself. When Kuber had set out to have a new city built for himself, his first and foremost stipulation had been that it should not be like Lanka—possibly because any resemblance would act as a reminder of his ignominious ouster from there. As it turned out, Alanka was almost a mirror image of Lanka, the only major difference being that the new city shone white like silver, as against the yellow glitter of gold of Lanka. Both were on par as far as opulence was concerned. Ravana mentally complimented Kuber for his exquisite taste.

The trip was, however, wasted, for, Kuber was away. 'Coward!' Ravana thought to himself, unwilling to even consider that it could be a genuine reason that had taken Kuber away. Ravana decided to take in the beauty of Alakapuri while there and roamed the streets, markets and gardens. As he sat by a brook and let his senses feast on the chirping of birds, the sound of gurgling waterfalls and the scenic beauty of the place, his attention was caught by the sight of a beautiful maiden walking by and plucking flowers. She was dressed to allure.

Lust kindled in Ravana's bosom and he approached the lady with his proposal. She was courteous, but firm in rejecting his advances. When he insisted, she said that Ravana was a father figure for her and that he should protect her and her integrity rather than attempt to sully her with unwanted attention. Ravana laughed. 'I, a father figure to you! How did you arrive at that relationship, may I ask?' he said in mock civility.

'I am Rambha, an apsara from Indra-loka. I am married to Nalakoobara, son of Kuber. Kuber is my father-in-law. You, Lord of Lanka, are Kuber's brother and so stand in the same position as far as I am concerned. I advise you to respect that relationship,' she said, her voice only increasing the desire in Ravana.

Ravana laughed again—derisively this time. 'Look at the devil quoting scriptures! These rules apply to manavas who marry once and have but one husband for an entire lifetime. You are an apsara, not bound by any such rule. So please do not insult my intelligence with all this talk of morals and ethics. Who does not know that Indra has used you often to distract rishis from tapasya. You may be married, but you are not a pativrata by any stretch of the imagination. You know very well that in this realm, only passion decides relationships and not social codes,' he said and pulled Rambha by her hand. He ignored her pleas for mercy, and used his superior physical strength to subdue her.

After satisfying his lust, Ravana flew off on Pushpak.

Nalakoobara found his wife in a distraught, dishevelled state. She burst into tears at the sight of her husband and told him how she had been ravished by Ravana. Nalakoobara consoled Rambha and cursed Ravana for this rape. 'Ravana, should you ever take a woman against her wishes, your head will burst into a million pieces and you will die instantly,' he cursed.

The directly addressed curse resonated through Pushpak—a feature that had hitherto pleased its recent owner. Now it irritated him. Who does this fellow think he is, cursing the mighty Ravana as if he were a mere mortal! However, being the son of a pious Brahmin and having seen many such rishis during his lifetime, Ravana knew better than to brush their curses off lightly. He shrugged in resignation. The end had been pronounced upon his propensity to take women as fancy took him, irrespective of their consent and willingness.

Ravana fell into a pensive reverie. He had accumulated an impressive basket of curses. The first one had been uttered by that Nandi—Shiva's vaahana and doorkeeper, who had taken offence to being called 'monkey-faced' by him, and had stated that a monkey would cause his death. Then there was that tapasvin woman who had gone into a huff just because he had caught her by the hair. She had said that she would take another birth and become the cause of his death. She did turn into an ayonija inside a lotus, which her ashes had converted into. Luckily, he had been able to get rid of her in the sea, with help from Prahasta, without anyone getting wind of it. Now it was this apsara's husband! Well, such is life. The strong and mighty ones end up having a lot of enemies. But of course, he had nothing to worry about, blessed as he was by Brahma and Shiva with so many boons. Weak manavas and scatterbrained vanaras could not really harm him, he told himself, stamping his foot that such a thought should even enter his mind. Nonetheless, he would not force his attentions on unwilling women, he said to himself as he directed Pushpak to head home.

The very thought of home soothed his nerves; he remembered the melodious song wafting up to him from the Ashoka vana, and decided that he would investigate the source of that singing at the earliest.

chapter 19

'*N*arayana, Narayana!' the familiar chant in the familiar voice brought Saraswati out of deep thought. She opened her eyes at the same time as her lips parted in a beatific smile of welcome. Simultaneously her hand rose to motion Sage Narada to a seat close by.

Narada smiled back at her and settled comfortably into the indicated high-backed aasan with another chant of 'Narayana, Narayana.'

'It has been a long time since your last visit here, Narada. What brings you this time—is it another conference that you want?' He shook his head even as he joined in her light laughter at this reference to the last conference he had organized between Brahma and an illustrious array of pundits and seers of various disciplines. 'You should have taken me into confidence about your motivations in bringing over that crowd of argumentative seers,' Saraswati said, her mind darting back to that day of unending discussions on all manner of subjects, organized because Narada had wanted to prevent Brahma from descending to the earthly plane to grant boons to Dashagreeva and his brothers.

'I really did not have time. The sages were very worried at the prospect of those three rakshasa brothers attaining near immortality, and pita shree was all set to grant them what they wanted,' he responded.

'And we managed to check only one of them,' Saraswati said. There was a tinge of regret in her tone.

'Vibheeshana with his desire to live a dharmic life was no

threat to peace on earth. Only Dashagreeva, who now calls himself "Ravana", secured what he wanted. Kumbhakarna has been as good as completely neutralized with sleep, thanks only to you because you realized the purpose of all those debates in the nick of time.'

The two fell into a light, bantering conversation about who had said what and how at that tedious conference. They said things that neither would say to anyone else under any circumstances. While nothing of substance was said by either, the conversation reflected the special bond the two shared. Narada respected Saraswati for her complete and flawless knowledge. Saraswati, on her part, considered her knowledge to be incomplete without the valuable insights from Narada, gleaned by him during his tireless journeys through the three lokas, and which he shared with her without any reservations. Her very presence filled him with joy and contentment. He did not tire of admiring her pristine beauty. She was always draped in a spotless white saree. Narada often wondered whether it was the glimmer of the interwoven gold and silver threads that created a halo-like aura around her or if it was her inner light that shone through the fabric, imparting that magical sheen to it. And the large and bejewelled 'tatankas' she often wore in her ears! How rhythmically they swayed when she spoke! The ethereal designs of various hues cast on her cheeks by the precious gems gave the impression of a smile playing on her lips even when Saraswati sat silently.

Music was a shared passion for them. They enjoyed discussing music and their experimentations with their respective veenas. Their veenas were identical, gifted to them by Brahma on account of their deep and abiding love for music, but Saraswati considered her veena, which she called Kacchapi, superior to Narada's Mahati. They loved these divine instruments so much that they had made them a part of themselves, never leaving them aside even for a moment. Narada had a tendency to strum Mahati when he needed to think fast to get out of tricky situations. He also used its lilting sound as announcement of his arrival, synchronizing its notes to his chants of 'Narayana, Narayana' as he strolled on his ceaseless rounds of various lokas.

In addition to music, almost every other subject under the sun was grist for elaborate analysis. Their debates were mutually enriching—Saraswati's theoretical insights becoming elements for practical experimentation for Narada during his trips to various planes of the universe, and Narada's experience helping the personification of knowledge. They were, in a manner of speaking, two sides of a coin, each complementing the other, giving structure and substance to ideas.

'So, how are Vishravasu's three sons dealing with their boons from the Creator?' Saraswati asked as a natural corollary to their discussion on that mega congregation.

'Fine, I suppose,' Narada responded and took a moment to arrange his thoughts before he continued. 'Actually, I came here hoping for help and ideas from you regarding the eldest of the three. He has become a law unto himself and is causing a lot of trouble all around.'

'You surprise me, Narada. I had heard that Lanka is amongst the best administered countries; that its riches compare with the best in the Deva-loka and that its citizens are happy and content.'

'Your information is correct as far as Lanka is concerned. Ravana is a quick learner; he learnt about statecraft and administration from his pitamaha Sumali and manages Lanka beautifully. He also has an able prime minister in Prahasta, who held the same position in Lanka when Malyavant was king. What is of concern is his thirst for power and the havoc he causes in the process of conquering other lands. He has built himself a formidable reputation in warfare and there is hardly a king in Bhoo-loka who dares to stand up against him. So much so that kings surrender to him without a fight and he takes off with all women who take his fancy. In the jungles, he troubles hermits—extinguishes their yagnic agni by throwing animal carcasses, and despoils the tranquillity and sanctity of ashrams in a thousand ways,' Narada shook his head in despair, absentmindedly running his fingers along the strings of his veena, causing a whispering melody to spread across the room. He looked at the goddess of learning with imploring eyes: 'Please suggest some way of reining him in—manavas are desperate for help.'

Saraswati flicked a hand—indicating that the problem on hand was not major. 'I am sure there are people who are stronger than Ravana. It would be easy for you to instigate him to fight them or the other way around. Defeat would teach him the necessary lesson. Another solution could lie in getting his brothers to put sense into his pompous head.'

Saraswati realized the gravity of the situation when Narada, instead of teasing her for her rather obvious suggestions, shook his head sadly. 'I did consider these options, amma. Of his two brothers, Vibheeshana is much younger than Ravana and therefore propriety prohibits him from putting too much pressure on the elder brother. And Kumbhakarna is awake for only one day in six months and so cannot exert sustained pressure through counselling. This means that we cannot look for constructive help from the brothers.

'There are three elders who wield some influence on him—his grandfather Sumali, mahamantri Prahasta and his mother Kaikasi. The first two are of no use to us, because they are the ones who fuel his thirst for power and instigate Ravana to conquer the world. Kaikasi has her limitations on account of being a woman. She does try to mellow down her son, but Ravana does not pay heed to her advice in these matters.'

Saraswati did not like the worried frown on Narada's face. She knew that the issue was grave and needed to be addressed urgently and effectively. She needed time to think just as Narada needed to think. But for Narada to think, he needed to let go of his worry. Saraswati set to work in this direction, choosing Narada's address of her as 'amma' as the means to divert him. 'Why do you call me "amma" Narada? Why not by name as I call you—after all, are we not siblings? And, if you must treat me as mother, why not address me as "matru shree" as is the normal practice?'

Narada gave her a smile, letting her know that he understood her intent. 'You know the meaning as it applies in the Bhoo-loka. A mother's love for her children is the most beautiful emotion in that world. It makes one yearn for such love. I have not had the opportunity to experience such love, being a mind-born son of Brahma. So, on occasion, when I feel particularly perturbed, I address you thus and draw solace. And you, despite being a mind-child like me, are the epitome of maternal affection. It comes naturally to you.'

Narada's characteristic mischievous twinkle returned to his eye as he continued: 'Do you realize that you are very special—you are the only girl-child that pita shree created!

'And now, here is the answer to your question. I did try to pit Ravana against a mighty foe. Mind you, it was not easy to find such a foe, given Ravana's strength. There is hardly a manava who can match this rakshasa king, and you know that, on account of the boons from Brahma, he is protected from harm from deva-danava, yaksha-kinnera, gandharva-kimpurusha and other such exalted beings.

'I had to scout far and wide before I found Kartaveerya-Arjuna, a king of immense strength. His strength is distributed amongst his thousand arms. Of course, it was much simpler to goad Ravana to fight him,' Narada's smile and sparkling eyes spoke volumes.

Saraswati's interest was piqued. 'Did the fight take place? When?

And what was the outcome?'

'The fight ended the way I wanted, but without achieving my intended purpose,' Narada's words only increased his listener's curiosity.

'This is not fair, Narada! You are testing my patience,' Saraswati complained.

'Do not be cross with me, amma. You know that I share everything with you. This is how it happened,' Narada said and launched into the story.

'After identifying Kartaveerya-Arjuna, I went to Ravana. He was in the Ashoka vana, his favourite haunt in Lanka. This is one place where Sumali and Prahasta do not disturb the king, which gave me a chance to plant my seed in his mind. I pumped Ravana's ego by praising his strength and marvelling at how he had conquered all kings. I told him that there was one king in the Bhoo-loka, however, who claimed superior strength and that he should be taught a befitting lesson.

'Ravana bit the bait and was ready to challenge Kartaveerya-Arjuna immediately. I accompanied Ravana to seek out this king. We came upon him while he was frolicking with his numerous wives in the river Narmada. His bodyguards patrolling the riverbank said that their king could not be disturbed for any reason as he was drunk and engaged with his wives. Ravana flared up in rage and started killing all the guards and then challenged Kartaveerya-Arjuna to a duel. What followed next was unbelievable. It was all over before I could even blink an eye! The king merely extended an arm, grabbed Ravana by the scruff of his neck and pulled him into the waters. In a moment, Kartaveerya-Arjuna was yojanas away, walking against the current and pulling Ravana after him. The mighty Ravana looked like a spider being washed away in a flood.'

'Oh!' Saraswati exclaimed, knowing that the story was far from over and waiting for Narada to continue.

'I learnt that the king threw him into a dungeon in his palace,' Narada said, shaking his head to convey his disbelief.

Saraswati waited with bated breath.

'I could not believe my eyes some time later when I saw none other than pita shree making his way to Kartaveerya-Arjuna and seeking Ravana's release, citing his illustrious descent from himself.'

'What!' disbelief sounded clearly in that one single word that escaped Saraswati's lips.

'Yes, that was what happened. Kartaveerya-Arjuna, who had by then forgotten the encounter with Ravana in the Narmada, went to check in his dungeons and, finding Ravana there, handed him over to Brahma. Ravana quickly left the palace, barely stopping to thank the Lord for securing his release. I am sure that I do not have to tell you that Ravana has not mentioned this episode to anyone,' Narada concluded with a wry smile.

Saraswati and Narada sat silently for a while, each lost in thought. 'Why did the Creator act thus?' Saraswati wondered aloud.

'I did ask pita shree for an explanation, given the fact that Ravana had gone back to his old ways of troubling manavas with a renewed vengeance. He said that there was a larger role that Ravana was to play and that the sequence of events would be in jeopardy if he were to be taken out of circulation.'

'I can understand that. But something must be done to teach this mighty rakshasa king a lesson so that he stops pestering innocent and helpless humans,' Saraswati said with a thoughtful look in her eyes. 'Narada, I suggest that you do not stop your efforts to put some sense into Ravana's ten heads. There must be others who can make Ravana realize that he is not invincible and stop him from using brute force just to please himself.' Narada nodded his head, signalling complete agreement with the sentiment.

'Narayana, Narayana!' Narada chanted as he rose to leave.

chapter 20

'*N*arayana, Narayana!' the chant was familiar, but its tone lacked its usual geniality. Saraswati, who opened her eyes to greet Narada, noticed that the usual spring in Narada's step was missing. Nor was there that characteristic mischievous smile on his lips. In fact, he did not even give Saraswati his customary salutation. Instead, he wearily deposited himself in his usual aasan—more by habit than by volition. His fingers moved across the strings of Mahati, but produced no musical notes—a clear indication that his mind was elsewhere.

Saraswati strummed Kacchapi—something she rarely did. She treated her veena with great reverence and drew notes from it only to create music. However, on this occasion, she plucked at it in a bid to perk up Narada and pull him out of his obvious mood of dejection.

Narada looked up. He met Saraswati's questioning gaze with a slight shake of his head. He still did not speak and his fingers continued to dance silently across the strings of his veena.

Saraswati waited, knowing that Narada would talk to her when he was ready. She played gently on Kacchapi, its soothing notes helping Narada to organize his thoughts and, in the process, lifting his spirits. Finally, he straightened himself and cleared his throat, the chant of 'Narayana, Narayana' escaping his lips involuntarily.

'I do not bring happy tidings, amma,' he said. Saraswati nodded, the tatankas in her ears swaying and creating enchanting designs of reflected light on her cheeks. Narada watched as if mesmerized and in a moment was his usual self. He smiled impishly at her and asked: 'Do you want all the details or will a gist of my failures suffice?'

'All the details, arranged chronologically,' she responded seriously and added, 'Do not omit anything, because I am sure, hidden somewhere along the way will be an opening to success.'

'Well, my search for someone capable of routing Ravana in a fight was rewarded soon enough.' Narada lifted a restraining hand: 'Do not throw a volley of questions at me. I will tell you everything. Just be patient,' he said and continued in the tone of one settling in to tell a long story.

'It was Vaali, the monkey king of Kishkindha. Besides his strength, the fact that he belongs to the vaanara race made him ideal for this task, because Ravana specifically omitted the nara and vaanara races from the list of beings he wanted protection against. Once again, instigating Ravana to pick a fight with Vaali was easy. However, Ravana found it extremely difficult to catch up with this king of legendary agility. You see, Vaali goes round the world everyday to give arghyam, the offering of water, to Surya. This he does with the waters of the four oceans around the globe, covering the distance before Surya reaches them to cause sunrise. Ravana finally caught up with Vaali as the monkey king reached the southern ocean to perform his ritual to the sun god. Ravana leapt on Vaali from behind, afraid that he might lose him if he waited for the other to complete his ritual.

'Vaali was caught unawares by this attack from the back and momentarily lost his balance. But his immense agility enabled him to recover within an eye-blink. He turned around and pulled off his attacker with his left hand. Focused as he was on completing his morning ritual to the sun, Vaali tucked his attacker under his arm without so much as a glance at him and proceeded with his sun salutation. Ravana had to struggle to free himself, despite his unmatched physical strength—as he was unable to breathe properly in the confines of Vaali's armpit.

'When he finally got a chance to draw breath, the moment was lost even before he managed to take half a breath as he found himself submerged underwater along with Vaali, who was taking a dip in the ocean to mark the completion of his salutation. Vaali then proceeded to the next ocean, Ravana held captive in his armpit; then to the next and then to the last. Each time, Ravana found himself sucked right back into the hollow under Vaali's arm, apparently without the vaanara even noticing it. Ravana was repeatedly dunked in the brine of the ocean and quite starved of life-saving air. He was ready to collapse into unconsciousness due to lack of oxygen when suddenly he found himself slipping to the ground.

'He breathed in huge gulps of air, and then stood up with some difficulty. As he was steadying himself, he heard Vaali address him in a tone of exaggerated surprise. "Ah, Ravana! What a pleasant surprise! When did you come? And please tell me what I can do for you."

'Amma, I, who had seen exactly what Vaali had been doing with Ravana all along, was impressed by this display of surprise. I was sure that Ravana would be defeated in next to no time, given his physical condition after the ordeal he had just gone through. While I would have liked a good fight—you know how I enjoy them, amma—I was quite pleased that I was about to achieve what I had set out to do.

'But then, it was my turn to get a surprise. I could see that Ravana was re-evaluating his position vis-à-vis Vaali. He realized that he was no match for the vaanara king either in strength or agility. So he concentrated on saving his reputation.

'"My dear Vaali! The mighty king of the vaanaras! Having heard so much about your legendary strength, I came from Lanka with a hand extended in friendship." Ravana then heaped praises on Vaali for his valour and strength and offered eternal friendship and support. He offered to seal this vow with agni as witness. Vaali accepted his offer of friendship.

'Thus ended my chance of instilling some sense of modesty and fairness in Ravana,' Narada ended his story. Saraswati remained silent and attentive, realizing that Narada had more to say. She was not disappointed. Narada adjusted a cushion behind him, took a deep breath and began again.

'I was determined not to give up on my mission and continued my search for people with the potential to take on Ravana. But as there was none such among the manavas, I thought it would be a good idea to make Ravana take on the devas. I believed a good fight would teach him to mind his own business and desist from troubling the helpless.

'This time when I met Ravana, I used a different approach. I ridiculed him for picking on weaker beings. Manavas, I told him, had enough troubles in life. They encountered old age, disease and hunger, and their lives were aborted by Yama at will. A real hero should pick opponents of equal or superior power, I told him and dared him to vanquish beings of higher realms. Why hesitate when you know that death will not come to you from them, I said. Conquer their lands. Better still, conquer Yama, the Lord of Death, I goaded him.

'Look at my folly, amma. I believed that I had come up with a brilliant idea, and I thought it would be befitting to have those victimized by Ravana see him vanquished. I collected an array of devas, gandharvas, siddhas and others and took them to witness this historic duel between the invincible Ravana and the Lord of Death. But alas!'

Saraswati's heart missed a beat. 'What happened?' the words escaped Saraswati, in spite of herself.

The question made Narada snap out of his reverie. He looked at Saraswati—her face had acquired a golden pink hue, an indication of her excitement and anticipation. Narada understood her unspoken wish—'You wish you had been a part of this action!' he said, his eyes twinkling.

Saraswati nodded vigorously, the glint of her tatankas filling the room with a riot of colours. 'Then see how it happened,' Narada said, tapping the central point between his˙eyebrows.

The story of Ravana's encounter with Yama played out for her.

(Ravana is in consultation with his chief advisors Prahasta, Sumali and Vibheeshana about his intended assault on Yamapuri. Vibheeshana is sitting silently, but his disapproval of the proposal is clear from his demeanour. The other two are excited and eager to plan for it.)

Prahasta: Victory over Yama! What an idea, Lankadheesh! Only you could have come up with such a fantastic proposal!

[How happy he looks, as if the war is already won, thought Saraswati.]

Sumali *(thumping Ravana on the back in a congratulatory manner)*: With victory over the Lord of Death you will effectively obtain the boon that Brahma refused to concede to you— immortality. Yes, you will have defied death itself with this feat, putra! I am proud of you. *(Sumali raises his hand in warning before continuing.)* I would, however, ring a bell of caution at the very outset. Yama is a deva, son of none other than the all powerful Surya and powerful in his own right. So we should not go on the offensive without adequate preparation.

Ravana: I am second to none, pitamaha, when it comes to strength or valour. Victory over death will make me immortal. I must take on the devas and teach them a befitting lesson. *(Pauses and looks at Vibheeshana.)* What is bothering you, Vibhee? Why are you shaking your head like you have a neurological disorder? Do you doubt my strength?

Vibheeshana: Bhrata, please do not even suggest that I doubt your strength and capabilities. I hold you in great respect, awe and admiration. However, I do not think you should invite a clash with the devas, who have the support and blessings of Lord Vishnu.

Ravana *(visibly angry and in a raised voice)*: Enough, Vibheeshana! I will not hear this cowardly talk even for a moment. How can you, my own brother, talk like this? It makes me wonder at times whether you are my well-wisher or enemy.

Prahasta: Calm yourself, Lanka Naresh! You asked for his opinion and he gave it. Consider it or reject it on its merits. You are the elder brother, you should protect your younger siblings at all times. That is your dharma. At the same time, I must confess that I agree with Sumali. Do not ever underestimate your opponent. We must get our forces into battle-fitness mode...

Ravana *(raises his hand and cuts Prahasta off mid-sentence)*: We do not need an army. I can handle Yama single-handedly. *(He preens his moustache to stress his point.)*

Prahasta: I know you can. We all know you can. But how can you be sure that Yama will not play some underhand trick to neutralize you? We must have our forces standing by to deal with any eventuality. You must heed our advice, Lankeshwara!

Ravana: All right, all right! But do it fast. I will give you just one week to ready the forces. *(So saying, Ravana leaves, swishing his angavastra in style.)*

(The scene shifts to Yamapuri. Ravana, flanked by Sumali and Prahasta, is leading a strong army mounted on chariots, elephants and horses, besides foot soldiers wielding a variety of arms like maces, bows and arrows, spears, swords of different kinds and so on. Yamapuri itself is a scene of bustling activity with the souls of the manavas and other jivas undergoing different types of punishments for their individual actions while alive.)

Saraswati found the scene distasteful and saddening, but continued to watch. Narada noticed the little frown on her face and ran a hand across his forehead to end the vision.

'There is no need for you to witness the gory details of the fight, amma. I will tell you what happened during this war that lasted one full week. The rakshasa sena sought to instigate the Yama-bhattas by obstructing their work and soon a full-scale war broke out between the two armies. Both sides suffered heavy casualties. Yama responded to Ravana's call for a duel and both fought valiantly, using the variety of arms and missiles under their command. It was an equally matched fight in all respects. Finally, Yama lost patience with the duel, which seemed set to go on forever.'

Narada took a deep breath before continuing: 'All of us who were watching the fight from the skies felt momentarily blinded by a lightning-like brightness. Then we saw Yama standing in full fury, with his kaala-dand, his baton of death, in hand. Amma, you are aware that the kaala-dand was bequeathed to Yama by pita shree and has the same power as the Brahma-astra. It brings certain death to anyone it touches and therefore is to be used only in the rarest of rare cases,' Narada paused dramatically.

Saraswati's voice was almost inaudible as she whispered: 'Then?'

'Pita shree appeared between them. He put a restraining hand on Yama's raised hand, which held the kaala-dand.

'"I urge you to desist from using the kaala-dand on Ravana. While I did leave it to your discretion to decide when to use it, there is a problem in this case that makes me seek your indulgence and lenience. Just as I gave you the kaala-dand as the surest missile to cause death, I gave a boon to Ravana, by the power of which his death cannot be caused by a deva. If you invoke the kaala-dand for Ravana, you will be pitting my missile against my vardaan. As a consequence, either the kaala-dand will be ineffective or Ravana will die. Either way, I will suffer the stigma of being an asatyavadi, one whose word is not valid. Would you like that disrepute to come my way?" pita shree asked Yama.

'Yama's hand wavered. He looked at Ravana, then at Brahma and then again at the rakshasa raja, and finally declared that the war itself was invalid and disappeared from the scene,' Narada concluded his narrative.

'What did Ravana do? What did pita shree say?' Saraswati asked, slowly letting out her long-held breath, indicating her relief at the outcome of the confrontation.

'Ravana declared himself victorious and returned to Lanka,' Narada said, and added: 'But our problem persists—how do we put sense into Ravana, so that he stays away from sadhujan?'

'Get him to fall in love,' Saraswati said with a twinkle in her eye and a smile on her lips.

*R*avana walking down the thoroughfares of Lanka was a rare sight. And a never-before seen sight was of the king of Lanka striding across the busy streets in broad daylight, that too with all his ten heads on display. Yet that was what the citizens of Lanka witnessed on one particular summer afternoon. Such was their disbelief at what they saw that traffic came to a standstill; people bumped into one another, stumbled and fell; many ran helter-skelter in fear, trying to find a safe hiding place.

Ravana continued to press forward, completely oblivious to the chaos he had unleashed. A breeze from the surrounding seas made the long, curly tresses on his ten heads stream out behind him and his clothing of fine silk billow around him. His twenty arms swayed back and forth vigorously to aid his quick step, making the loose ends of his angavastra flutter like the wings of a frightened bird.

Ravana strode on purposefully, lost in his own thoughts. He had left his ministers and counsellors debating the many weighty issues of governance mid-way through the court's session. He had simply motioned them to continue when they had looked at a loss as he rose to leave. He needed time to sort out his own problems.

Ravana headed straight to the Ashoka vatika—his favourite place for relaxing. None dared disturb him while he was there. Ashoka vatika was a natural forest and represented Nature's balance in the fullest. There were flowing water-bodies, cave formations and small hillocks, and the area was thick with vegetation. Animals roamed free, as none hunted them. Ravana was almost the only intruder there and he had several favourite spots within the expanse of the vatika: sometimes he would walk along its many brooks, sometimes he would climb hillocks, while at other times he would sit on the lush green carpet of grass amid the tall trees. The only man-made structure was a small temple dedicated to Shiva, where Ravana prayed, if he was so inclined while in the vatika.

On that day he chose to sit on a stone in a clearing amidst a clump of trees. The place reminded him of his childhood in Rishi-teertham; of how his mother would vanish for hours on end and they would find her sitting quietly on a stone bench outside an abandoned orchard. He felt he understood his mother like none of his siblings did. He knew what she had gone through to establish this rakshasa-raj and bring her family back. Luckily, she was now at peace with herself, happy with her Shiva puja and watching her eldest-born manage Lanka as also their family.

Ravana sighed and shifted position. His mother did not have as many problems with family as he did!

'Hahaha…' The garrulous laughter irritated Ravana. It was one of his heads on the left side laughing at him. 'Thinking too much of yourself, are you, Shamuloo!' it mocked Ravana. The usage of this pet name, the one his mother called him by when they were alone, irritated Ravana further. But this was how his various heads argued things out. The words thus spoken amongst his different heads were not heard by others, even if they were seated right next to Ravana. The five heads on the right generally dealt with questions of logic and statecraft and the heads on the left were more preoccupied with issues pertaining to relationships, morality and such like. So he let the mockery pass and articulated his concern.

'Right now, janani is herself turning into a problem, making things difficult for me. Her new-found love for that Vishnu is the root of it. She does not tire of telling me to make peace with that fellow. She says she worries that I may come to harm because of him! She told me that he is also god, just like Shiva! How do you

like that? How am I to deal with her?'

'Did you tell her how your duel with Vaali went?' this mocking question came from a head on his right side. It was a reminder of his earlier humiliation.

'What is the need to inform her of that? To worry her more and make her push even more for truce with Vishnu?' another head on the right countered.

'I agree that janani need not be told about the defeat. But it is definitely a serious issue. At the time of seeking boons from Brahma, naras and vaanaras were specifically mentioned as groups from whom I do not need divine protection. And now I find there is at least one vaanara who is immensely strong—one who could have easily crushed me to death under his arm. I think it was one of my rare moments of weakness. Anyway, there is no need to worry as I have befriended him.

'But, while returning after defeating Yama, I was accosted by Shani, who challenged me to a duel. He was angry that I had defeated his brother, Yama. This surya putra insisted that Yama had withdrawn from the fight in deference to Brahma's wishes and that I had no right to declare myself winner over him. He bragged that he was under no obligation to anyone—meaning Brahma, who had gifted the kaala-dand to Yama—and that I should fight him. Shani is a hefty fellow, whose movements are extremely slow. In fact, his slowness irritated me; even his speech was slow and laborious. I accepted the challenge and we started a free-style wrestling bout. It did not take me long to realize that I had underestimated Shani. But I finally managed to pin him down and sat on his back—he had said that he would concede defeat only if I pinned him on his back. But he directed his debilitating glance at me and drained me of all my strength. Shani then reversed our positions. But instead of claiming victory, he offered to concede to a tie if I released all the other planets that I had immobilized sometime back. Shani said the other eight planets were his siblings, as they all orbited the sun as a team and helped maintain balance in the universe. I agreed and got away. But my strength has not returned in full measure even now.'

'I just cannot understand how you can talk endlessly about such inane things and ignore the real issues. Strength is a physical thing, which increases or decreases periodically, depending upon a number of variables. The real issue is that I need a companion; a soulmate with whom I can share my innermost feelings, joys and fears; someone I can cherish and love.' This was said by the first head on the left side, which was keen to rubbish the chatter among the heads on the right side.

'You speak like a poet, not like a warrior-king!' mocked the second head on the right. 'You sound like a love-lorn lonely heart with no company whatsoever, when, in fact, there is an entire palace full of women waiting for attention.'

'True. But these women can only fulfil one's physical needs, whereas love transcends it. There is not one among these thousands of women whom I would want to marry, have children with and spend my life with. That is the kind of company I crave,' countered the head on the left.

Another head on the left spoke up: 'In fact, there is one such woman. I have not set eyes on her, but I often hear her mellifluous voice here in the Ashoka vatika. The very sound brings me a sense of peace and serenity, and makes me feel that I could spend my life looking at her. '

'So what has prevented you from seeking her out?' The question came from the right half.

'You won't understand.'

'I will, if you can explain cogently and justify your arguments with logic.'

'You see, there is this longing for the ideal companion; a

companion who will stand by one through thick and thin and to whom one does not ever need to say sorry for anything. That is the kind of understanding I seek from her. This voice that I hear, singing praises of lord Shiva, enchants me. It touches me somewhere deep inside. I feel this person could be the companion I am looking for.

'But, there is a problem in pursuing her, in seeking her out and making her my life partner. I cannot marry without first settling my two younger brothers. Finding a bride for Kumbhakarna is difficult, given the fact that he sleeps for six months at a stretch. Who would want a husband like that? And how I can I think of marriage for Vibhee and myself and leave Kumbha out? It would not be morally right.'

The head on the right nodded its understanding and appreciation of the problem. 'It is a problem all right, but not a difficult one to solve,' it said and continued: 'We have so many women at our disposal. Select one of them and make her tie the knot with Kumbha. Vibhee too can select a wife for himself.'

'I cannot believe that you can suggest such a thing. But I'll let it pass. For it is beyond your comprehension that the bride's consent is as important as one's own when one enters sacred matrimony. Marriage is not about having a "woman". Anyway, this apart, there is another dimension to the problem.

'There is Surpi, now a widow. I feel terrible even thinking and talking about finding life partners for us three brothers, when our only sister has lost her companion. What makes it worse is that I was responsible for Vidyutjihva's untimely demise. Had I not insisted on his leading that expedition to the mainland when he was under the influence of madira, he would not have fallen off the drawbridge and been eaten by the alligators in the moat. The sound of Surpi's wails that day still ring in my ears. She needs to be settled before I can contemplate wedlock for any of us,' sighed the head on the left.

The heads on the right fell silent, sharing Surpanakha's sorrow, as did the heads on the left.

But surprisingly, it was not complete silence that prevailed. A couple of heads from both sides were indulging in an exchange of their own. The issue that engaged their attention was not of a personal nature, however. The debate was academic and revolved around the effect the Ashoka vatika had on Ravana. These heads noted that there was something in the air in the vatika that soothed the soul and lifted one's spirits—one always felt happier and healthier after spending a little time there. Could this be the effect of the foliage? Would it be possible to obtain the same effect by taking select herbs from the vatika and administering them to the sick and ailing? What type of physical and mental problems could be addressed with such herbs? And so on.

Ravana noticed that the effect of the vatika that was being debated had, in fact, worked on him already. He felt much better; the irritation and frustration that had made him come to Ashoka vatika had left him. New thoughts were taking shape in his mind.

Ravana relaxed. He began the process of withdrawing his many heads. He sat there with half-closed eyes, letting ideas crystallize and action plans emerge. A smile played on his lips as he fancied that a melodious voice was reaching out to him.

chapter 22

'*N*arayana! Narayana!' the surprise in the chant was obvious. Narada could not believe his eyes and hastened his step to catch up with the object of his amazement. 'Narayana! Narayana!' he chanted, louder this time to reach the ears of Ravana, who was now just a few steps ahead of him.

Ravana paused in his stride and turned around, but neither greeted the other nor did Ravana give any indication that he welcomed the visitor. Narada could not believe what he saw in front of him. Was this really Ravana? Of course he was, but there had been an unbelievable transformation in his appearance. Ravana, Narada knew, loved the good things in life. He dressed well—in the finest of silks his weavers could create, with a liberal interweaving of gold, silver and gems; he loved jewellery—gold embellished with sparkling gems adorned his arms, neck and waist, not to mention the array of crowns on his ten heads. His love for fine food and drink and beautiful women was the stuff of legend in Lanka. But today, he presented a completely different picture. He was wearing a coarse loincloth with an angavastram tied around his waist to keep the loincloth in place. There was a complete absence of jewellery—barring the strings of rudraksha beads around his neck and arms. His luxurious mane of shoulder-length curls was soaked with dhatura milk and matted into a coil atop his head. Bhasma—ash—was smeared on his forehead and chest. Even his stylish footwear, specially crafted for him with precious stones studded into fine leather, was missing. Instead he wore wooden sandals.

There was a reason why Narada was so very surprised by

Ravana's attire. Besides being unusual, this appearance defeated the very purpose of his seeking out the king of Lanka. He had planned to set Saraswati's proposal into action by suggesting that Ravana find a suitable girl to marry. He had planned to speak about Mandodari as an ideal partner for the king.

Mandodari was the girl he had spied in the Ashoka vatika several times. This kanya from Matsya-loka had been frequenting the idyllic environs of the vatika for quite some time now. Initially, she used to be accompanied by her sakhis, but later began the practice of visiting the vatika on her own. Her interest in the owner of the property was evident from the fact that whenever Ravana came to Ashoka vatika, she would hover in the vicinity, observing him closely but without showing herself. She, however, ensured that he felt her presence by either singing softly or leaving signs of her having visited the Shiva shrine.

Narada had started observing Mandodari's movements after Saraswati recommended shifting Ravana's attention to romantic matters. Narada was convinced that Mandodari would make a good wife for Ravana, and only earlier that morning had spoken to her in this regard. While she had maintained the decorum and bashfulness natural to kanyas, Mandodari had acknowledged that her heart was with Ravana and that she would like nothing better than to live the rest of her life with him.

Narada had offered to be the go-between, stressing that there were a couple of problems that would need resolving before their union could be sealed. One was Mandodari's insistence that her father—Mayasura—would have to agree to the proposal. Herein lay the problem, Narada had pointed out. Mayasura, king of Matsya-loka, was a staunch Vishnu devotee and Ravana considered all Vishnu devotees to be his personal enemies. Mandodari's face had fallen as she saw her love reaching nowhere. This was a major difference and neither Ravana nor her father would consent to the marriage, she had despaired. There was no problem in this world that had no solution, Narada had told Mandodari and had urged her to trust him to manage matters.

It was while Narada was contemplating possible strategies to solemnize the Ravana-Mandodari union that this encounter with Ravana happened. It was obvious that the time was not right to broach the subject. So he proceeded to quiz Ravana on the why and wherefores of his present avatar.

A volcano of anger burst forth from Ravana. Using the choicest of expletives for Vishnu, Ravana said that this hater of Shiva and all his followers had conspired to wreck his mother's daily pooja. Narada, who under normal circumstances would have shut his ears with his customary chant of 'Narayana, Narayana', kept wiser counsel and urged Ravana to disclose all details.

'You know that janani is a devout Shiva bhakta. Since coming to live in Lanka, it has been her practice to pray to him at sunrise every day. She goes to the sea, makes a saikatalinga, performs her pooja, makes her offerings and immerses the linga in the waters before returning home. It is her belief that her offering at this pooja, consumed by me as prasad, protects me from all dangers. In fact, my morning rituals are not complete if I do not partake of that prasad. But today...' Ravana spluttered in rage: 'Today, traitors to Shiva and slaves of Vishnu conspired to ruin janani's Shiva pooja. They caused the waves to rise to unnatural levels to wash away janani's saikatalinga.'

'So...' prompted Narada, unable to make the connection between the disruption of Kaikasi's Shiva pooja and Ravana's present attire.

'Janani was heartbroken that her pooja had been ruined. She was also very upset that she was unable to give me the prasad of her offerings,' Ravana paused a while as if he was organizing his thoughts before continuing: 'I am determined to ensure that janani's pooja is never disturbed again. She should not have to make a Shivalinga with sand every day and be exposed to the danger of it being washed away before her pooja is concluded.'

'So...' prodded Narada, still unable to see any connection between Ravana's words and the change in his appearance.

'I promised janani that she would have Shiva's atmalinga, his soul, to offer prayers to. So I am off to do tapasya to obtain Shiva's atmalinga,' Ravana concluded, his voice reflecting his determination.

Narada was dumbstruck. Obtain Shiva's atmalinga? This was a prescription for disaster! Ravana had to be stopped from undertaking this foolhardy expedition. Should he succeed in securing Bhole Shankar's blessing—which was quite possible, given Shiva's easy approachability for his devotees—Kailash would become a dead place. It would mean that Shiva's soul could become captive in Kaikasi's poojagriha. What would become of Devi Maa and Kailash, he wondered even as he hastened to keep pace with Ravana, who had started to walk away. As the only one to be let into the purpose of Ravana's proposed tapasya, he had to act and act quickly to pre-empt this adventure.

'Do not waste your time, Ravana! What makes you think that anyone, even Shiva—called "Bhole Naath" with good reason— would part with his very soul?'

Ravana was unmoved by the apparent ridicule in Narada's tone. 'I promised janani Shiva's atmalinga and I will fulfil my promise,' he declared without even slowing his pace.

Narada could see determination in every step Ravana took. He continued to follow Ravana, hoping that some plan that would make Ravana give up on this expedition would occur to him. No worthwhile plan emerged despite Narada straining his mental faculties. He watched as Ravana selected a patch of thorny bushes in a dense forest and settled in the lotus pose right on a clump of thorns. He looked on as Ravana chanted 'Om Namah Shivayah'.

Narada realized that he could do nothing to disturb Ravana's intense concentration and so should escalate the problem to someone else. He hurried off, Ravana's chants of 'Om Namah Shivayah' echoing in his ears even as he neared Mount Kailash. He rushed on, still lost in his thoughts, and almost bumped into Maata Parvati.

'Narayana, Narayana,' he said apologetically and went on to explain the reason for his preoccupation and the purpose of his unannounced visit. 'It is a question of your pran-nath's atma, Shree Maata, and so it is for you to salvage the situation,' he concluded.

Concern writ large on her face, Parvati looked around wildly, as if a solution would present itself before her. However, the moment passed and composure returned to her countenance. 'Who but my brother Shree Hari can help me? I will go to Vaikuntha immediately,' she said.

'Narayana, Narayana,' chanted Narada in relief and stepped aside to let Parvati pass. 'Meanwhile, I will go and see how Ravana is progressing with his tapasya and do whatever I can to stall him.' So saying, he turned earthward.

'Narayana, Narayana!' the familiar chant escaped Narada's lips involuntarily, and there was a hint of helplessness in his tone. His eyes widened in disbelief and consternation as he saw Ravana lost in his own world of concentration. Ravana was dripping blood and his chants of 'Om Namah Shivayah' had given way to the spontaneous composition of a prayer in praise of Pashupati (which later came to be known as the Shiva-tandava stotram). He was strumming a unique veena that he had put together using his very guts as its strings and two of his heads as the base on which the strings were anchored.

The inevitability of the situation stuck Narada in the face. There was no questioning the intensity of Ravana's tapasya, nor its outcome. Shiva would appear sooner than later and grant him whatever he asked.

It was impossible to tell whether Shiva preceded or followed Narada's thought, but he was suddenly there, drawing Ravana out of his trance. The greater surprise for Narada was that he was accompanied by Parvati, who he thought had gone to seek Vishnu's assistance.

With his body smeared with ash, Shiva was a radiant sight. He was wrapped in a tigerskin; rudraksha beads and snakes adorned his neck, arms, wrists and even ankles. In his right hand he held his trishul, his dhamaruka tied to its staff at the top. The crescent moon atop his coiled and matted locks competed for prominence with Shiva's brightness. His two eyes beamed benevolence and his third eye, placed vertically in the middle of his brow, was closed. Parvati, standing to his left, was a picture in contrast. Her wheat-pink skin added lustre to the golden yellow saree that draped her slender body. She was heavily bejewelled, with a tiara placed upon the crown of her head, large gem-studded earrings and a similar ring in her shapely nose, several necklaces of varying lengths and design, armlets, bangles and a golden waist-band. Even her feet were adorned with jewellery—rings on her toes and anklets made pleasant sounds with her every movement.

Narada, who had quietly taken cover behind a nearby bush to conceal his presence, looked closely at Devi Maa's face for clues. He noticed that her cheeks shone with a heightened tinge of red, but it was her eyes that held his attention. The large almond-shaped eyes that generally brimmed with vaatsalya, reflected a variety of competing emotions. She appeared proud to have the protective arm of her consort around her shoulder; awed at the sight of this mighty rakshasa, whose power of tapasya was sufficient to draw the very soul of Parameshwara; reassured that this calamity would not befall her; yet scared and nervous that something might still happen and she would come to lose the sheet anchor of her life.

And underlying all these was a look of defiance, a resoluteness that she would remain one half of Ardhanareeshwara—half male and half female—that she would not be torn away from the one whose one half she literally was.

'You pleased me, Dashagreeva!' Shankara said, his voice full of compassion and vaatsalya. It was no accident that Shankara had called the tapasvi 'Dashagreeva' and not 'Ravana', which was the name he himself had given. The two severed heads of Ravana returned to their place on his shoulders, the guts went back into his abdomen and all the blood was absorbed into his body as if it had never flowed out. Ravana rose to his feet and folded his hands in salutation.

Narada, who was despairing that Shiva would give away his atma at Ravana's request, froze at the words that fell on his ears next. 'You, with your ash-smeared body, are an eyesore beside this apoorvasundari, this matchless beauty. She deserves the life of a queen. I will make her my queen and give her all the luxuries she can dream of. I seek her from you.'

chapter 23

arada had a bird's eye view of the foothills of the Himalayas. He had made himself invisible and was flying bird-like in search of his quarry. He spotted them soon enough—Ravana was walking jauntily, with Jagat Maata following him a couple of steps behind. Narada continued on his path, not letting the two out of sight. His heart went out to Parvati, who was dragging her feet with difficulty, her head downcast. The droop of her shoulders spoke volumes about her mental frame. Ravana, on the other hand, had a swagger to his stride—the walk of one who has just won a prize.

Narada knew he was losing time. He had to formulate his strategy for confronting Ravana and ensuring the relinquishment of Shiva's consort. After considering various options, Narada decided that his chance of success would be enhanced if he managed to surprise Ravana, and he landed behind the foliage near a bend in Ravana's path.

'Narayana, Narayana!' he chanted and stepped right into Ravana's path, managing a head-on collision between them. 'Narayana, Narayana!' he chanted once again, rubbing his forehead gingerly. Thrown slightly off balance by this unexpected obstacle, Ravana took a moment to regain his composure.

'Oh! It is you, pitamaha,' he said, his tone clearly indicating that he was not happy to see Narada.

'Narayana, Narayana!' Narada's signature chant this time held an overdose of exuberance. 'What a pleasant surprise, Ravana! Are you returning with the fruit of your austerities? I would like very much to have a glimpse of Shiva's atmalinga before you present it to your mother. But wait, what is this? Your hands are empty and you have a woman walking with you! Don't tell me that you did not do tapasya at all, and that you were actually searching for a wife for yourself!'

Narada would have continued in this manner had he not been interrupted by an impatient Ravana. 'Stop jumping to all kinds of conclusions, Muneendra. And I am sure I do not have to tell you how one should conduct oneself in the presence of women.' So saying, he dragged Narada a few steps away. 'Devi, sit here for a moment and rest your tired legs. I'll join you in a minute,' he said over his shoulder.

'I could not have asked for more, Muneendra! I got Parvati for myself as reward for my tapasya. I know that Shiva will follow her. I will keep this personification of beauty for myself and give Shankara to janani for her pooja. Are you jealous of my good fortune?' Ravana spoke in a triumphant voice.

'Not jealous, but definitely sceptical. For I do not think anyone, including Bhole Naath, would part with their companion, whatever the reason. I feel a trick was played on you and you were fooled into thinking that you were taking Parvati with you.'

Ravana shook his head emphatically. 'None can fool me and I know that Shankara does not fool his bhaktas, leave alone a devoted bhakta like me.'

'I am not convinced, Ravana! There has definitely been some trickery involved. Let me speak to this lady. I am sure that I can discover her true identity. You know that I have magical powers. I can make anyone shed their assumed personalities. However, I need to be alone with that person.'

Narada's words and manner injected a germ of doubt in Ravana. Come to think of it, Shiva had appeared only too ready to give away Parvati, which was not normal. It would be nice if he could reassure himself that he had not been tricked, Ravana thought and signalled to Narada to make the necessary enquiries. He then moved away, putting more distance between himself and the woman who had been following him.

Parvati had her back to him when Narada approached her, showing her lack of interest in what was transpiring between the two men. Narada walked around to face her, so as to keep Ravana within his sight.

'Ah, it is you, Narada! Come here to laugh at my predicament, have you? Is this a joke that you and Vishnu decided to play on me? First you come and tell me that Ravana is about to seek Parameshwara's atmalinga and then, when I go to seek Vishnu's help in foiling this bid, he promises to prevent it. Oh, yes! He kept his promise. And how did he do it? By making that rakshasa ask for me! I hope Vishnu is happy at seeing me separated from my beloved!'

Parvati's tirade was understandable, even though quite unexpected. Narada tried to put a stop to this angry outburst so that they could consider ways of getting out of this situation. He also did not want her words to reach Ravana's ears. But her seething anger made her blind to Narada's gestures for silence.

'Vishnu will also taste the pangs of separation from his beloved! He will be born on earth to experience the pain that I am going through now.'

She regretted her words the moment they were out. Overcome with remorse, Parvati started to apologize for her hasty curse on Vishnu.

'Do not fret so, maate! Your anger is understandable and quite possibly, your words are prophetic in the larger cosmic scheme of things. In fact, I am here as the bearer of Narayana's apologies to you for having put you in this predicament. Let me explain briefly how all this came to pass. The moment I heard Ravana ask for you as the fruit of his tapasya, I rushed to inform Vaikunthavaasa of the development. He, of course, knew of it, as it was he who had influenced Ravana's thoughts and tongue. The Lord explained to me that this was the only option that occurred to him in the short time available. He has now sent me to secure your release from this bondage.'

'How will you do that, Narada?' There was despair in her voice.

'Nothing is beyond you, maate! You are the shakti that runs this universe. Do not let this unsavoury circumstance cloud your thinking. You know that you are capable of taking different forms as per the demands of a situation. At all times you are the Jagat Janani, taking the form that your bhakta's need. You have slain several rakshasas by taking on a fierce aspect and the required physical attributes. Given the fact that Ravana asked for you on account of your physical beauty, arguing that you and Eeshwara do not match on that score, you can easily play the same trick on Ravana.'

'And how will I do that?'

'Easy, maate! I will chant your mantra, invoking you as Bhadra Kali and urge you to show yourself in your avataar, and you will assume that form in answer to the prayers of this bhakta.'

Even as Narada was completing his sentence, Ravana walked towards them with the question: 'Well Muneendra! Have you found out who this Maaya Swaroopini is?'

Narada's lips began to move in a silent incantation in praise of Maata Bhadra Kali, even as he nodded a response to Ravana. 'Maa, please show us your real self,' he said.

The bejewelled and benevolent visage of the Mother of the Universe transformed into a fierce form—with large protruding eyes, long unkempt tresses that hung like huge ropes down her back, a garland of skulls and bones around her neck and a full skirt of hay around her torso. In her right hand she held a heavy, bloodstained sword and in her left hand she held a severed head, the blood still dripping from its neck.

Ravana stopped in his tracks. His mouth gaped. A wordless sound escaped him. He was clearly stumped.

'Who wants to make me his queen?'

The taunting question, spoken in a voice that sounded like a thousand donkeys braying at the same time, made the two men want to run for cover. Narada gave in to the impulse and turned on his heel and would have run for it, had Ravana's hand not gripped him hard. Ravana answered for both, making a great effort to remain cool and composed. Through clenched teeth he said: 'No one. Go away to where you come from.'

No sooner were the words out of Ravana's mouth, than a whirlwind built up where the woman stood and the next moment, the dust cleared and it was as if there had never been anything or anyone there. Ravana looked at the empty space for a moment before he let go of Narada's hand, let out a long-held breath slowly— making a hissing sound in the process—and started to walk away.

Narada too let out his breath, a silent prayer mingled with it as it escaped his lips. He turned his eyes heavenward and folded his hands momentarily. His lips parted in a half-smile as he complimented himself on the success of his mission. Then he looked at the receding figure of Ravana and remembered that he still had something more to achieve. He hurried after Ravana, calling out to him.

Ravana neither looked back nor slackened his pace. 'Putra, putra!' panted Narada as he finally caught up with him and placed a restraining hand on Ravana's arm. 'Where are you going?' he asked in the same breath. Ravana continued to stride along, ignoring Narada.

'Hasty actions taken in a fit of anger never yield proper results. You know that, don't you, putra,' Narada said, continuing to use the filial term in a bid to secure Ravana's submission to his counsel.

His words succeeded in slowing Ravana's pace somewhat.

'I am going to that keeper of burial grounds to teach him a lesson for double-crossing me,' Ravana's voice showed his anger.

'I understand how you feel, Ravana, but still repeat my advice to you. Decisions and actions that arise out of anger often lead to disastrous consequences. I am not suggesting that you accept the trick played on you and do nothing to seek retribution. But first you need to control your emotions and deliberate on the choices available to you.' Narada took a sidelong look at his companion to assess the impact of his words and was happy to note a thoughtful expression replacing the white rage. 'Come, let us sit in the shade of this tree and devise our course of action,' he said, gently propelling Ravana to a nearby banyan tree. Ravana settled on a clump of roots, sullenly looking at the ground, trying to achieve a modicum of composure, using pranayama as the means to do so.

Narada sat nearby, thinking on how to achieve his objective, which was, in fact, twofold. It was imperative that he prevented Ravana's return to Lanka for the moment, as that would set him once again on his mission to secure Eeshwara's atmalinga. He could not hope to be this lucky the next time. The second part was to somehow arrange a marriage for Ravana, which would take his mind off wars and conquests—this was the plan Saraswati and he had together thought up. He wished he could quickly come up with a plan of action that would serve both purposes.

'I did not expect this kind of underhand action from Shankara,' Ravana's tone showed how let-down he felt. 'If only I knew where he hid Parvati,' he added wistfully.

'What would you do then? Mount an offensive to get her?' Narada asked, looking closely at Ravana.

'No, Muneendra! You have helped me overcome that instinct with your sage advice. I cannot thank you enough for that. For, had I given in to that impulse, I would have started an endless war. You know that I cannot die at the hands of devas, and devas, because of the amrit they consumed, also cannot die. I would have spent all my time and energy in a sapping war.'

'I am glad I was of help. And I am here to be of more assistance to you, should you feel so inclined,' Narada said in a tone intended to secure a positive response.

But Ravana's mind was on other things. 'I have to avenge this trick played on me. I will locate Shiva-patni wherever she is hidden and make her mine. Only then will I consider my mission accomplished and rest in peace,' he said resolutely.

'How will you find her? You don't even know what she looks like!'

'That is true. But believe me when I say I will know her when I see her. Come to think of it, I think Parvati herself is interested in me.'

Narada fought hard to keep his voice even and not betray the turmoil Ravana's words had ignited in him. 'And what has made you come to this conclusion?' he asked slowly.

'Perhaps you never saw it, but there is a small Shiva shrine that I had built in the Ashoka vatika, so that I would not have to miss out on Shivaarchana when I was in the vana. Since no one is allowed into the vatika, the shrine is not cleaned regularly. Recently, however, I noticed that someone has been cleaning the shrine. I know it is a woman, because sometimes I hear this person sing. I have never set eyes on her, even though I have tried; possibly because she possesses superhuman powers. It is the sweetest and most mellifluous voice I have ever heard. I am convinced that that person is Parvati and that she comes to the vatika to feast her eyes on me.'

Narada's heart jumped with joy at this reference to Mandodari. He knew he would achieve his objective, and began to fine-tune his game plan. He turned slowly to Ravana, choosing his words carefully: 'And what makes you think she goes there for you?'

Ravana's eyes twinkled mischievously. 'It is difficult to put it into words and besides, you would not understand these things, pitamaha, since you are a celibate brahmachari.'

Narada nodded his agreement with this statement, even as he tried to frame a question that would bind Ravana to his intent to wed the lass he thought was Parvati but was Mandodari. 'If I—a celibate brahmachari—understand you correctly, you say you will marry this girl whose sweet voice tells you that she loves you,' he said, his tone half questioning, half stating.

'Yes, I will marry her. But I have to first find out where that Shiva has hidden her,' he said.

Narada nodded once again. 'You can leave that task to me. I told you I am here to help you in every way I can,' he said and added: 'Let me concentrate and find out where this Parvati of yours is.'

chapter 24

'There is a problem,' Narada said. His voice displayed no emotion, but the manner in which he sat down at some distance from Ravana was calculated to convey fatigue of the body and mind. His eyes, however, were very watchful, as they viewed Ravana from under lowered lids.

'Now what?' Ravana's manner and voice showed exasperation and a trace of nervousness. He had been sitting under this coral reef for a long while, and the subterfuge it involved irritated him. It was distasteful and completely out of character for this warrior rakshasa king, who considered valour his second nature. He would take any situation head on first and then think. But here he was, hiding like a thief! All for his life's love, and for having taken the wily Narada as his guide and accomplice!

'Your Parvati says she will not take any step without the consent of her "father",' Narada said, stressing the last word.

'Oh, Muneendra! This charade is going too far! We know, and she knows that this asura king is not her father; she does not belong here,' Ravana rose and began pacing up and down, wringing his hands behind his back, where he kept them locked in an attempt at self-control. He stopped mid-step and turned to Narada abruptly: 'Is this another of your favourite games, kalaha-priya?'

'Narayana! Narayana!' Narada chanted as he rose with his hands covering his ears, as if to shut out the words. 'This is a great return for my efforts, Ravana! I think I should not have agreed to be the matchmaker for you. I am a brahmachari whose life is dedicated to loka-kalyan. It was my folly that made me want to help my putra find true love in his life, knowing full well that I am not suited for the task. I do this for you and you call me "kalaha-priya". Narada's every word oozed pain, and he turned as if to walk away.

Ravana was beside him in a trice, a restraining hand placed apologetically on Narada's shoulder. 'I am sorry, pitamaha! Please pardon me. I have been hiding amidst these creepy coral reefs ever since we arrived here. I am impatient to be united with my beloved. My eagerness to meet her in person has been growing by leaps and bounds ever since you informed me that she reciprocates my feelings of love. That is why I cannot comprehend what problem can keep us apart.'

Narada led the lovelorn Ravana back into the seclusion of the coral reef. He guided Ravana into a sitting posture. 'Knowing how determined you are to marry this lass, I am doing all I can to seal the alliance. She insists that we seek her hand from her father. I had hoped to avoid a meeting between you and Raja Mayasura, given the diametrically opposite views you both hold on certain issues. You are a Vishnu-dweshi and he is a vocal Vishnubhakta. Your wedding plans could fall apart if an argument crops up in this regard.'

'The smart devil! Shiva, who portrays himself as "Bhole Naath" to his devotees, has turned out to be quite a devious fellow! He found a Vishnubhakta to hide Parvati from me!' Ravana wrung his hands, looked at Narada and muttered: 'Why must Parvati continue to play the dutiful and obedient daughter? Does she have no feelings for her strong and valiant lover, who, for her sake, has been hiding like a thief in this slimy little hole?'

'I cannot answer these questions. If you want to go ahead, we have to seek an audience with the king and make a proposal for his daughter's hand. We can hope for his consent, if you will let me do the talking, and do not needlessly bring up the names of either Shiva or Vishnu,' Narada spoke curtly and waited for

Ravana's nod before striding off in the direction of the royal palace to send word about his presence in the region and desire for a meeting with the king.

Ravana looked at the receding figure of Narada and was overcome with gratitude for him. He was going to such immense trouble for him. 'Pitamaha!' he called out on impulse.

Narada stopped and turned around, fatigued on account of the numerous trips he was making through the unaccustomed watery environs showing even in this small movement. He raised a hand and parted his lips as if to say something, but changed his mind and returned to where Ravana was sitting. 'What is it? Is something bothering you, vatsa?' he asked kindly and then added, a tinge of doubt in his tone: 'Or is it that you have changed your mind?'

Ravana stood up, his head and shoulders slightly hunched to fit into the cramped cave he was hiding in. 'No, pitamaha! I just wanted to thank you. You have taken such pains on my behalf; I do not know how I can ever repay you for your kindness.' Ravana's face and tone both reflected his gratitude.

Narada waved a hand dismissively, but his eyes twinkled mischievously. 'You don't have to repay me for anything. You call me "pitamaha" and in that capacity, it is my duty to help you in any way that I can. But do remember to spread the word that I am not "kalaha-priya" as the world likes to paint me. Even you call me that sometimes, don't you,' Narada said in a mock taunt.

Narada's reference to filial relations reminded Ravana of his own two brothers. He took a small step forward, coming partially out from under the overhanging coral cliffs and placed his arm around Narada's shoulders. Perplexed at this action, Narada tried to guide Ravana back into the coral cave, urging him not to give himself away at this crucial juncture.

'Pitamaha, I know the great effort you are making to help me realize my heart's desire. I can neither thank you nor repay you enough. Your wisdom and ability to strategize encourage me to be bold and seek your help in finding suitable wives for my two brothers also. I feel I am unequal to this task on my own, particularly in Kumbhakarna's case, because of his peculiar circumstances. Which girl would want to marry a man who sleeps for six months at a stretch? But you, who travel around the worlds, would be able to find a suitable mate for him, I am sure!'

Narada laughed indulgently. 'I am flattered at the faith you show in my abilities, Ravana. But please remember, I am yet to complete negotiating your matrimony successfully. And now, be good and return to the safety of your hiding place till I return.' So saying, Narada removed Ravana's hand from over his shoulder, gestured for him to stay out of sight and walked away resolutely in the direction of the royal palace.

Ravana settled back in the coral alcove, his eyes following Narada till a bend in the path took him out of sight. He was confident that Narada would be able to persuade this danava king to give Parvati's hand to him in marriage. For a moment, he was irritated that he was forced to participate in this charade of seeking the bride's father's permission and having him give away his daughter in 'kanya-daan', when the bride here was Parvati and not who she pretended to be—Mandodari, daughter of Mayasura. Well, all this trouble was worth the final result, he mused.

Ravana's heart once again filled with gratitude for Narada. He had not only saved him from getting stuck with that monster that Shiva had tried to palm off to him as Parvati, but had also helped him locate the real Parvati, hidden cleverly by Shiva in the house of a Vishnubhakta. Narada had also taken the trouble of escorting him to Matsya-loka and acting as the go-between for him and Parvati.

The journey into Matsya-loka had been tough, but Narada's presence by his side had made it much easier. Narada had used his magical powers to facilitate his breathing in this watery world, and had guided his first foray here. And it was Narada who had devised the strategy that had enabled Ravana to confirm that this girl was indeed the one who had taken his heart long ago in his own Ashoka vana. The plan was brilliant in its simplicity. Narada had arranged a meeting with her and had engineered a walk with her that took them close to the coral alcove where Ravana was concealed. Ravana had been able to identify her from the electrifying vibrations that reached him—just the way it had been back then in Lanka. And the fleeting glimpse of her face through the veil over her head and the lilting gurgle of her laughter at something her companion said had sent his heart lurching with longing for her.

The next step of the three-phase action plan had been the trickiest of all, as it had involved securing the lady's consent for his proposal. He had had to curb his recurring urge to bite his nails to cope with the suspense. He had wondered whether Narada, a brahmachari who had never dallied with a damsel, could achieve the goal. His doubts were set at rest the moment he saw the wide grin on Narada's face when he returned after spending quite a while with Parvati alias Mandodari. Oh! How happy Ravana had been to learn that she reciprocated his feelings for her and that she was willing to spend the rest of her life as his wife. The caveat of course was that her 'father' agreed to the union.

And this was the issue that Narada had gone to tackle now—to get 'father Mayasura' to consent to their wedding. Ravana fervently hoped that this too would be accomplished without a hitch. How pleased janani would be to have none other than Parvati as a daughter-in-law.

Narada shaking him by the shoulder and repeatedly calling out his name brought Ravana out of his daydream. It took him a while to return to the present and for the import of Narada's words to sink in. The meeting with Mayasura had gone off exceptionally well, with the king being very pleased by the fact that a great sage like Narada had graced his home and had come bearing a wedding proposal for his daughter. Narada had spoken highly about the prospective groom, his illustrious lineage, his accomplishments and above all, how keen he was to forge this relationship between them. 'Naturally, the king wants to meet you once before formally accepting our proposal. I told him that it would take a couple of days for me to bring the groom over for the meeting,' Narada said and, looking at the expression on Ravana's face, added with a chuckle: 'You did not expect me to tell him that you were hiding amidst the coral reefs, did you? I had to pretend that I had to summon you from Bhoo-loka, which would take some time.'

'It is all right for you to keep up all these pretences, pitamaha. But think what will happen to me if I have to stay in this cramped position for two more days! I will lose my ability to stand straight ever again,' Ravana complained.

'No need to worry on that score, putra! Mayasura has invited me to be his guest till your arrival here, and has allotted guest accommodation for me. I am sure I will be able to hide you there. You will have good food, a comfortable bed to sleep on and space enough to stretch your legs,' Narada said and smiled at the look of relief that came over Ravana's face.

'Would you also arrange a meeting for me with...with her?' Ravana was surprised at the spate of unaccustomed emotions that swept over him. He was somewhat nervous, somewhat bashful, somewhat excited, and elated. There was something about Mandodari that touched his heart in a manner that had never happened before. He smiled, surprised that he was slowly getting used to Parvati's other name.

'Certainly not,' Narada was curt. 'I do not want you to be discovered before time and have all my efforts washed away in the swirling waters of the Matsya-loka. And, if you really want this wedding to happen, you will follow my instructions strictly.' Narada looked at Ravana's crestfallen face and softened his tone. 'Let us wait for this meeting with Mayasura to be concluded successfully. Then we can decide what to do. But till then, please be very very careful, and do nothing that could spoil our plans.'

'I am sorry, pitamaha! I promise to be careful and not do anything without your permission till we meet my father-in-law and get him to agree to our proposal.'

Narada smiled. 'Then stay here, while I go and see where I am to stay while waiting for the bridegroom's arrival. Then I will return for you and take you there in secrecy.'

Ravana nodded and watched Narada walk down the by now familiar path to the royal palace. He felt happy and suddenly, the fatigue and tension of the past few days seemed to catch up with him. He let his shoulders slump and his head droop and fell into a fitful sleep, dreaming about the comfortable bed he would soon have to sleep on. And it would not be long before he would have the company of Mandodari in his bed, he thought, smiling in his sleep.

chapter 25

'I wish you could stay here for some more time.'

Narada smiled. 'These are words you should say when your father is leaving you in the new environs of your in-laws' house, Mandodari, not when a grandfather on your husband's side is leaving your parental home.'

'No pitamaha! I feel guilty at the subterfuge I indulged in to marry the man I love. I pretended to be someone I am not. I die a thousand deaths each time Lankadheesh addresses me as "Parvati". It seemed all right then and your presence and support gave me the courage to go through with it. Now I am scared that I might be found out and that he will desert me. I am scared as to what will happen if my father learns the truth,' Mandodari said, her head bent and hands wringing the edge of her long bridal veil.

Narada placed a reassuring hand on Mandodari's shoulder, and lifted her chin up with his other hand. 'There is no subterfuge, child, none at all. You are the girl that Ravana wanted to wed, his only confusion was about the name. Your husband can call you by whatever name he chooses, there is nothing wrong in that. In fact, there is a tradition in the Bhoo-loka wherein a girl is given a new name in her matrimonial home. This given name becomes her identity in her new home. In your case, your husband calls you by two names. In due course, he might come to use your actual name more.'

Mandodari smiled and nodded her head, even as her eyes betrayed a thin film of moisture. 'I wait for the day when my husband will love me as myself and not under the impression that

I am somebody else,' she said and added after a slight pause: 'I do not have words to thank you for giving me my life's love. With you here, I did not for a moment feel that I was doing anything wrong. But now that you are going away, I am no longer sure.'

'Do not fret so, my little one! What has happened is what has been ordained. You and Ravana are made for each other. And for helping me achieve this, I will give you a special blessing. You will never experience widowhood,' Narada placed his right hand on Mandodari's head. Then, he turned and walked away.

Mandodari continued to stand there even when she could no longer see Narada, lost in thought, particularly about the permanence of her conjugal bliss. The past month still seemed like a dream to her. She had lost all hope of her love for Ravana reaching its logical end, as it had been a long time since he had visited Ashoka vatika. So much so that she had stopped going to the vatika and was pining for him when, out of nowhere, maharishi Narada had come to seek her out. She had been so thrilled to hear that Ravana loved her fervently and had come to seek her hand in marriage from her father that she had readily agreed to the plan suggested by Narada. She so longed to be Ravana's dharmapatni that she did not think much of keeping two little secrets—one from Ravana and another from her father. Not letting her father know that Ravana was a staunch Vishnu-dweshi was understandable, but that she should not object to being called 'Parvati' by Ravana miffed her. Narada had explained that when Ravana had fallen in love with her, he had thought of her as Parvati, the name he had given his 'swapnasundari', his dream girl, and now he loved the name as much as he loved her. This was a small thing to do for a man who had come across the worlds to wed her.

As her luck would have it, Mayasura had liked Ravana so much that he had been only too happy to accept Narada's proposal. The wedding had taken place almost immediately and the festivities had lasted for almost a week.

Life with her new husband was all that she could have wished for. He made her feel special in every way and left her in no doubt as to how much he cared for her. Ravana had agreed to spend another month in Matsya-loka before returning to Lanka with his bride. Narada, however, had pleaded preoccupations and had taken his leave. While Ravana and the king had bid their adieus at the entrance of the royal palace, Mandodari had accompanied Narada to the gates of the palace.

Mandodari snapped out of her reverie with a jolt as she remembered Narada's admonition. He had told her not to leave her father and husband alone together for long stretches of time to avoid the possibility of any major argument developing between them. She turned on her heel and started walking briskly towards the palace, hoping that her husband and father had not gotten into any serious discourse about contentious issues. She had barely reached the first bend in the picturesque path when she bumped into Ravana, who had come looking for her.

'Where did my darling get lost? I thought you had gone off with Narada Muneendra,' Ravana said in mock complaint and put a hand across her shoulder, drawing her close.

'I wish he could have stayed with us longer.'

'I understand how you feel. He has really exerted himself to bring us together. Even now, he is on a mission to help me find suitable brides for my two younger brothers.' Ravana noticed the puzzled look on Mandodari's face and went on to explain: 'There are certain special circumstances that call for intervention and pitamaha is best suited for the task on account of his globetrotting lifestyle. My brother Kumbhakarna is an invincible warrior and a master strategist, but sleeps for six months at a stretch. We want to find a girl who can adjust to this situation.'

'And Vibheeshana?'

'Vibhee is more like a recluse; not very interested in marriage or women. He needs a wife who understands him and can be a companion to him at the intellectual plane. I persuaded pitamaha to help me find brides who will make my brothers happy. I expect him to bring news in this regard by the time we reach Lanka. Then I can consider my responsibility as the elder brother duly discharged.'

'There is something more that you want to do to feel fully satisfied as the head of the family, I can sense that in your words. Would you like to share it with me?' Mandodari asked in a hesitant, cajoling tone.

Ravana looked at his new wife with admiration. How quickly she had learnt to understand him and his innermost thoughts! 'I have a sister; her name is Surpanakha. She is very pretty and I always think of her as Chandramukhi. Recently, she lost her husband in an accident. I am indirectly responsible for that accident and Surpanakha is very upset about it.'

'How can you be responsible for an accident?' Mandodari said, knitting her brows in incomprehension.

Ravana took a deep breath, as though preparing himself for a confession that was being forced out of him. 'I have not admitted this to anyone till now, and I do not know what makes me do so now, but the truth is that I am responsible for his death. I know I am. I forced Vidyutjihva—Surpi's husband—to undertake a journey across the oceans when he was clearly not up to it. At that time, however, it seemed like I was doing the right thing. I am sure you know how it is…there are a thousand things that need to be done for the smooth functioning of administration.

'There was an emergency and Vidyutjihva was the correct person to resolve it. Speed was of the essence, but he was at a madhushala, drunk on intoxicating spirits. He was in no fit state to stand on his own without support, leave alone perform a task. I lost my temper and forced him to leave immediately, ignoring his condition. He slipped and fell into the deep waters of the moat as he was crossing it. He was eaten up immediately by alligators and sharks. Surpi has not been herself since then. And I am to blame for it,' Ravana said, burying his face in his hands.

Mandodari, who had led Ravana into the relative privacy of a shrubbery and seated him on an artfully crafted bench there, remained silent for a while. 'Nath,' she said softly, placing her hand gently on his arm. 'No one can change what has happened. Blaming yourself is not going to help either. Your real worry is that Surpanakha is widowed and is lonely. This situation can be changed by getting her married once again, isn't it?'

'How I wish it was so simple! But it is not—for various reasons. One is that the law in Lanka does not permit widows to remarry. This law had to be put in place under intense public pressure. Lanka's citizens have no objection to anyone—male or female—cohabiting with any number of partners as long as one is unmarried. But once anyone ties the knot, it is for life.'

Mandodari nodded. Ravana continued to speak without looking at her. 'Surpanakha has a free spirit that does not accept rules and regulations. The reason she remained loyal to Vidyutjihva was because he understood and respected her and satisfied her in all ways. After she lost her husband, she has become more wilful and vengeful.' Ravana's voice dropped to a whisper; he was talking to himself, forgetting his wife beside him. 'Lanka is no longer the right place for her. She should be where she feels completely free, with no restrictions.' Ravana's face brightened suddenly as a thought struck him. He sat up straight, looked at Mandodari and declared: 'I know what to do. I will send Surpi to Janasthana.'

Mandodari looked confused, even as she wanted to share in her husband's enthusiasm for this place. Ravana patted her hand and smiled. 'Sorry, priye, for flying off like that about matters you do not understand. I will explain. Janasthana is a part of Dandaka Aranya. It is currently being managed by my cousins—Khara and Dushana. They are the sons of Kumbhinasi, my mother's cousin sister. They nursed a grouse that they were not being given the importance they deserved and started creating problems. My options as to how to deal with them were limited on account of our relationship. So I sent them to Janasthana as managers charged with the responsibility of monitoring events and developments that have a bearing on Lanka. I provided them with some manpower to satisfy their egos.'

Mandodari nodded, marvelling at her husband's ability to deal with tricky issues, but still not understanding how this fitted in with the peculiar problem of her sister-in-law.

Ravana was elated. He stood up and slapped his thigh in a self-congratulatory manner. 'Priye, you are wonderful. Your mere presence by my side has enabled me to resolve an issue that has been bothering me for a long time. Surpi can go and live in Janasthana; she can oversee her two younger brothers and live like a queen there. There she will be able to take on any number of lovers without fear of social repercussions,' Ravana pulled Mandodari to her feet and gave her a tight hug. 'Come, let us go in. Your father will be wondering where we have disappeared to,' he said and set off at a brisk pace.

His thoughtful mood still prevailing, Ravana slowed his pace after a while, stopping to wait for his wife to catch up with him. He slipped a hand around her shoulder as they both continued their walk at an easy pace. Ravana began to speak again, pouring out his innermost thoughts. 'You know, Mandodari, I never thought I would come to like your father so much. Initially, I looked on him as a hurdle that I had to cross to reach my prize—which is you, my dear!' Ravana squeezed his wife's shoulder. So engrossed was he with his own thoughts that he failed to notice that Mandodari did not respond to his words.

His own thoughts shifted as he remembered Narada's word of caution to him. 'Do not discuss Mayasura with your wife. Remember that he deserves your gratitude and respect as your father-in-law. His being a Vishnubhakta does not change this position. Be nice to him during your stay here as his guest,' he had said.

As his thoughts revolved around Narada and Mayasura, another picture formed in his mind—that of his own father, Vishravasu. How similar Mayasura and his father were, he mused. Even before he realized it, he was articulating his thoughts. 'I am surprised that your father should remind me of my own father, even though on the face of it there is hardly any similarity between them—one is a king administering a kingdom and the other is a muni who has renounced this world.'

Mandodari was glad that her husband had provided her with the opportunity to change the course of their conversation. 'What is he like? Do tell me about that great man,' she urged.

'I have not seen him in many years. Not since I came to live in Lanka... But you are right, he is a great man. Besides being the father who gave me life and body, he was my first guru. I wish I had been a more devoted student; I could have learnt so much more from him.'

'I have not known any muni, except Narada Muneendra. And you must agree that he is not like any conventional muni,' Mandodari said.

'I do agree with you on that,' Ravana laughed, bringing a smile to Mandodari's lips. 'My father is a real, or, to put it in your words, a "conventional" muni. He never lost his temper, he gave whatever was sought of him and stayed committed to his lifestyle. It was not a small thing that he married my mother, a rakshasa kanya, because she desired it, even though he was perfectly happy with his existing wife and son.

'And such was the inspiration he provided that matru shree, that is his first wife, accepted janani as her own sister. She helped bring us up. And I love her most for the understanding and sympathy with which she treated my wilful and moody sister.' Ravana felt that he was possibly boring Mandodari with all these details about his family. He turned to apologize for his chatter, but was immediately caught by the pallor on her face and her unsteady gait.

'Priye, are you alright? Are you tired? Come, sit here for a while and rest,' he said and tenderly walked Mandodari to the nearest stone bench on the pathway. He noted that, for the first time in all this while he had known her, Mandodari did not protest at being treated as a dainty and weak person. In fact, she leant against his shoulder and closed her eyes, making Ravana feel helpless.

chapter 26

'She is a liar!' Ravana shouted, pointing an accusing finger at his wife. His stance, as he stood with feet apart, was defiant.

Mandodari, who was trying to merge into the background by positioning herself behind a tree, made an effort to shrink even further back. Her eyes were smarting with unshed tears. She had never felt so humiliated in her life. To be called a 'liar', that too by her own husband in front of his mother—she could not have dreamt of a worse nightmare. The implied accusation contained in this epithet was that she was an imposter, pretending to be someone she was not. The words hurt like a thousand arrows piercing her body and soul. The only consolation she drew was that they were in her mother-in-law's private garden with no servants or attendants in the vicinity.

'Use that hand to close that unholy mouth of yours,' Kaikasi shook a finger at her son. Her voice was soft and dangerously even and conveyed her displeasure eloquently. 'Have you given up on the very basics of civilized behaviour? Do you not know how a wife is to be treated by the one who pledges to protect her under all circumstances? Or have you given the go by to even these sacred vows you took with agni as your witness?'

'Janani!' Ravana interrupted his mother with a raised hand. 'You heap accusations on my head without even considering the facts that stare you in the face. In fact, you do not even have to exercise your mind to deduce the meaning of these facts. All you need to do is to make this double-tongued snake confess,' he said, throwing a challenging look at the tree behind which his wife stood.

'So be it!' responded Kaikasi and, turning to the same tree, called out: 'Come here, child! You have nothing to fear.'

Mandodari swallowed hard, fighting the tears that threatened to break free, moved by the kindness in her mother-in-law's voice. She stepped out, her attempt to stand straight and square her shoulders not escaping either observer. She walked up to Kaikasi, concealing her clenched fists in the folds of her saree, her eyes downcast, yet conveying her readiness to answer any question. She scrupulously avoided looking at Ravana and stopped a couple of steps from Kaikasi.

Kaikasi rose from her seat and took a step closer to Mandodari. She placed one hand on the younger woman's shoulder and used the forefinger of the other hand to lift her chin up, forcing her to look straight into her eyes. 'This pig-headed son of mine has been raving that you are Parvati, Shiva's wife. What have you to say?'

'No, janani! I am Mandodari, daughter of Mayasura, the strongest king in the Matsya-loka. I swear by the unborn child of Lankadheesh that I am carrying in my womb,' she replied with all the dignity she could muster, her right hand placed protectively over her belly.

The words, spoken in the softest of voices but with unmistakable resoluteness had a numbing effect on all.

It was as if time stood still as each was transported into their own inner worlds.

Kaikasi bit hard on her lips to stifle the gasp that threatened to escape her. Her panic-stricken gaze darted from her son to the girl he had brought home as his bride and now claimed was none other than Parvati, consort to her beloved deity, Shiva. Had her son committed the ultimate blasphemy of bedding the mother of the cosmos? And, if what this girl said about her pregnancy was true, what divine punishment was in store for her and her son? She could only hope that her son had been misguided about the identity of the girl he had married. She also knew that Ravana, who never lied to her—no matter what the situation—was not twisting the facts when he said he had sought Parvati from Shiva. Only Shiva, the Mahadeva, could help her. She slipped into a silent prayer to Shiva, seeking guidance and pardon.

Mandodari would have given anything to bite back her words. She was, if it was possible, more shocked than the other two at the words that had escaped her lips. It was the last thing she had wanted to say in her defence. It made her appear like a weak woman who sought forgiveness citing her condition as her excuse. She had not wished to announce her pregnancy in this manner! She did not know why she had, or what had made her swear on her unborn child. She looked at Ravana, her loving husband of a little over three months, and wondered dully if this was the same person whom she had fallen in love with and married for a lifetime of togetherness.

No, she had not erred in her judgement or choice of mate. Her close and intimate association with Ravana since their wedding had convinced her of that, and today's spat—however distasteful it might be—had not altered her conviction in this regard. In fact, her respect and admiration for him had multiplied manifold since stepping into this enchanting land of Lanka. He had personally escorted her around the magnificent city, showing her its gardens and architecture, and even his favourite Ashoka vatika, which had brought back memories of the secret visits she had made to it just to feel Ravana's presence.

She cast a furtive glance at Ravana from the corners of her lowered eyes, her heart sinking at the stoniness of his demeanour. How had the love evaporated from his eyes to be replaced by such anger? Even hatred! Did he hate her? Even if she was fooled by her own love for him into believing that he reciprocated her feelings in equal measure, her assessment of Ravana as a tender and caring person was not the creation of a besotted imagination. She had felt it first-hand when he had taken her to meet his brothers. She had noticed him tiptoeing into Kumbhakarna's chambers and speaking to him in whispers even though he knew that his brother's slumber could not be disturbed by a hurricane or a thousand elephants trumpeting at the same time. Nor had she imagined the gentleness in his touch as he had stroked his brother's hair and forehead. He demonstrated a rare protectiveness towards his youngest brother, Vibheeshana, with whom he had serious ideological differences. She herself had taken an instant liking for the soft-spoken Vibhee, her respect for him going up for the tenacity with which he held on to what he considered was 'dharma' and his refusal to be cowed down by his elder brother's towering personality.

Was this man, who was breathing fire from his every sinew, the same as the husband for whom love was second nature? Had he not given ample evidence of how much he adored her? Was it her imagination that had led her to think that, underlying his casual bantering voice when talking to Surpanakha was his boundless and indulgent love for his only sister? The way in which Ravana cherished his sister made Mandodari yearn for a brother who would cherish her and stand by her through life's ups and downs. She had felt their bonds of love when Ravana had first introduced her to Surpanakha and sensed that Surpanakha perceived her as a potential rival for her brother's affections. Ravana had understood and empathized with his sister's apprehensions and had devoted himself to addressing them. He had put into motion the plan he had worked out while honeymooning with Mandodari in her father's home. Ravana hoped that Surpanakha would find a mate of her liking in Janasthana and through him, regain her verve for life.

In fact, they had just bid their adieus to Surpanakha before coming to see the raj-maata. Ravana was particularly happy that Surpanakha had selected Trisira to accompany her. Trisira was a trusted lieutenant of Ravana's and a rakshasa of rare strength. In addition, he was extremely presentable and a master of the art of wining over women's hearts. He also possessed a free spirit like Surpanakha and Ravana hoped that a romantic relationship would bloom between the two in Janasthana. The conversation had been easy and light till the elder woman had delved into Mandodari's childhood and parentage.

Mandodari came back to the here and now as she felt Ravana's contemplative eyes on her. She knew that her troubles would vanish if she pretended to be who her husband imagined her to be. But she did not want to base her life on a lie. Nor was she ready to forsake her parentage. She was as proud of her father as Ravana was of his ancestors. Her father had sacrificed a lot to bring her up. He had chosen to devote all his time and attention to Mandodari after her mother was summoned back to Amaravati by the king of the gods, Indra. It had been a tough choice for her mother, an apsara, who had willingly given up her life in Indra-loka to wed the man she loved. But Indra had punished her for her transgression, ordering her to choose between either returning to Indra-loka or becoming a stone statue in Mayasura's palace. She had chosen the first option as that would stave off Indra's ire for the moment and also keep alive the hope that she would reunite with her family sometime in the future.

Ravana was staring at the dipping sun on the western horizon, Mandodari's words echoing in his mind. Ravana could not believe his ears! He would be a father soon! But alas! The words that should have brought the greatest joy to him came at a moment and in a manner that was anything but joyous. He did not know how to react, he was so confused.

Confusion did not sit well with Ravana, whose ten brains resolved the trickiest of puzzles in a trice. However, in this instance, his logical and computing skills were unequal to the task of understanding and assessing a woman's inner feelings and motivations. Why did his wife insist on identifying herself as Mayasura's daughter even now, when she was securely married to him and was in the impossible-to-breach Lanka? Who and what did she have to fear?

He was sorely tempted to look at his bride, but willed himself to continue gazing at the setting sun. His face assumed a comparable tint of red as he battled his inner confusion. He was determined to resolve his own turmoil and decide how he wanted to deal with the situation at hand. He loved Mandodari dearly and would do anything to wipe out these past few words spoken between them. Did it really matter who she was, as long as she was the companion he cherished? He knew the answer, but still needed time to come to terms with the fact that she had tricked him into believing that she was the Parvati. Then again, had she really tricked him?

Suddenly Ravana's resolve broke and he looked at her. His heart went out to the girl he loved so dearly and was his wife now, standing as if she was an accused in a king's court. She returned his look, and Ravana felt his confusion melt into nothingness. He knew that subterfuge was not in Mandodari's character. He alone was responsible for misconstruing facts, blinded as he was by his ego that made him imagine that Mother Parvati would fancy him.

Even before the thought really formed in his mind, Ravana was kneeling in front of Kaikasi with folded hands. 'Please forgive me my trespasses, janani!', he said and turned to face his wife with another apology on his lips. But Mandodari was on the ground next to him even before any word came out. She placed a finger across his lips as if to say that words were not necessary between them.

Ravana rose to his feet, pulling Mandodari along with him. 'Janani, I have been a vain fool and that is the only reason why all this has happened. Now I have to do something immediately—I have to go and secure pardon from Shiva. I leave my wife and my unborn child in your care.'

He was gone before either woman could respond.

chapter 27

*K*umbhakarna stretched, turned on his side, yawned as he sat up and set his feet on the floor. He felt refreshed and ready to take on the world. He looked at his attendants, their faces showing the same familiar expression of apprehensive attention. His brows knitted as he tried to recall that additional something that had roused him from his six-month-long slumber. He looked around in a bid to remember the unusual stimulus that had accompanied his waking. The roll of his eyes was enough to set the retinue of attendants shivering, much to his exasperation. He lifted his arms in irritated frustration, only to drop them. The slapping sound this action generated struck a chord and he knew that it was a sound—a thunderous sound—that had woken him.

Once again his brows puckered in incomprehension. For, he was in no doubt that he had heard thunder. No, it was more like the rumbling of a thousand thunders at the same time. He also knew that it was somehow out of place. It was neither the rainy season, nor was there the lightning that accompanies such loud thunder. Kumbhakarna made a mental note to investigate this odd phenomenon during the day. He stretched once more, that simple action sending shudders down the spines of almost everyone in the cavernous bedroom. This reaction never failed to alternately amuse and irritate him. Just as he was about to take a step towards the door, it burst open and a messenger rushed in, slightly out of breath on account of the excitement that permeated his entire body.

'Great news!' the words escaped the messenger's lips before he caught sight of the vertical visage of Kumbhakarna and quickly made an about-turn in a clear bid to get out of the room.

'Announce the news,' Kumbhakarna stopped him in his tracks.

'Yes, Your Highness!' the messenger wrung his hands before primly stating that Maharani Mandodari had just delivered a male child, heir to Ravana's throne. He bowed deeply and walked backwards at a surprisingly brisk pace and was gone even before the news sank into Kumbhakarna's mind.

Kumbhakarna almost sprinted to Mandodari's quarters, close on the heels of the messenger who had brought him the news. Even as he reached the main entrance of Mandodari's palace, he heard the sound again—the sound of a thousand thunders at the same time. He smiled as comprehension dawned—it was the newborn baby crying. He was also amused at the sight of the numerous female attendants trying to do several things to shut out the deafening roar. 'Can I hold "Meghnaad", my precious first nephew?' he asked even as he greeted and congratulated his sister-in-law with his eyes.

Kaikasi, who was attending to Mandodari, turned with a happy expression on her face. 'Greetings, Kumbha! You have come at the right moment and have fulfilled your bhrata's responsibility of naming his offspring. See, Meghnaad wants to be held by you,' she said pointing to the baby in the cradle next to his mother's bed.

Kumbhakarna moved into the room, going first to his mother and touching her feet in obeisance and then turning to focus on the infant in the cradle, who had his arms outstretched. Kumbha, however, stopped midstride and turned to greet Vibheeshana, who had arrived just then. The two brothers hugged affectionately and together turned their attention to Meghnaad, who began howling as if in protest at being thus ignored.

Attention was snatched once again from little Meghnaad by the chant 'Narayana, Narayana!' heralding the arrival of the venerated Maharshi Narada. Ravana's two younger brothers turned quickly to welcome the guest, as did Kaikasi. Even Mandodari sat up straight in her bed, pulling a sheet over her legs.

'Narayana, Narayana!' Narada entered and raised his right hand as blessing in acknowledgement of the greetings from the first family of Lanka. 'Ah! I seem to have come at a very auspicious time! The family, nay, the whole of Lanka is celebrating the birth of Ravana's heir.'

'Please bless Meghnaad,' Kaikasi brought the infant over for closer inspection by Narada. 'What brings you to our humble abode, maharshi? It is well known that your visit to any place is never without a purpose,' Kaikasi said as she deposited the baby back in the cradle.

'Narayana, Narayana! I am an aajanma brahmachari, who has given up all things worldly. I have no purpose beyond loka-kalyan wherever I go. I come here to deliver on a promise I made to your eldest son, Kaikasi. He had asked me to scout for suitable brides for Kumbhakarna and Vibheeshana. I acted on his bidding and come here with good news of success. And, since Mandodari was with her husband when he sought my help, I would like to disclose the details in her presence,' Narada said and settled comfortably into an aasan shown to him by Kumbhakarna.

'Oh! I am so happy! I request you, Muneendra, to disclose all details without further delay. Where are the girls? Do they have a lineage that compares with our illustrious forefathers? Are they pretty? Are they accomplished in various arts?'

Narada raised both his hands in surrender, thus putting a brake on Kaikasi's barrage of questions. His teasing laughter that accompanied the gesture, however, made it clear that he was pleased with her response.

The happy smile on Kaikasi's lips faded when Kumbha's voice boomed: 'Who is talking of marriage for me? I, who wake for only one day in six months, am no good to anyone, leave alone a wife,' he said and turned a mocking gaze towards Narada and added: 'But

I do not underestimate this ghotak brahmachari's devious mind. He must have found some hapless girl to commit herself to a life of boredom and loneliness. But I will not allow it,' he declared.

Kaikasi put a restraining hand on Kumbha's arm. He fell silent, but continued to glower. Vibheeshana felt rather discomfited by this conversation about his marriage, which was taking place right in front of him, but his chest swelled with pride at the principled stand taken by Kumbha. He glanced at Narada, wondering what kind of a bride he could have chosen for him. If she was a true blue-blooded rakshasa kanya, he knew that he would have immense ideological differences with her on account of his total adherence to dharma. He also did not relish the idea of settling with a wife when his elder brother remained single. Vibhee hoped he would be able to extricate himself from this situation without being rude to the venerated sage. He looked up at the sound of Narada's tinkling laughter and was relieved to see that the sage was not offended by Kumbha's rudeness.

'Your two younger sons underestimate my capabilities, Kaikasi devi! I would have you know, mighty Kumbhakarna, that I have gone round all the seven lokas in my search for suitable matches. I have traversed the seven oceans and combed the nine dweepas before making my selection, which, I am sure, will receive your approval,' Narada paused for effect. He knew he had the complete attention of his audience and announced dramatically: 'I brought Vajrajwala from Mahar-loka for Kumbhakarna and Sarama from Satya-loka for Vibheeshana.'

'What? You have brought them here with you?' Kumbha almost jumped out of his seat.

'I am amazed, Muneendra; truly amazed that you should take so much trouble for us and also to hear that there are so many other lokas and that there is life there,' Vibhee's voice reflected his surprise.

Kumbha looked at Narada with narrowed eyes, trying to gauge him. He could not believe that bhrata had asked this kalaha-priya muni to find a wife for him—that too without consulting him! 'Do not be taken in by his sweet talk, Vibhee! This muni is a trickster. He never does anything without an ulterior motive. He is that wily Vishnu's spy and is here only to harm us in bhrata's absence. Huh! Scouted the seven lokas, did he? He would have caught the first hapless woman he saw and brainwashed her into believing his outlandish tales.'

Kaikasi was flabbergasted. Could this son, whom she considered to be the most balanced of her children, be using such harsh language with a globetrotting sage like Narada? She would not allow it. 'Kumbha!' she said in a dangerously even voice, conveying her warning clearly.

This entire exchange was lost on Vibheeshana, who had been distracted by the muni's talk about different lokas. 'Please tell us more about these lokas. Pita shree taught us something about lokas, samudras and dweepas. It all sounded like fairy tales then. What kind of life exists there?'

Narada turned to face the youngest son of Vishravasu, giving Kumbha time to marshall his emotions.

'You know that we live in the Bhoo-loka. There are six other lokas. Bhuvar-loka, Suvar-loka, Mahar-loka, Jana-loka, Tapo-loka and Satya-loka. There is life in all the lokas, in different forms. Although life in some lokas is very close to the life in Bhoo-loka, it is actually not possible for the life forms of one loka to survive and thrive in another loka, the conditions are so different. In fact, it takes a lot of tapas-shakti to move from one to another loka.'

'Ah, there you are! On the one hand you tell us that life is different in different lokas and that movement is not possible between lokas, yet on the other you want us to believe that you brought two girls from different lokas to marry us and live here with us?' Kumbhakarna looked around triumphantly at having exposed the lie of Narada.

Narada smiled and stopped Kaikasi from rebuking her son. 'He has raised a valid point and it gives me great pleasure to elaborate somewhat on my efforts to accomplish the task entrusted to me by Lanka Naresh.'

Narada looked Kumbhakarna straight in the eye and spoke earnestly. 'Identifying Vajrajwala and Sarama as the right partners for you was a simple task for me. The greater and more complicated part of my work was to convince the girls to transit to Bhoo-loka and lead totally different lives as the wives of rakshasa kings. After that was done, we had to effect suitable mutations in the physical and physiological aspects of these beings—alien as they are to the atmosphere here—so that they could survive in the Bhoo-loka paryavaran. This took time, but I am glad we made it here on your waking day so that we do not have to wait for another six months to perform the wedding rites and rituals.'

'I see. But do tell us how you convinced these girls—I do not know if I can call them that—to undergo such a torturous experience just to find husbands!' Kumbha was still unconvinced.

'There are problems of one or the other variety in every galaxy. Sarama is a being from Satya-loka. Her father, Sailusha, is a ruler there. Sarama was to inherit his throne, but there was a grave danger to her life from her father's enemies. Sailusha was ready to make compromises with the contenders to the throne, but Sarama's commitment to dharma made it impossible for her to agree to this plan. When I spoke about Vibheeshana and how much he values dharma, Sailusha agreed that it would be best for his daughter to marry him. He convinced his daughter and so she is here now,' Narada paused and asked Vibhee if he would accept Sarama as his wife.

Vibheeshana nodded, feeling happy and shy at the same time.

Narada turned to Kumbhakarna. 'I do not think that a narration of Vajrajwala's situation will satisfy you. I suggest that you talk to her directly and understand the circumstances that led her to make this choice to accompany me as a potential bride for you.' So saying, Narada led a slightly calmer Kumbha to the front courtyard, where there stood an ethereal being.

Kumbha stood transfixed. Narada had returned to continue his conversation with Kaikasi, and Kumbha did not know how to approach this stranger, who apparently wanted to be his wife. He was surprised to note that despite being an alien, she looked like a normal human being.

She possibly felt his gaze on her and turned around. 'Are you Kumbaran?' she asked.

'Yes, my name is Kumbhakarna. Your name is Vajrajwala, Narada Muni said.'

'Yes, and I am sure you want to know who I am and what I am looking for in a marriage with you,' she said. There was a pronounced nasal twang in Vajrajwala's words, as if she was speaking through her nose.

The complete absence of guile and even maidenly modesty in her manner surprised Kumbha. He quite liked her directness. He nodded.

'Narada said I should tell you everything about myself. I come from Mahar-loka. The Sutala stratum of that galaxy, surrounded by the Sarpi Samudra, is where I lived before I accompanied sage Narada to the Bhoo-loka. My parents are from the Guhyaka race and were masters in all sixty-four art forms.'

These were strange details that made no sense to Kumbha. He was still geting used to her nasal speech and jerky hand movements as she spoke. He noticed that she had two, or even three rows of very small teeth, which was possibly why her words had an airy quality. She continued with her narration.

'There is a strange custom among the Guhyaks. The first child of every married couple must be a male. So, if a couple has a girl child first, they are ordained to throw it into the ocean to appease the snakes therein. It is believed that, by doing so, the couple will have a male child next. Parents who refuse to sacrifice their first-born daughter are turned into stone.

'And that is what happened to my parents. They ran away from their home into the jungles and kept me hidden in a cave. They thought the world of me; they thought that I glowed like a diamond, which is why they named me "Vajrajwala".

'But one day their luck ran out and we were discovered by the king's spies. The royal priest and sorcerer tied me to a tree in front of our house. They chanted some mantras and sprinkled water around the house and went away. When I managed to free myself, I found my parents turned into statues.

'I swore that day that I would bring my parents back to life. I launched on a course of severe austerities to please the elements and secure powers to undo the sorcerer's curse. I did succeed in gratifying the elements, but failed to achieve my objective as they did not have the power to counter the curse.'

Kumbhakarna was impressed. This girl, left all alone in a jungle with her parents turned into stone, had fought back. He liked her guts and grit. 'That is sad. Is that why you decided to come here and get married?'

'No. The elements told me how I could revive my parents. I was told that my tapasya had generated certain powers in me and that I could use these powers to achieve my objective.'

Vajrajwala emanated a mystifying fragrance and Kumbhakarna found himself drawn to her irresistibly. He did not know how or when it happened, but they were holding hands as they walked along the winding paths of Mandodari's garden. 'Tell me about it, please,' Kumbha said, feeling happy and light-headed that this beauty was confiding her most intimate secrets in him.

'I should marry a man whose shakti from tapas is equal or more than mine. This man should not have cohabited with any woman till his marriage to me. Even as I live under the same roof with him, physical intimacies between us should not exceed once in a year. When I marry such a person, I will be able to deliver a male child on the same day as the wedding. And the birth of this male child will bring my parents back to life.

'Sage Narada said he would lead me to such a person and brought me here. I am a woman with a mission, Kaikasi Kumara, and would feel honoured if you will allow me to serve you in whatever condition you are in,' Vajrajwala breathed in deeply, as if relieved to have disclosed her purpose honestly.

Kumbhakarna felt humbled in the presence of this delicate girl, whose abiding love for her parents had shaped her life. He was struggling to articulate his thoughts and feelings when he heard his name being called by Narada and his mother.

Within minutes, the two marriages were solemnized. And even before Kumbhakarna could come to terms with the day's fast-paced developments and the fire in the homa-kund had cooled, Vajrajwala declared that she was pregnant. And lo and behold! She delivered a set of healthy twins before the day was out. Kumbhakarna's joy knew no bounds. He was so thrilled at their likeness to him that he named them 'Kumbha' and 'Nikumbha' to rhyme with his own name. He went to bed a happy man, promising his wife of a few hours that she would never have to face unwanted attention from him—ever. The last thought on his mind before he slipped into his slumber phase was that his sons would inherit his physical strength and their mother's mental strength.

chapter 28

Spring was in the air. All the vegetation in the picturesque Ashoka vatika was in full bloom, and the air was thick with myriad fragrances. Birds chirped in gay abandon and the sounds of distant waterfalls were so musical as to lift the spirits of the most despondent of beings.

All this beauty was lost on Ravana who sat pensively on an artistically carved and comfortable seat in the shade of lush green trees. His life had undergone several changes since his return to Lanka after the successful completion of his penance for Lord Neelakantha. The resident of Mount Kailash had been so pleased with Ravana's tapasya that he had not only granted an unconditional pardon for coveting Maata Parvati, but had also gifted Ravana divine weapons of defence.

Ravana had returned a very happy man and his happiness had multiplied manifold on learning of the marriage of his two brothers. That there were three boys of the next generation in the family was another good tiding that gladdened his heart. And, how happy he had been to be in Mandodari's elevating company!

Lost in his thoughts, Ravana looked with unseeing eyes at a movement he perceived at his feet. It was a tiger cub, exploring the strange combination of smells arising from the dead hide of Ravana's footwear and the living skin of his feet. He kicked the cub hard in a sudden burst of irritation, sending it several feet across the grassy meadow. It hit a tree and stayed there limply, yelping pitifully in pain.

Ravana's lips parted in a queer kind of satisfaction. The yelping of the cub somehow soothed his own hurt. For, truth betold, he was hurt; hurt by Mandodari, whom he loved dearly. Ravana recalled the events of that fateful day vividly. He was hurrying to his wife's palace after a particularly stressful day in the court when a group of extremely beautiful women, attired to attract male attention, accosted him and engaged him in flirtatious banter. He was flattered immensely when he realized that some among them had entertained him before he had married Mandodari. It was a heady feeling when they told him how much they missed his company and how upset they had been at being abandoned. How could a youthful and virile king, a dilettante, let go of all his lovers just because he was no longer single, they asked and begged him to give them his company for just a little while. He went with them, telling himself that it was not chivalrous to turn down their request. And oh! What a lovely time he had with them that evening! It refreshed his memories of the times when he had had so many beauties in his bed at the same time! He was served the best of sura, he was entertained with music and dance.

He was in a slightly inebriated state, but very happy when he reached Mandodari's palace. His wife was the perfect spoilsport. While she did not utter one negative word, she behaved as if he had committed an unforgivable crime. In fact, she came up with some pious platitudes about it being his 'dharma' to keep these women happy and well-provided for. However, according to Mandodari's concept of 'dharma', discharging his duty by these women would bar him entry into her own private palace! Was it not her 'dharma'—as his wedded wife—to give him company in bed whenever he wanted it? Ha! What convenient use of this word 'dharma'!

He was angry and confused. What was his wife, whom he loved very dearly, talking about? It was common, it was normal, it was accepted practice for all kings to keep concubines. In fact, there were many kings, and not very powerful ones either, who married several women and declared them all to be queens. All these queens did not seem to have any problems with one another, and no problem at all with the king. So, what was Mandodari objecting to? In fact, he had thought that she was merely playing hard-to-get because he had spent time with other women and had left her alone that night; he had been confident that her anger would subside by morning. That did not happen and Mandodari's calculatedly 'proper' behaviour in public and cold-shouldering him in private bothered him so much that he had responded by spending more and more time with the women he had abducted during his various conquests. In fact, he had launched a fresh series of wars only to add to his harem. Mandodari maintained an outward calm but he knew by the look in her eyes that she was unhappy. He was sure that she would return to him one day.

Ravana's thoughts turned to his only son, Meghnaad. He was a strapping youth now and had successfully completed his education and training under Guru Shukracharya. Kumbhakarna's twin sons, Kumbha and Nikumbha, treated Meghnaad as their guide and elder brother and accompanied him at all times in everything. When Shukracharya had brought the trio back to Ravana after they had graduated in all aspects of rakshasa warfare, the proud father had decided to test their learning by sending them to conquer Indra.

He had chosen Indra for the test because of his own experience with his attack on amaravati, when Indra had fled from the battlefield. A convincing victory by his son would remove Ravana's lingering feeling that he had left that task half-done. There was another reason—one that Ravana did not admit even to himself. Smarting as he was under Mandodari's continued rejection of his amorous advances, Ravana had begun to derive vicarious pleasure from doing things that his wife did not approve of. War with devas in general and Indra in particular, would be something that she would thoroughly disapprove of. And letting young Meghnaad lead the attack would hurt her even more. Yes, Ravana wanted to hurt Mandodari as much as she had hurt him!

Even as his lips curled in a snarl at the memory of his wife, a worrying thought pierced his heart. Had he exposed his only son to needless danger just to spite her? Ravana shook his head to remove this thought from his mind.

'Janaka!'

Had he heard right, or was he imagining Meghnaad's voice? Ravana was not sure and he shook his head once again, only to hear the word once again, this time louder—the trademark booming voice of Meghnaad could not be mistaken. He turned and saw his son bounding towards him. He was closely followed by Kumbha and Nikumbha, with Guru Shukracharya walking at a more leisurely pace behind them.

'My child!' Ravana hugged him in a rare demonstration of affection. That Meghnaad had appeared before him just when he was doubting the wisdom of his decision filled Ravana with relief. His son's body felt strong as a rock and the triumphant look on all their faces told Ravana that there was good news in the offing.

Kumbha and Nikumbha competed with each other to tell the tale of the epic war. Ravana barely heard what they said, his eyes feasting on his son. This war had turned the boy into a man. There was a distinct confidence in the way he carried himself. Head held high and shoulders thrown back to show off a wide chest, which carried a hint of manly hair. Ravana proudly thought that his son looked exactly as he had at that age. He had the same chiselled features, sharp nose and flowing, curly hair. Even his walk and the way he held his mace over his right shoulder was so like Ravana.

Ravana snapped into the present when he heard Guru Shukracharya take over the narration from the two ebullient youngsters. 'Meghnaad defeated Indra convincingly, Dashagreeva. He wanted to show his catch to you and tied him up and hauled him into his chariot. It was a gratifying sight, particularly for me, as I have been trying to train danava and rakshasa youth to overpower devas so that our supremacy over them is established beyond doubt.'

'What great news this is! Where is that trickster and wily Indra? I will lock him up in a dark dungeon and then see how Vishnu deals with that,' Ravana's eyes shone and he smacked his lips in anticipation of the torture he would subject Indra to.

'Brahma intervened. He urged Meghnaad to free the king of devas if only to avert chaos in the universe. He promised to grant boons to Meghnaad in return,' Shukracharya said, stroking his flowing white beard.

'And what did you seek from our forefather?' Ravana asked his son, joy overflowing from his entire being.

'I asked for immortality, janaka,' Meghnaad spoke for the first time, his voice displaying a combination of pride and regret.

'I sought the same from him so many years ago. And he would have told you that absolute immortality is against the law of nature. Right?' Ravana chuckled.

'Yes. He said he would grant me virtual immortality in as much as I would remain invincible in war. The only condition is that I should make a fire offering to the presiding deity of Lanka, Maa Nikumbila, before going to war. On completion of the yagna, Brahma said a supreme celestial chariot would appear and I would become invincible in any battle,' Meghnaad announced with pride.

'Brahma also decreed that Meghnaad would henceforth be called "Indrajeet", meaning one who has conquered Indra,' Shukracharya said before disclosing the caveat Brahma had laid down to Meghnaad's invincibility. 'Not completing the yagna will make Indrajeet vulnerable in war and whosoever destroys this yagna will also be the one to kill him.'

The word of caution failed to dampen Ravana's mood. He told Guru Shukracharya to make an announcement about Meghnaad's victory in the royal court the next day, signalling an end to their interaction. With Shukracharya gone, the father led the three boys for a celebration of their coming of age. He left them at the entrance to the palace of pleasures, which housed the scores of women who entertained him every day. Tonight, he needed neither madira nor mahila to relax. News of victory over Indra was his most potent intoxicant.

Ravana turned in the direction of his own quarters. He walked at a leisurely pace, enjoying the cool night air and reliving every word of what he had just been told.

'Bhrataaa...' The piercing sound cut short his reverie. Ravana thought his mind was playing tricks. How else could he hear his sister, who was far away in Janasthana? 'Bhrataa...' He heard the familiar voice again, still not able to comprehend if he was hearing right or imagining it. Even so, he stopped and turned to investigate.

Then he saw her—his beloved sister Surpanakha, running towards him with hands outstretched. He walked briskly towards her and stopped short when he got a clear look at her face. Was this grotesque being, her face smeared with blood and crying piteously, his lovely little sister?

chapter 29

'Shut up, Shamuloo!' Surpanakha shouted. Ravana's jaw dropped in shock. Such a display of anger was unthinkable from any younger sibling, leave alone a sister who was years younger. He also noticed her address of him as 'Shamuloo' the pet name that his mother used for him on rare occasions and one that he thought was unknown to anyone else in the family. However, it did not matter now, given the gravity of the issue under discussion between them.

'You are supposed to be the learned one, the strongest and bravest of all. In reality you are only a pig-headed bull with no capacity for serious thought. What good are your ten heads, when together they do not add up to the intelligence of an ant? When faced with a crisis, you can only think of war and the use of brute force for you to prevail.'

Surpanakha continued to rave and rant in this fashion for a while. Ravana tried neither to counter nor stop her. He understood that his younger sister was venting the accumulated frustrations of long years. It was remiss of him not to have checked on her personally, he mused as he slowly walked around the couch on which she was reclining after being ministered to by expert surgeons and physicians under the able supervision of Guru Shukracharya. Even as they conversed, Ravana could see the healing happening under the layers of balms applied around her repaired ears and nose. Traces of the pain Surpanakha was undergoing showed on her face. Ravana ran an affectionate hand over her head. The simple gesture had a dramatic effect. Surpi broke down and copious tears started running down her cheeks.

'What kind of life have I had, bhrata? Such a waste!'

Ravana walked around the couch and sat on a low stool in front of her, cupped her hand between his two hands and looked into her eyes. 'I was not educated—kept out of the classes that all my brothers attended. Instead, I was burdened with housework; I hated it. And now, I live the life of a sloth; eating is my only pleasurable activity. See what overeating has done to me!' she paused for breath before continuing: 'I was happy with my marriage. I enjoyed life when Vidyutjihva was with me. His death changed everything for me.'

Surpanakha looked her brother straight in the eye: 'I could not even live in Lanka, the rules did not permit that. How fair are these rules? Rules that allow you to cohabit with hundreds of women even as you are married to one, and punish a woman if she opts to have another partner!' She fell into a thoughtful silence and Ravana sat there, patting her hand. When she resumed, it was as if she was talking to herself, even as she addressed her brother.

'I know you care for me, bhrata. That is why you sent me to Janasthana—so that I could find another mate to be happy with. There was none—not one with whom I could have shared an intimate relationship. I had actually stopped looking for such pleasures. And then, suddenly, out of nowhere, comes this strange being, captivating me. He is unbelievably attractive, and I know I can be happy with him. I cannot decide whether he is a deva, gandharva, danava, manava, yakshya, kinnera or something else entirely. Whatever his race, he rejected me. And why did he reject my love? Because he is already married, and is committed to having a single wife—eka-patni vrata—that is why. I tried to overcome this hurdle by killing that wife of his, and his brother chopped off my nose and ears. Told me that he had spared my life because I was a woman!

'Should I take this humiliation quietly? No, I will not let anyone insult me.' Surpanakha straightened to look Ravana in the eye. 'I admire you, I always did—for your strength, affection, understanding and above all, your courage; courage to attain what you want. I did the same to get this man for myself. I instigated Khara and Dushana to overpower him and bring him to me. Believe me, bhrata, he is no normal mortal, this man who calls himself Rama, son of King Dasharatha of Kosala.

'I saw him fight. He single-handedly killed each one of our fourteen thousand-strong army! Not a single arrow wasted, every arrow dealing a deathly blow. And what speed! Unbelievable! I could not see his hand as it moved back and forth, taking arrows out, threading them onto the bow and shooting them off. And he doesn't shoot one arrow at a time. He lets off scores of arrows in a single salvo; his speed multiplied whenever he was even grazed by our missiles. He stood like a rock in the middle of the battlefield...'

'Stop praising the enemy so, Surpi!' Ravana interrupted her seemingly unending eulogy of this man's prowess with bow and arrow. He got up and started pacing back and forth. 'I know why we lost. Our men in Janasthana have become lazy. They have done nothing but eat and sleep for years. So impotent have they become that even good-for-nothing hermits have not been scared into leaving the Dandaka vana.

'I admit that I have neglected Janasthana for some time. I will now take matters into hand and set everything right. I will kill this man and wipe out all traces of human settlements in and around Janasthana.'

Surpanakha caught him by the hand as he passed by her side. 'There you go again! Has nothing of what I said just now penetrated your thick head? Believe me when I say that Rama is invincible. You cannot win in combat with him. And moreover, I don't want him killed. I want him; I want to marry him. What we need is strategy, not strength. I have already worked it out. We have to separate that husband and wife. You can either add her to your harem or replace your wife, Mandodari, with her. I know how things have been between the two of you, but that is up to you,' Surpanakha did not bother to meet her brother's surprised look at her mention of his strained relations with his wife, and continued.

'The separation can happen only through abduction. Think how and with whose help you will achieve this. And now, please leave me to get some sleep. The potion that vaidya gave me is making me drowsy,' she said, slipping into a comfortable supine position on the couch and closing her eyes.

Ravana sat down once again. He felt shaken. How perceptive was this baby sister of his! While he sat on the throne and ruled over half the world, thinking no end of his abilities, this girl, carrying the angst over the denial of education and equal rights in her childhood and banished to the jungles in the prime of her life on account of widowhood, showed a better grasp of life. She had kept tabs on him without any formal machinery at her disposal, knew what she wanted and more importantly, knew how to go about achieving it. She had come seeking his help, and he must measure up to her expectations. Ravana pulled himself up to his fullest height, determination writ large on his countenance. He stepped out, conjured up Pushpak and took off across the oceans.

Minutes later he landed. Pushpak's vibrations disturbed the monk sitting in meditation inside a cave. He was huge for an ascetic and his muscles rippled with every movement. 'Ah, Ravana! Welcome. Your unannounced visit at such a late hour indicates that you have a mission of considerable importance. How can I help you?' he asked.

'Mareecha, son of Tadaka! My friend! You guess right. Only you can help me in this task I propose to undertake,' Ravana's tone was calculated to secure compliance with his request and Mareecha responded with elaborate hospitality.

'You look fatigued, Ravana. Please sit and rest. Honour me by accepting the fruits I offer you as nourishment.'

It was as he bit into the succulent fruits placed before him that Ravana disclosed the purpose of his visit. He made it a point to remind Mareecha that the latter owed him a favour for the help Ravana had given him when he had needed it. It had been a long time ago and Ravana did not even know the details of Mareecha's troubles. It was his grandfather Sumali who had brought Mareecha to Lanka for asylum so that he could recover from grievous mental and physical injuries. Mareecha had spent some months in Lanka, leaving after his health was restored.

'Mareecha, my two cousins—Khara and Dushana—as also other brave commanders like Trisira, Mahakapaala, Sthoolaksha and Pramaadhi, not to mention fourteen thousand brave soldiers, have been killed in Janasthana by one fellow called Rama. I want revenge. I am told that one way to punish him is to abduct his wife. I want to achieve this with the help of your amazing shape-shifting capabilities.'

Mareecha froze. It took him a while to wet his parched lips and get some words out. 'Oh King of Kings! The Greatest of Rakshasas! I cannot imagine who would have suggested this plan to kidnap Rama's wife. But I can tell you that he is your greatest enemy, masquerading as a friend. And I will speak like a true friend and well-wisher, even though my words may not be flattering. The task you want to achieve—separating Sita and Rama—is as impossible as separating heat and light from the sun. I have experienced the power of Rama twice and know what I am saying.

'I once laboured under the impression that I was invincible—I had the strength of a thousand elephants and looked like a huge mountain. The very earth that I walked on shook with every step I took. Naturally, I was very proud of myself and drew great pleasure from torturing men and animals alike. Sage Vishwamitra was my favourite target and I laughed when he brought in a twelve-year-old boy to protect his ashram and yagna. My brother Subahu and I sauntered into the ashram just to enjoy the reaction of the ashram inmates. Ravana, I swear that I saw this boy, Rama, lift his bow and shoot just once. When I regained consciousness, I was drowning in an ocean. I was rescued by your pitamaha Sumali, who took me to Lanka for treatment and recuperation.

'I learnt later that Subahu had died instantly. You can imagine how angry I got with this chit of a boy, so immature and untrained in archery. I went looking for him near Vishwamitra's Siddha ashram. I had two other shape-shifting rakshasas with me and we took on the guise of wild beasts to attack Rama. By now he had been trained by the maharshi and he shot three arrows in one go. The arrows were raining fire and, realizing the danger, I ran away. But an arrow managed to find me and once again, I was thrown across the ocean. Ever since, I have lived in mortal fear of Rama, his very name sending shivers of panic down my spine. My sincere advice to you is to give up this foolhardy scheme.'

Ravana, whose impatience with Mareecha's long account extolling Rama's strength and valour was growing by the minute, could not take it anymore. 'Enough Mareecha, enough!' he said, trying hard to keep his temper under check. 'Just because I come to you seeking assistance, does not mean you can praise my enemy. Also, I am sure I do not have to tell you how to talk to your king, that too, a king who gave you a fresh lease on life. I command you as king to do my bidding or pay with your life for insubordination,' Ravana thundered.

The next moment he regretted his outburst. For, truth be told, he had no 'plan B' to fall back on if Mareecha refused to help him. So, he took a deep breath, injected a note of persuasion into his voice and added: 'On the other hand, if you help me pull off this abduction, rest assured that you will be rewarded suitably.'

Mareecha had seen enough of life to understand the inner

workings of Ravana's devious mind. But he had no interest in any material gifts that Lanka Naresh could give him. Fear of Rama, nay, his very name, had become a part of his being. He saw the bow-bearing Rama even in his sleep. He had adopted a hermit's lifestyle, working on gaining control over his breathing and mind, so that he could overcome his fear of any word that began with the letter 'ra'. But now, Ravana threatened him with death if he did not do his bidding. And participating in any scheme that Ravana proposed meant certain death at Rama's hands. In effect, it was death for him either way. He could only choose his killer. Mareecha decided there was dignity in having Rama as his slayer. He looked at Ravana and nodded.

Ravana's lips parted in a triumphant grin. He grabbed Mareecha by the hand, bundled him into Pushpak and ordered the craft to head to Dandaka vana. En route he explained his plan and Mareecha's role in it.

Pushpak touched ground a little distance from Panchavati, where their quarry was. Mareecha transformed into a beautiful deer, its golden coat with sparkling silver spots calculated to captivate. He pranced around for a while, showing off his moves, before disappearing in the direction of a hut in the middle of a clearing. Ravana conjured up the saffron robes of a sanyasi, complete with a danda and kamandala. He draped the angavastra carefully around his torso so that his battle scars were well-covered and positioned himself behind a bush that afforded him a clear view of the front yard of the kuteer.

Ravana did not have to wait long. Sita emerged from the hut and began gathering flowers. Ravana gasped, completely floored by the beauty and grace of this woman. He noticed two men in the background repairing a fence only when Sita turned towards them and waved. One of them, who was possibly Rama, walked over to her and peered in the direction of her pointing finger. 'Ah!

The golden deer effect!' thought Ravana with satisfaction.

The couple was soon joined by the other man and there ensued a debate of sorts, with all three periodically either looking or pointing to where the deer had been spotted. It was clear that the second man did not agree with whatever the other two were saying. Ravana's body stiffened in suspense. He relaxed and breathed easy only when he saw Rama pick up his bow and arrows and leave and the other man take up position near the wicket gate. Sita collected her flower basket and went indoors.

The waiting was becoming intolerable. It seemed like ages before Ravana heard what he was waiting for. 'Ah, Sita! Ah, Lakshmana!' he heard Rama's voice call out in pain. Ravana's eyes darted to the kuteer even as Sita emerged and ran to the young man guarding the wicket gate—Lakshmana—who remained unaffected by the screams. Ravana experienced another bout of uncertainty as Lakshmana did not rush off into the jungle in panic—as Ravana had expected he would. He watched helplessly as the duo engaged in an argument of sorts. Sita was gesticulating wildly towards the woods and speaking animatedly and Lakshmana's gestures conveyed that he was trying to calm her down. But, what was wrong with him? Why was he not going to rescue his brother? More importantly, what should he do if Lakshmana did not leave his post and instead, Rama returned to them? Was his plan doomed?

Ravana perked up suddenly when he noticed Lakshmana cover his ears, then fold his hands in a salutation before turning on his heel and rushing off in the direction of the distress call. In a way, he was happy that Lakshmana had delayed his departure as this had left Sita in a particularly distraught state. His chances of success with Sita in such a state were better.

Ravana adjusted his top cloth carefully before stepping out from behind the bush. He walked up to where Sita stood by the gate, looking anxiously into the depths of the jungle beyond. '*Bhavati bhiksham dehi*!' Ravana called out softly, holding out a jhola that hung from one shoulder.

Sita turned with a start. She had not encountered any bhikshus since coming to Panchavati, but saw nothing amiss as her mind was filled with concern for her husband's safety and well-being. 'Welcome, mahatma! Please be seated while I bring some fruit for you,' she said and turned towards the kuteer.

As Sita stepped out of her courtyard with the offerings, Ravana gripped her hair and let out a loud guffaw. 'The fruit that I am interested in is you, my dear Site!' he said and in a trice, lifted her off her feet, deposited her in Pushpak and became airborne. Sita's cries for help were drowned by his triumphant laughter.

As for Mareecha, he could fend for himself if he managed to survive Rama's arrows!

chapter 30

*R*avana sat staring at his reflection in the mirror. What he saw did not displease him. It was a handsome face with chiselled features and his curled and upturned moustache and thick, curly and dark hair made him look very attractive indeed. He had strong and well-developed biceps and his muscular torso narrowed to a slim waist. Lankadheesh preened his moustache in a regal gesture and turned slightly to admire himself from all angles. Artistically crafted jewellery adorned his neck, arms, wrists and waist, adding lustre to the dhoti of fine yellow silk.

Ravana's shoulders drooped in dejection as the one question that had been bothering him for months surfaced once again. Why was Sita not attracted to him? He felt a fire spark through his entire body at the very thought of her beauty. He must possess her soon if he wanted to prevent this fire from consuming him. His train of thought broke when a dwarapalaka entered with a messenger in tow.

'Prabhu, I bear a message for you from Prime Minister Prahasta. The Council of Ministers is ready to deliberate the issues listed in the day's agenda and is awaiting your arrival. A chariot is waiting to make the trip with your esteemed presence in it,' the messenger spoke his well-practiced lines with his head bent and hands folded in reverence.

Ravana waved him off with an impatient hand. 'Tell Prahasta to begin. I will come there in a while.' The messenger and the doorman bowed even lower and withdrew.

Ravana lost interest in admiring himself. He walked over to

the window and looked with unseeing eyes at the sprawling green of his garden. He wondered what it was about this woman he had forcibly brought to Lanka close to ten months ago that ignited all his senses. He had not felt like this even for Mandodari. Was it Sita's rejection of his advances that had strengthened his determination to win her over? But she was not the first woman to have rejected him! He had abducted thousands of women from various lokas and not all of them had fallen into his lap without protest. There was something about Sita that disturbed his senses.

'I have not seen a bigger fool than you! And what kind of a ruler are you—you cannot even fulfil one single request your own sister makes of you. You do not care for me,' Surpanakha had burst into her brother's private chambers, brushing aside the guard at the entrance. The mix of indignation and tears was calculated to force Ravana into doing her bidding.

The intrusion irritated Ravana, but he could not display it, as that would only cause his sister to throw a temper tantrum. 'Do not be ridiculous Surpi,' Ravana used a controlled tone to ward off any emotional onslaught by his sister. 'What have I not done for you? You should be proud that I took your advice and spruced up our communication network. I also took note of your complaint that our soldiers have become sloppy and instituted rigorous training programmes for them. What more do you want?' Try as he might, he could not hide his impatience.

'Huh!' Surpanakha grunted in disdain. 'Our plan to kidnap Sita was executed to weaken Rama so that you could vanquish him in war and bring him to Lanka for me. You have all but given up on her. And I am ashamed that this mighty brother of mine has not been able to break one woman. Can't you make a woman submit to you?' Surpanakha's tirade showed no sign of ending, and Ravana could take it no more.

'Shut up,' he screamed, the sound reverberating through the

palace and bringing all activity to a halt. 'Since when have you appointed yourself as my master? Do you think I am so weak as to govern my kingdom and manage my empire on the advice of a woman? I have been very lenient with you because you are my only sister. You have abused that position for too long and I will not tolerate it any longer. Be informed that I do not wish to set eyes on you ever again.'

Surpanakha looked taken aback at the virulence of her brother's response. It was unexpected from this brother, whose affection had been the mainstay of her life for so long now. She looked at him dumbly for a moment before turning on her heel and storming out. Ravana was as surprised as his sister at the words that had issued from his lips, but knew this was not the time to attempt a repair of relations. He shrugged his shoulders and once again turned to the window, his eyes looking into the distance this time.

His thoughts returned to Sita once again. It was as if she had occupied his entire body, mind and soul. He could think of nothing else. His entire being ached for her. One kind word, one little gesture to convey love—that was what he longed for. The retinue of women who filled his palace of pleasures had exerted themselves collectively to keep him engaged and entertained. They had plied him with the best of wines and other intoxicants to take his mind off Sita. They had even visited her more than once to impress on her the advantages of accepting Ravana's love. Some had focused on the dangers of rejecting him. Sita did not stop shedding tears for her husband; nor did she consent to any proposal that came her way.

Ravana saw Sita in his mind's eye, and the memory of the blade of grass she had placed between them to show what she thought of him angered him even more. Trina, grass, is considered worthless and so not used in any worship or pious activities. By placing a single blade of grass in front of him, this woman, who was his captive, had told him that neither he nor his opinion mattered to her.

He had gone to see her early that morning, determined to appeal to her sense of reason and justice. He had told her how it was normal practice for rakshasas to abduct anyone who took their fancy and violate them to fulfil their sexual appetite without waiting for consent from the other party. 'But have I lifted one little finger in this direction? No! That is because I love you. I am waiting for you to come to me willingly. I am ready to marry you and make you my maharani, demoting Mandodari from that position. Recognize my strength and power and be my partner. Do not waste your transitory youth crying for a worthless man like Rama. Admit that he cannot even breach Lanka, leave alone vanquish me in war and take you back,' he had spoken in a very persuasive tone.

It had had no impact whatsoever on Sita. She had placed a blade of grass deliberately between them before addressing Ravana, making him marvel at the firmness in her voice despite not having touched food or water in all the ten months she had spent sitting under the very same banyan tree in the Ashoka vana. Sita's implied insult to him in that simple action of placing a blade of grass in front of him was not lost on Ravana and he had had to struggle to keep his anger in check. However, her voice when she spoke was calm and even.

'I am a married woman and committed to upholding my dharma as a pativrata. You are a king. It is your dharma to respect and protect all women as you would protect and respect your own womenfolk. Coveting other people's wives will only lead to your downfall. All your riches and physical strength will not make me surrender to you. What strength and courage are you flaunting, when you stooped to stealing a woman when her husband was away? You know that you cannot stand up to Rama and win.

Understand that your welfare and the welfare of your people lie in returning me honourably to Dasharatha-nandana,' she said.

'You are taking advantage of my soft approach to you, Sita. I warn you, do not test my patience any further. It is only because I have fallen in love with you that I am giving you the chance to come to my bed willingly. Remember that nothing stops me from using force to get what I want. It has been ten months since I brought you here. I will give you two more months to change your mind, failing which, I will either use force to have my way, or have you killed by these very rakshasi guards and make a feast of you,' Ravana had threatened.

Ravana's reverie was broken by the arrival of Jambumali. Jambumali was the son of Prahasta and was training in statecraft under his father. Ravana knew that only an emergency would have made his prime minister send his son thus. He rushed to the conference hall with Jambumali close behind.

Ravana's mood sobered when he saw the worry on every minister's face. Something serious had transpired, he knew. Prahasta spoke. 'There is disturbing news, Prabhu! A monkey was spotted in the Ashoka vana this morning. Our guards there became alert when they saw this monkey conversing with Sita and they questioned her. She provided only vague answers, but I am informed that the captive has been in an upbeat mood since then, which raised suspicions. Then came the news that this monkey has been on a destruction spree, smashing buildings and uprooting trees. We need to decide on a course of action to stop this vandalism.'

'Prahasta, you surprise me. You deemed it fit to disturb me to deal with this "monkey business"? All you needed to do was to send a couple of foot soldiers to finish off this rampaging animal,' Ravana allowed his irritation to echo in his voice.

'Your Highness! That was tried with disastrous results—all our soldiers were crushed under the boulders this monkey hurled at them. All of us here have come to the conclusion that this is not a normal, or natural, monkey. It is more likely that he is here at the behest of some deva—it could be Indra, Kubera or even Vishnu. Hence the decision to seek your guidance,' the prime minister said.

'I am not convinced by your argument, but I agree with you that we should increase the intensity of attack so that this monkey learns its lesson. Let us send a battalion with our five second-rung commanders leading the attack,' the king said. Ravana's suggestion was endorsed and a battalion, led by Viroopaksha, Yoopaksha, Durdhara, Praghasa and Bhasakarna went to restrain the marauding vanara. These commanders were held in high esteem for their combat skills, strategy and statecraft.

Barely had the Council of Ministers settled down to deal with other important pending matters of state in consultation with the king when further bad news came—the entire battalion had been injured grievously and the commanders had been forced to withdraw. They appeared in person before the king and admitted that it was not possible to check the vanara, and said that they had had to retreat in the absence of permission to kill the offender.

Ravana could not believe that an entire battalion, led by such skilled commanders, had failed. This fact strengthened the theory that they were dealing with a shape-shifter, deputed by some antagonistic power. The council felt that it was imperative that this monkey be caught alive and questioned about his true identity. Ravana's son Indrajeet was the unanimous choice to undertake this task.

Indrajeet was summoned, the problem explained and his views sought. Indrajeet nodded his approval of the suggested strategy, but rejected the offer of an army to assist him. 'I alone am enough to deal with this challenge,' said this master of illusory warfare.

Ravana and his ministers tried to carry on with routine work after Indrajeet left, but made little progress on account of their preoccupation with what the young prince could be facing in the virtual battleground. They heaved a collective sigh of relief when he returned, with the monkey in tow. Ravana noticed that his son had used the powerful Brahma-astra to capture the intruder and felt a wave of anger sweep over him. 'Execute him,' he ordered, his eyes raining fire.

'No! Your Highness!' Vibheeshana was instantly on his feet with his objection. 'We need to establish his identity and the purpose of his actions before taking any decision as to what would be a befitting punishment,' he said.

Ravana made little attempt to hide his irritation. 'Very well. Let us do what is right as per our senior minister's concept of "dharma",' he said, sarcasm dripping from every word. 'Prahasta, question him,' Ravana said, pre-empting any chance of Vibheeshana undertaking this exercise.

Prahasta walked up to the captured offender. 'Speak without fear, and speak the truth. Your appearance as a monkey is unconvincing as the amount of damage you have inflicted in the city is beyond the capability of an ordinary monkey,' Prahasta's voice hardened a shade as he realized that the monkey was not really under the spell of the Brahma-astra. Why was he pretending to be under its influence, he wondered as he shot his questions, prefacing them with a warning that any deviation from the truth would invite death penalty. 'Who sent you here? Indra, Varuna, Kubera, Yama or somebody else? What is the real purpose of your coming here?'

'I am a monkey by birth. This is not an assumed form. My name is Hanuman. I came here to see Ravana. I caused some damage to attract attention, and the rest was done in self-defence when I was attacked. I have not been sent here by anyone mentioned by you. I am here to do an errand for Shree Rama on orders from my master Sugreeva. The entire vanara population of the Kishkindha kingdom has been despatched to locate Shree Rama's dharmapatni

Sita, who was abducted from Panchavati.

'I have seen that devi here. I know that all of you here are well-versed in dharma-shastra. Lankadheesh Ravana has acquired immense powers through tapasya and is blessed with riches. It does not behove a person of his stature to forcibly keep somebody else's wife. That the lady concerned is Sita, wife of Dasharatha-nandana, spells the dissolution of your kingdom. I would advise you to honourably restore Sita to her husband and save yourself from certain doom.'

Every word Hanuman uttered multiplied Ravana's rage. 'Execute him!' he shouted, his face a dangerous shade of red.

'No,' the vehement objection came immediately from Vibheeshana, who had once again jumped to his feet. 'Bhrata, it is against all tenets of dharma to treat a messenger thus. Please remain within the limits of dharma when dealing with a doota,' he said, his stance—legs planted slightly apart and hands resting on his hips—indicating his determination to challenge his brother's decision.

Prahasta, who was quite used to confrontation between the brothers, stepped in with practiced ease. 'Vibheeshana is right, Ravana. The shastras prescribe several alternate ways of sending a befitting message through the messenger. You can have his head shaved, subject him to lashing, branding and some other punishments. We can decide what suits us. Also, if we finish off the messenger, we lose the chance of sending a stern message to our enemy.' He looked from one to the other brother, a silent appeal for peace in his eyes.

'I have one more question to ask Hanuman,' Prahasta said. He walked slowly and deliberately to the vanar, who stood with his hands tied behind him. 'Why did you pretend to have been struck by the Brahma-astra?' he asked, his unblinking eyes not leaving Hanuman's face for a moment.

'Out of respect for the Creator,' Hanuman replied, impressed by the mantri's keen observation. 'I have a vardaan from Brahma that nobody will have the power to tie me down.'

Ravana missed this brief interaction between Prahasta and Hanuman, on account of his preoccupation with trying to decide on a stiff punishment for Rama's messenger. 'Monkeys are very proud of their tails. So, set his tail on fire and set him free to go,' he ordered.

Ravana came out of the palace to watch the rare and funny sight of a monkey with its tail ablaze, running away in agony. All his ministers followed him. The group was amazed to see the monkey flying around Lanka, holding his burning tail in one hand as if carrying a torch, showing no signs of pain or discomfort. He went around the city setting fire to vegetation and anything else that could catch fire. Amidst the chaos caused by the widespread blaze and the attempts to douse them, Lanka-dwellers watched the monkey leave the island's shores and fly off across the ocean.

*K*umbhakarna awoke to a strange feeling—as if someone or something was waiting for him. The air in his sleeping chamber was somehow different and his entire being stiffened in defence. He kept his eyes closed and focused on his sense of smell and hearing, in a bid to get some hint of what awaited him. He felt that the room was warmer than usual and, combined with the sounds that penetrated his senses, he decided that there were a lot of people in the room. Who were they, and why were they there? Was the gathering friendly or otherwise? And more importantly, how did they all get past his security apparatus?

He opened his eyes slowly, trying to look around without letting on that he was awake. It was a wasted attempt, as he could not see anything beyond the tip of his nose, but he was relieved to hear the familiar voice of Durmukha, a minister in Ravana's court. Durmukha announced that Kumbhakarna had woken and a burst of chatter greeted him. Kumbha sat up and was surprised to see so many ministers. Vajrakaya, Mahodara, Shardula, Durmukha, Vajradamshtra and Vajrahana—all senior ministers and trusted representatives of bhrata Ravana were there. His eyes then fell on Ravana and Prahasta, who were standing a little apart from the others, apparently in deep discussion, and who now turned in his direction.

'To what do I owe this never-before honour of the crème of Lanka's intellectuals coming here to witness my awakening?' he asked half in jest.

Prahasta spoke. 'Recently, a small monkey made its way into

Lankapuri and created havoc. Now we have information that an army of manavas and vanaras is readying to mount an attack on us. Ravana wanted to discuss this looming danger to our kingdom and it was the king's decision that we await your waking day.'

Kumbhakarna looked around the room. He knew that this brief account of the problem omitted vital details. His suspicion was confirmed when he looked at his elder brother. 'Wait! I seem to have missed some details. What I do not understand is how a monkey could have reached our land? And even if it did and managed to cause a lot of damage, how is that related to this impending attack by manavas and vanaras?' he asked, looking straight at his brother.

'That monkey had come looking for the woman I had abducted from Dandaka vana,' Ravana responded, but still did not meet his brother's eye.

'I see,' Kumbha said and looked around for more clues. He noticed the absence of Vibheeshana in this brainstorming group. 'Where is Vibhee?' He returned his gaze to his brother, waiting for an answer.

Ravana shuffled his feet and turned a little away from his brother. It was Indrajeet who spoke on his father's behalf. 'Vibhee uncle questioned Janaka. Not only that, he insulted Janaka in a full court and told him to return Sita with full respect and seek Rama's pardon. He praised Rama's virtues and said that all the yodhas and mahayodhas of Lanka would be wiped out by Rama and that Janaka himself would not be able to escape Rama's wrath, even if he hid deep down in Paatala. He did not even consider the fact that I was present there. I, who trounced Indra himself and have such boons from Brahma as to make me virtually immortal. I held my silence with great difficulty, respecting his age and stature as my father's brother. I was satisfied only when Janaka took exception to his behaviour and told Vibheeshana to leave Lanka immediately.'

'So, where has he gone?' Kumbha asked and looked from

Ravana to Indrajeet.

'He has most probably defected to the enemy camp. He left with his wife Sarama and his four assistant ministers—Anala, Panasa, Sampati and Pramati,' Ravana said, stealing a glance at his younger brother. His expression unnerved Ravana and he tried to defend his action. 'He was a coward, unfit to be a scion of Pulastya. He was trying to undermine the morale of our army. If it was anyone but my own brother, I would have beheaded him immediately.' Ravana stole another furtive glance at Kumbha and realized that his words had not had the desired effect. 'Do you also want to fault me for past deeds and go and join the enemy?' he screamed defiantly.

'No bhrata! Whether I agree with your actions or not, I will stand by you till my last breath. That, for me, is my dharma. Nonetheless, let me tell you that your action was wrong. Now it seems that we have no option but to fight Rama and his army. I promise you that I will pulverise this army of weak manavas and vanaras and finish off Rama. Once he is dead and gone, maybe his wife will agree to submit to you.'

Prahasta cleared his throat. 'I had sent some spies to gather information on the enemy's strength and strategy. If you want, we can summon them and hear what they have to say.' He clapped his hands together without waiting for permission from either brother. Ravana, who had already heard some of these reports, had withdrawn into a sullen silence.

Shuka, who seemed to have been standing by, stepped in, his body bowed at the waist in a show of respect. 'I entered the enemy camp in the form of a parrot. The mood is very upbeat. The only bit of information I was able to learn about their strategy is that they plan to build a bridge across the ocean so their entire army can cross it to reach Lanka. It is for Your Highness to take a decision on whether to meet the enemy in combat or hand over Sita and make truce.'

'How dare you even suggest truce,' Ravana thundered. 'Indra, Varuna, Yama and Kuber have all lost against me. What is a mere human like Rama? He does not have any idea about my strength, otherwise he would not have launched this misadventure,' he declared.

Another spy, Vichitrakaya, stepped in. 'I have the latest information from the enemy camp, Prabhu! They have managed to complete the construction of the bridge across the ocean in just five days. The construction was supervised by Nala, the son of Vishwakarma. I watched its progress from several vantage points, disguised as a vanara. They completed the construction of fourteen yojanas on the first day, twenty yojanas on the second, twenty-one yojanas on the third, twenty-two yojanas on the fourth and the last twenty-three yojanas on the fifth day. This hundred-yojana-long bridge ends at the Suvela mount in the foothills of the Trikoota range. The bridge is ten yojanas in width, and almost the entire army was involved in carrying the material to build it from the mainland. Currently they are resting. It is not possible to assess their numbers—they are too many and they are constantly on the move.'

Mantri Sarana moved one step towards his king. 'There is something that Vichitrakaya has not mentioned, but that I gleaned from his account, my lord. His assessment is—and I agree with it—that it is impossible for us to win if we go ahead with this war. Based on my wisdom of centuries in statecraft, my sincere advice to you is to make truce with Rama by returning Sita and save Lanka from certain ruin.'

Ravana squared his shoulders defiantly. 'I will never agree to this proposal,' he said, trying to make it sound like a matter of principle, but actually unable to bear the thought that he would have to give up Sita. A plan seemed to take shape in his mind and turning to Kumbha, he ordered him to draw up force deployments and formations with the assembled ministers. He himself stepped out, taking Mantri Mahodara with him.

Ravana set a brisk pace as he walked towards Ashoka vana, explaining his strategy to his companion. 'Mahodara, I confess to you that I am besotted by Sita. I had hoped to bring her around with my gentle and caring behaviour. I resisted the desire to force her into submission several times. The reason for this is a curse from Nalakoobara, son of that Kubera, to the effect that my head would burst into smithereens if I ever forced myself on anyone. He cursed me a long time ago when I raped an apsara.'

Mahodara nodded, waiting for instructions regarding the action sought from him now. Ravana placed a friendly arm around the minister's shoulders before continuing: 'I must have Sita, but by making her submit to me. We need to create an illusion for this purpose.

'You have considerable powers of magic and illusion, which I have always admired tremendously. Use these powers to create Rama's head. I will use that to convince Sita that her husband is dead. I am sure that she has been resisting my advances because this fellow is alive and she fears repercussions. The death of Rama and my valour implied in this event will make her grant me the favours I seek.'

Mahodara was flattered enough to agree to the plan, even though he harboured doubts about its efficacy. He decided to comply with the king's orders rather than seek confrontation at this point. 'I understand, Prabhu! You proceed to Ashoka vana and engage Sita in conversation; prepare the ground and I will be there right behind you to do what is required.'

The very thought that Sita would soon fall into his embrace made Ravana forget his travails on the war front for the moment. His heart beat faster as he imagined Sita in his arms. He had waited for this day for close to eleven months. Ravana quickened his pace, impatient with every moment that kept him away from his sweetheart.

Then, out of nowhere, Ravana felt the presence of his two brothers with him. Vibhee seemed to warn him that the woman he had kidnapped was a venomous snake who had set foot in Lanka only to finish the rakshasa race. Kumbha, Ravana imagined, was angry with him, but he was unable to understand whether it was for inviting the war on Lanka or for having abducted Sita. A slight shiver of fear ran through his body at the thought of possible defeat, not to mention the death and destruction that would be caused by the war. Ravana shrugged in a bid to drive the fear of Rama out of his mind. *He is a manava, and so death cannot come to me from him.* But a niggling doubt crept into his mind—*was it humanly possible to construct a hundred-yojana-long bridge in five days?*

Ravana's thoughts changed course once again as he entered Ashoka vana and Sita came within view. 'I bring news for you, Sita. Your husband—what is his name—yes, Rama, he is dead—killed by my soldiers,' he sang happily.

Sita could not believe her ears. Was this true? Her eyes filled with tears, but she remembered to pluck a blade of grass and place it between her and her captor. Whatever his strength and stature, he held no charm for her. She would remain true to her pativrata dharma.

'I knew you would not believe me unless you had proof. I will tell you how I engineered his end. Your husband managed to reach this shore with his army of monkeys. While they slept at night, we mounted a lightning attack. My worthy son Indrajeet, Commander Mahaparshva, Minister Mahodara and Kumbhakarna's sons Kumbha and Nikumbha led the attack and wreaked havoc on them. Many were killed and many others ran away in fear. Mahodara sliced off Rama's head. That monkey—Hanuman—is dead too. Their camp is a river of blood,' he said, providing graphic details calculated to fill Sita with despair—despair that would make her opt for his company.

'I do not believe you,' Sita tried to hold on to her faith in Rama.

'I knew you would not believe me. So I had Mahodara bring Rama's head for you to see. Once you are convinced and have cried over his death, we can talk about ourselves. Your reservation that you are a married woman doesn't hold water now. Now you have no excuse to reject my love. Marry me and be happy. I will make you my maharani. All the riches and luxuries that you can dream of will be yours just for the asking.'

Mahodara walked over in response to a signal from Ravana. In one hand he held a head that resembled Rama and in his other hand he held a bow. It was Rama's, he claimed.

Just as Sita was fighting the impulse to swoon, telling herself that she needed her wits about her to deal with the situation, a messenger came unannounced. Ravana's anger flared at this intrusion, but he held his tongue when he noticed that the messenger was from his mother's palace.

'Prabhu, I beg for your indulgence. Raajmaata Kaikasi seeks your presence urgently on a matter of utmost importance. A chariot is waiting to take you there,' the messenger said and waited, indicating that he was under orders to ensure compliance.

Ravana felt frustrated that the moment he had waited for for eleven months had been thus ruined. His irritation showed in the swish of his angavastra as he turned and left. The very next moment, the magically conjured head and bow disappeared as if they had never been there.

chapter 32

*H*e strode down the thoroughfares of Lanka, impervious to the curious glances from passersby. He walked against the wind as if challenging it to impede his progress. His dhoti and angavastram billowed behind him and both seemed to be engaged in a valiant struggle to stay in place. However, his preoccupation was such that he did not notice when his angavastra slipped off his shoulders. The fine red silk fabric dragged after him for a while before it parted company and was blown away in the westerly sea breeze. While his face remained an inscrutable mask, a close look revealed eyes reddened with tears threatening to break free. His eyes burned, his head ached and his entire being was in agony.

He had not expected this from his mother; janani had always supported him in whatever he did. She was so proud of him and his achievements, and always found excuses for his excesses. In a perverse way, she quite liked the streak of wildness in him. Even when his wife Mandodari had barred him from her private chambers for having sexual relations with other women, janani had sided with him. She had told her daughter-in-law that maintaining a harem was a royal prerogative. The queen should accept it gracefully and in fact, should try and secure beauties for his pleasures.

Was this the same person who had chastised him today for bringing Sita to Lanka? Abducting women who took his fancy was a sign of the king's virility—she had agreed with that view till now! She had not been so upset even when he had brought Mandodari home and presented her as 'Parvati', Shiva's consort. Janani, who generally addressed him either as 'Ravana' with great pride or as 'Shamuloo' with great affection, had today addressed him as 'Dashagreeva'. It was as if she had been trying to invoke his father's spirit and impose the rishi's values of dharma.

This alone would not have affected him so deeply. But she had also made him out to be a perfect villain, responsible for every ill that plagued Lanka. She had faulted him for Surpanakha's departure from Lanka. This was news to him. He had not seen his sister since the day they had argued over Sita. How was he to know that she would react in such an extreme manner? It was bad enough to know that Surpi had gone away without so much as informing anyone about her whereabouts, but for his mother to hold him responsible for it broke his heart. Did she not know how much he loved and cared for his sister? He could not decide what bothered him more—Surpi leaving Lanka without giving him a chance to set her life on a happy course, or janani holding him guilty of the crime of driving out the daughter of the house.

Janani had also declared him responsible for Vibheeshana's going away. 'You ordered him to leave,' she had screamed, tears rolling down her cheeks. 'My baby, my little baby, punished so harshly by his own bhrata,' she had wailed. Surprisingly, it did not seem to bother her that Vibheeshana had indulged in the worst kind of crime against the throne—he had praised the enemy of Lanka, thus humiliating the throne and the king who occupied it. As if that was not enough, his youngest brother had gone and joined the enemy ranks now. Why did that not upset her, make her angry? Vibheeshana would not have done that had he, Dashagreeva, paid heed to his sage advice to return Sita honourably to Rama—that was her argument.

The agony of being scolded like a little boy by his mother was compounded by the presence of Mandodari in the background. Only a couple of days ago, Mandodari—his wife and maharani of Lanka—had visited him in his living quarters, raising his hopes of the restoration of conjugal rights. As it turned out, her mission had been to persuade him to make truce with Rama by handing Sita over to him unharmed. Now it seemed that she had managed to co-opt her mother-in-law in this game plan. Nothing else could explain his mother's scathing attack on his actions.

When he saw Mandodari leaving janani's rooms, he instinctively knew that she would go to Ashoka vana to meet Sita. He had rushed out after her, determined to stop her, leaving his mother shouting after him. Surprisingly, he could not find Mandodari. Then, suddenly, his desire to find her and prevent her from going to Sita was gone. He did not want to see anyone or talk to anyone. There was a loud buzzing in his head, which made him want to pull his hair out. He felt blinded by the roaring, ringing sound. He could hardly stand erect on account of it. He swayed wildly from side to side, clutching his head and pressing hard on his ears. His arms felt powerless and press as he might, the noise in his head only seemed to multiply in intensity.

Oh! What was happening in his personal life! All the women he loved had turned against him—his mother and wife openly opposing his choices and his ebullient and carefree little sister going away without a word. And Sita, the one woman whom he wanted more than life itself, stayed steadfast in rejecting his advances. What upset and hurt him more than all this put together was the fact that Vibhee had left him to join forces with his sworn enemy. Vibhee, whom he had rocked in his arms as a baby and cherished all his life, had done this to him. There was nothing and no one to cheer him.

Ravana felt very lonely and in an odd way, frightened. Would he be able to protect and preserve this empire he had built? Or would it all be lost over one woman? Would he survive this crisis? Was Rama really as powerful as he was made out to be in the reports reaching him? What kind of a man was this Rama? What had he to offer a beauty like Sita? What did she see in him that she remained so completely devoted to him, even though he had subjected her to a harsh life in the jungles without the basic comforts? Ravana would have considered himself the luckiest man in the world if she had reciprocated his ardour for her. She would have been solace enough for him under these trying circumstances.

Of course, he had Kumbha, his brother who held family loyalty topmost in his thoughts and actions. Irrespective of what he thought and said, he would always honour the king's wishes. He had had very violent arguments with Kumbha on almost every waking day of his brother's. The verbal duels encompassed an entire gamut of issues, but in the end they always resolved their differences—their fraternal bond never took a beating. In contrast, Vibhee hardly ever raised his voice in front of him. He would stare at him with disapproval dripping from his eyes and sulk when his views were overruled. And on the one issue on which he knew that his eldest brother was adamant, Vibhee had chosen to desert the brother and endanger the very security of the land that was home to his family and a majority of rakshasas. 'I will discuss this with Kumbha forthwith and make him talk to the other family members. I must go immediately and find him,' he thought.

Raucous laughter rang out, bringing Ravana out of his reverie. Who was laughing, and why? Ravana strained his eyes to try and find the source of that mirthless laughter. He could not understand why it was so dark. And who were all those people sitting in the shadows? What were they all saying? He looked around wildly, trying to get his bearings. Then realization dawned—he was sitting on his throne in the main court hall of the royal palace. He narrowed his eyes and peered around him again. Why was everyone sitting behind pillars, and why were they not making speeches in an orderly manner? Why were they whispering to one another? Their collective whispering reached his ears like the sea at high tide. He peered again, shielding his eyes with a hand, and realized that there was no one else in the cavernous hall except for him. The people he saw were tricks his imagination was playing on him in the gathering dusk.

But how did he get there? And why was his crown lying on the ground so far away from him? Another realization dawned—the laughter was coming from him. All his ten heads were out and engaged in animated discussions. That was the cause of the chatter he had imagined was emanating from amidst the shadows. That all his heads had appeared without his volition was a surprise, but Ravana let it pass. 'Tell me, why are you all laughing,' he asked.

'It is your guilty conscience that makes it seem like laughter to you, Dashagreeva. We were discussing the serious predicament we are in,' said the third head on the right.

'First of all, stop calling me "Dashagreeva". I am Ravana. This name was given to me by Shiva and that title I have carried ever since. That is the reason why I have stopped wearing all these heads in public,' Ravana said. Then, ignoring the derisive laughter from all the other nine heads, he asked a question that was more to the point. 'What predicament are you talking about?'

'I am glad you understand that there is a difference between "Dashagreeva" and "Ravana". Nonetheless, I will spell out the difference, because you need to be reminded of it. Dashagreeva is the learned son of sage Vishravasu Brahma, well-versed in all the arts and a master of different aspects of life. And Ravana is a proud ruler, who has lost all respect for the opinion of others. He has become a selfish, power-hungry person who uses his powers as a ruler to satisfy his ego and keep his subjects in perpetual fear of him,' said the second head on the left.

'What nonsense! I am the same! "Dashagreeva" was the name given to me by my father when I was born and "Ravana" is the title bestowed on me by Shiva. Who would not be proud of such an achievement? That is why I like being addressed as "Ravana" rather than as the other one,' he countered.

'No Dashgreeva! It is not just a matter of what you like to be called. Before you gained this title, we all stood together and considered every issue from all angles before a decision was taken. Do not forget that that was a major reason why Lanka flourished in those days,' said the first head on his right.

Ravana turned and looked at the head. He did not like the way in which it stared back at him fearlessly, and he felt like dealing a tight slap on this face—just to teach him basic courtesy.

'What a fall for "Ravana"! The King of Lanka stands all alone today, forsaken by everyone.' This was the third head on the left. Ravana felt helpless in the face of this confrontation. In the gathering shadows of the durbar hall, it seemed as if each head, when it addressed Ravana, came to stand on its own in front of him.

'I am not alone. I have the awe-inspiring army of Lanka. I have my family and my council of ministers,' Ravana surprised himself with this defensive posture.

'You are and you know it, Dashagreeva. Do not fool yourself and do not try to fool us.' This was the second head on the right, which continued without waiting for a response. Ravana noticed a murmur of agreement from several other heads. 'Your youngest brother and sister have both left you. Janani has accompanied pitamaha Sumali to do tapasya; they left when you refused to listen to reason.'

Ravana's heart missed a beat. Pitamaha Sumali had retired from his life at the royal court several years ago, and had been living happily in his homeland Lanka. That he had come out of his seclusion and taken his daughter away at this critical juncture was a worrying bit of information. 'What about Kumbha? He is with me. Did you not hear him say so this morning?'

'Yes, we did,' said another head, speaking for the others also.

'His waking day is over and you will not have him by your side for the next six months. You will have to face this war with Rama all alone.'

'That is hardly a matter for concern. My army is full of great warriors who have bested even devas. Any one of them is enough to finish off this cobbled-up army of monkeys,' Ravana was all bluster.

'Indeed!' mocked a couple of heads on either side. 'Why was this great army of yours unable to contain one single monkey that came to Lanka? You have not even been able to fully repair the damage that he inflicted on Lanka in a single day. And now an entire army is at your gates, ready to take over this land.' Ravana noticed the slight shake of head that accompanied this statement.

'Dashageeva, what world of illusion are you living in? An able ruler has a proper assessment of his enemy's strength. He should be ready to make peace when the other side is stronger, or when the enemy is of comparable strength, but our strength is waning. An able ruler has to wait for an opportune time and hit the enemy when circumstances are favourable.

'You know this, Dashagreeva. Nobody needs to tell you this. But you are blinded by passion and unable to see even the most basic and obvious issues. Think! Is it really possible for manavas to build a bridge across the ocean? Is it not clear that this manava, Rama, has help from other, powerful quarters?

'The central point of contention is the abduction of Sita. Rama has come to wage war against us to avenge that. The war can be averted if you return Sita to her husband.'

Ravana made a visible effort to keep his anger in check. 'I am surprised that such advice should come from you, who are a part of me. How can you even suggest that I admit to fearing Rama and so return Sita? Is it in my character to accept defeat? I prefer to break rather than bend. I lust for Sita and will not consider any option till I satisfy my lust.

'As for building that bridge, that is no big deal. Anyone could have done that. But remember, no one who sets foot on Lanka with aggressive thoughts will leave this city alive. Rama and his entire army will be finished within the blink of an eye.' He could see that his other minds were not convinced, and decided to make another appeal.

'Did I invite this war? No! In fact, I tried to avert it. I sent a message to Sugriva, the king of the vanaras, on whose strength and support this neecha manava is banking for victory over us. I told him that there was no enmity between the two of us. So he should not put his people at risk by forcing a war on them merely to help one single man satisfy his vanity,' he said, using a conciliatory tone.

'Dashagreeva, you know very well that this is all bluster. Your commanders, generals and soldiers are all in mortal fear of this impending war after the havoc Hanuman caused in Lanka. They are not saying it to you out of fear of reprisal. Do you need to be reminded that the morale of the force is as important as actual strength and skill?'

Ravana scoffed. 'Some amount of anxiety and insecurity is normal among common soldiers before they go into battle. Their morale is built and boosted by the leader. I have not yet addressed the forces. Once I tell them that they are the best in the world and that vanaras do not possess intelligence enough to strategize for war, they will be reassured and will fight with a positive frame of mind. Killing a couple of manavas and a horde of monkeys will be child's play for the rakshasa sena.'

Nine heads shook together, rejecting Dashagreeva's postulations. 'You are making history, Dashagreeva. You will be remembered as the great one who secured a homeland for rakshasas and also as the one who annihilated the race of rakshasas from the face of the earth. If that is what you want, so be it,' it was as if his heads had exhausted all their arguments against war.

Ravana was exasperated. 'Nothing can stop me from going to war. I will not be a coward and make compromises with the enemy. If Sita has not come to my bed willingly, I will force her to by leaving her with no other option. If Rama is really as strong as everyone seems to think, then I would rather die in the battlefield like a brave warrior,' he declared.

The silence that met his words made him very angry. 'Victory is mine,' he thundered, the sound piercing through the darkness. For, suddenly, the hall was flooded with early morning sunlight and Ravana found himself standing all alone.

'*W*e have won! We have won!'

The victorious chant of three robust and full-throated voices was heard a fraction of a second before the door burst open, revealing the happy faces of Indrajeet, Kumbha and Nikumbha. Ravana, who had risen from his simhasan even before the door opened, rushed down the dozen odd steps to envelop his son in a bear hug, unmindful of the blood, gore and dust that covered Indrajeet's body. He did the same with Kumbha and Nikumbha, before turning around and announcing once again the same bit of news: 'We have won!'

The others in the council hall—Prahasta, Anukampa, Vajradamshtra, Viroopaksha, Mahaparshva and Vajramushthi, all senior military advisors—were also standing, relief combined with varying degrees of surprise, if not disbelief, showing on their faces. They nodded vigorously when Ravana urged his son to share the details with them. 'Please give us all the details, putra!' Ravana said and led the three young lads to seats near the throne.

'There is nothing to say by way of details, janaka, because it is the outcome that matters. The outcome today is that your two sworn enemies—Rama and Lakshmana—are as good as dead. Life is slowly ebbing from their unconscious and inert bodies. I am glad to have proved myself a worthy son to you, janaka,' Indrajeet said. The overt display of modesty that won him beaming smiles of approval from the elders in the room also papered over an important detail—that the victory had not come easy; that Indrajeet had had to use his magical powers and wage war through invisibility to achieve this victory.

'Oh! Bhrata is being modest, janaka-bhrata!' interjected Nikumbha.

'Nikumbha is right, janaka-bhrata. It was a tough and exciting fight. The vanaras are not to be underestimated for their martial skills, and their sheer numbers posed a challenge to us,' Kumbha added.

Ravana looked at Indrajeet with great pride and noted that the twins still retained their childhood habit of taking over a narration from each other. Though born on the same day as Meghnaad, Kumbhakarna's children remained childlike in their behaviour and hero-worshipped their cousin.

'Bhrata Meghnaad first targeted that monkey Angad for his insulting behaviour of yesterday,' Nikumbha said, and Kumbha launched into mimicking Angad, who had come as an emissary just the day before. 'I am Angad, son of Vaali and crown prince of Kishkindha. I come here to you, Lankeshwara, as a messenger of King Sugreeva. My Lord, who is a friend to Rama and Lakshmana, urges you to make peace even now. Return Sita unharmed to Rama or face a complete wipeout of your family,' Kumbha pranced around the room, jumping high and around pillars, much like a monkey, and triggered mild laughter in the room, easing the tension-filled atmosphere a little. Even Ravana, who found the mention of Angad distasteful at such a happy moment, could not suppress his laughter at Kumbha's antics.

'We should not have let that monkey get away yesterday, particularly after he damaged janaka's palace,' Nikumbha said, contining his twin's narrative. 'Our work would have been so much easier today.'

'What happened? Indrajeet, give us all the details of how the fight went today and how you finally neutralized the two manava brothers. Is Angad dead or alive?' Ravana's voice was so sharp that the twins immediately quietened down, looking at their cousin for guidance. Ravana's brow knitted in anger as he recalled the manner in which Angad had escaped the previous day from the entrance courtyard of his seven-storey palace, damaging some of the beautiful pillars with his bare feet. It was a shame that it had happened in front of a huge gathering of Lankan citizens in the thousand-pillared courtyard. They had just put their stamp of approval on the proposal for war against the vanara army and Ravana had been gloating over his oratorical skills in painting the manava-led vanara army as aggressors.

Indrajeet noticed the lines of worry on his father's face. 'There is nothing for you to worry about, janaka. The war is over. There is panic and chaos in the enemy camp. They will slither away by morning.'

Ravana continued to look at his son, forcing him to disclose further details. He could see that the prospect did not appeal to Indrajeet. It was grudging praise that he gave the enemy. 'The enemy was a highly motivated force, janaka, and very unorthodox in their tactics. They also have the advantage of huge numbers. At the outset, I targeted that Angad, who spoilt the mood at our public rally yesterday. He is a powerful fellow and it took some skill to put him on the defensive. However, I had to leave Angad and rush to assist the others in countering the marauding Rama and his brother. They were inflicting heavy casualties on our soldiers. I took them on and managed to wound them seriously, but their arrows were quite bothersome. I wanted to finish them off as quickly as possible and so used the tiraskarini tactic to become invisible and shower missiles upon them.'

'You should have seen the confusion that erupted in the enemy ranks when they could not see bhrata and yet his missiles were killing them by the dozens,' Nikumbha chipped in, adoration for his brother clearly showing.

Indrajeet ignored the interruption and continued: 'I used the naga-pasha astra to knock down the two brothers. They fell unconscious and the snakes in the astra are squeezing the life out of them even as we speak. Nothing can dispel the astra's grip of its victims. They will be dead within a couple of hours and the monkeys will leave by morning,' he concluded.

Ravana and his ministers nodded in agreement and were congratulating the prince for his valiant action, when the door burst open once again to let in a messenger. 'I seek your pardon for rushing in without waiting for permission, Your Highness! But here is urgent and important news that you must hear immediately,' he said, bowing deep. 'The manava brothers have recovered and there is jubilation in the enemy camp,' he announced.

'What? How? How is that possible?' Indrajeet was confused.

'A giant eagle came flying in from the north and the wind stirred up by his wings neutralized the snakes that bound the manava brothers,' the messenger said.

The mood in the room changed immediately. Ravana waved the messenger out and sat down in the nearest seat. 'This is that rakshasa-hater Vishnu's handwork, I am sure,' he said dully, his mind racing for ideas and strategies to overcome this unexpected hurdle.

'I agree. Vishnu must have sent in his mount, Garuda, to save these men,' Prahasta said.

'I have decided that I will go onto the battlefield tomorrow and finish off these minions of Vishnu,' Ravana declared.

'No,' Prahasta cut him short. 'It would be shame for all of us if we sat here and let you take the initiative. We will stick to the strategy we finalized yesterday and face the enemy with measured strength. Indrajeet had almost achieved the objective, but for this intervention from Vaikuntha. Now we have a better assessment of the enemy's strength and his support. So we will proceed with greater care,' the prime minister looked around to gauge the reaction to his words and saw heads nodding in agreement all around.

Prahasta continued: 'I suggest that Indrajeet commence a yagna for Devi Nikumbila. You know that the successful completion of the yagna brings forth a magical chariot for Indrajeet, which makes him invincible in the battlefield. While he is performing the yagna, we will lead the attack in groups and try to finish off the enemy. If we cannot finish off the enemy before the yagna to propitiate the kula devi is completed, then we will at least hold the enemy in check till Meghnaad comes riding in on the magical chariot and takes the enemy to its nemesis.

'Prabhu, I suggest that you and Virupaksha monitor developments from a central control room, and ensure that supplies reach our forces. You should also get some people who understand herbs and can be employed to tend to our injured soldiers.'

Prahasta looked around with unseeing eyes, his mind running through a checklist of things to be done to manage the logistics of war. For, it had been a long while since Lanka had mounted an offensive. Thankfully, Surpanakha's warning about Lanka's army having rusted due to disuse had pushed them to put their forces through refresher training and get them in fighting shape.

Prahasta continued: 'We will need to increase patrolling at the four gates. I will supervise patrolling at the east gate; Mahaparshwa and Mahodara should man the south gate; Suka and Sarana will have the north gate; and Anukampa and Vajramushthi will augment patrolling of the west gate.' Prahasta looked around for suggestions and objections. There were none and everybody rose silently to comply with the new responsibilities entrusted to them.

Life for Ravana from that moment on became a dazed blur. There was hardly any good news from the battlefield—something that was difficult for the mighty Lankadheesh to digest. Developments took place in such quick succession that he hardly had time to adjust to the fast-changing situation. One part of his mind noted that this was the first time that he was trying to defend his territory. On all previous occasions when he had gone to war, he had been the aggressor. That had given him the advantage of selecting the timing of the attack, giving him the upper hand and enabling him to operate from a position of strength. The situation had also kept his forces in high spirits. The current mood of despondency among the soldiers was so new that he did not know how to dispel it.

Also, after the first day, when Indrajeet almost killed Rama and Lakshmana, there was not one bit of good news from the battlefront. All his mighty commanders, whose every step caused the earth to quiver, fell like spineless blades of grass, unable to withstand the fierce arrows showered by the two humans who led the army of monkeys. The monkeys, whose intelligence he had ridiculed, turned out to be fearless warriors. The brute strength of the rakshasa army failed to instil fear in them. A major chunk of the vanara army lacked formal training in martial arts, but this was more than compensated for by their agility and ability to use anything and everything as a missile; their extreme motivation and commitment was also inexplicable. The number of chariots, elephants and horses that were crushed under the boulders rolled down on them by the monkey army was legion.

After the first couple of days, when he was able to dismiss the loss of life on his side as part of war, Ravana found himself getting alternately angry and sad at the number of deaths his army suffered. The death of rakshasa leaders like Mahaparshva, Vajradamshtra, Mahakaya, Vajramushthi, Suka and Sarana was also telling on Ravana's ability to counter the unabated enemy onslaught. He was thus forced to let Prahasta lead his army and was torn by anguish when not only Prahasta, but also all his assistants—Narantaka, Kumbhahana, Mahanaada and Samunnata—were killed in battle.

Ravana's grief at the loss of Prahasta was deep. He had been a father figure to Ravana and had guided the new king through the initial phases of organizing and administering the new rakshasa homeland. His commitment to Lanka and Ravana were complete and uncompromising. He had supported the king's every action, and managed his critics within the council of advisors. Over the years, the two had developed a great working partnership. And now, he was gone. Oh! How lonely he felt!

Left with little choice, Ravana ordered that Kumbhakarna be woken up. Within minutes of this order, Ravana had an unexpected visitor—Mandodari. One look at his wife and Ravana felt like a different person—somehow energized. But this feeling was rather misplaced, as the purpose of her visit could only be to fault him for the prevailing situation. Ravana squared his shoulders instinctively, readying himself for a duel of words. However, her voice, when she spoke, was conciliatory rather than confrontationist.

'Nath! Please do not force Kumbha to wake up in the middle of his sleep cycle. You know that it will spell doom for him,' she said, with not a trace of the distance that had developed between them over the past so many years now. Ravana realized, much to his own surprise, that nothing had changed between them. He loved her just as much as he had when he married her and he knew that his wife's love had not waned either.

'I have no choice, Mandodari. And do you really think that I would do anything that would cause harm to Kumbha, my younger brother, whom I love dearly? He has the strength of a thousand elephants. He has routed so many gifted and powerful beings without shedding a single drop of his own blood. And here the enemy is a couple of impoverished manavas roaming the jungles. He has but to walk onto the battlefield for both of them to drop down dead,' Ravana was seeking validation of his action from his wife.

'Please do not persist with this foolish logic that manavas are no match for rakshasas. If that were so, then why have so many of our commanders and heroes died at the hands of these two brothers? Can't you see, nath, that they are not ordinary manavas? They have assistance from the divine and they have justice on their side.'

With no plausible argument to counter his wife, Ravana turned away. Mandodari placed a restraining hand on his arm, forcing him to turn and face her. 'Nothing has worked well for us since you brought Sita here. Nath, I have seen her and know that she is a pativrata-stree. Please, be satisfied with all the lovely women in your harem and let this one return to her husband,' she urged.

'No priye, you know I cannot do that. It is a matter of my pride and prestige now. I would rather die fighting than give up now.' He, however, allowed her to lead him to a seat in a cosy corner of the room, feeling the strength that seemed to flow into him through her very proximity.

'I respect your stand. But I appeal to your sense of duty towards the citizens of Lanka. Would you not consider letting your pride go for the sake of Lanka, the homeland you built for rakshasas?' Mandodari knew the answer even before she completed her question. She retained her hold on his arm, and began stroking it absentmindedly. Ravana was sorely tempted to rest his head on her shoulder, but restrained himself out of fear that she might get up and leave.

It was some time before she spoke again, and when she did, she looked directly into his eyes, demanding an honest reply. 'Why are you not going onto the battlefield?'

'Because I am scared,' Ravana surprised himself with the answer. Mandodari, if she was surprised or disappointed with this response, did not show it. She continued to hold his hand in both of hers and simply waited for him to go on.

'Don't you see? All my commanders, whose strength, capabilities and skills in warfare are legendary, have died at the hands of these monkeys! And my rakshasa soldiers, who eat humans and monkeys for breakfast, are being killed by these same creatures as if they are flies sitting on a sweet! Obviously something is wrong—very wrong! Either we have fallen on extremely bad times or there is a grand plot against us,' Ravana spoke his innermost thoughts, secure in the knowledge that his wife would not be judgemental.

Mandodari's voice was full of compassion and understanding: 'You, my lord and my husband, are a mighty and powerful person. In addition to your natural strength and learning from your parents, you have the blessings of Creator Brahma. You have gifts of missiles from Brahma and Shiva. You have routed Indra, the king of the devas. You have commanded the planets in the galaxy. You can make oceans dry up and the wind stop blowing, and you can prevent the sun from shining. What can scare you? Nothing!'

Ravana shook his head. 'All this is true. But alas! My negatives outweigh these positives that you enumerated. I have collected an equally impressive list of curses for my excesses, and all of them have come together to spell doom for me,' he said. Tears pricked his eyes as he looked at this lovely woman, whose magnanimity in pardoning him and coming to stand by him in his hour of need he deeply appreciated. The next moment, he hid his face in the folds of her sari and felt comforted by the touch of her hand running through his hair as she cradled his head in her arms. Tears ran unchecked from his eyes as he bared his soul to her. 'When Brahma was granting boons to me, I was so drunk on my strength that I said I did not need divine help to protect myself from naras and vanaras. That is why it is a pack of naras and vanaras who are attacking Lanka.

'There was one king who dared to stand up against me in war, knowing full well the consequences. I ridiculed him and he prophesied that a descendent of his dynasty would come to avenge my transgression against peace-loving humans.

'Once I lost my temper with Nandi, Shiva's vahana, and called him a "monkey-face". He cursed me, declaring that a monkey would be the cause of my death. I laughed at him then, but see what is happening now!

'The more I think about it, the more convinced I am that Brahma has contributed to this plotting against me and engineered this army, which, on its own, stands zero chance of surviving even the most ordinary of rakshasas.

'And, did you know, Mandodari, that before I met you, I used to rape any woman who took my fancy. Their tears have turned into curses and I now think that this Sita is the incarnation of one of those women. She has come here to cause my ruin.

'So, don't you see that I will be killed if I go onto the battlefield? That is why I want to send Kumbha. He has a strong and pure character—he does not have the flaws that Vibhee or I have. He cannot be harmed by these men and monkeys. He has but to walk onto the battlefield for them to die of shock. Yes; that is what will happen; they will all die in next to no time when they look at the awe-inspiring figure of my adorable brother. They will die…they will all die…die they will…they will die…' Ravana kept muttering.

Mandodari used the edge of her sari to wipe the copious tears that rolled down his cheeks and the sweat that kept breaking on his brow, and tried to instil confidence in her husband. Time stood still for them and the announcement of Kumbhakarna's arrival jolted both into the present.

chapter 34

'*A*re you telling me that you will not lead the army in this war to save Lanka?'

Ravana's voice was silky soft as he posed the question, but the beetroot red of his face and clenched fists that showed the knuckles white, gave away his intense anger. Mandodari, standing right behind him, kept the tips of her fingers on his back, in a bid to help him control his temper.

Kumbhakarna was pacing up and down the room and his wife, Vajrajwala, who had followed him to Ravana's palace, stayed discreetly behind a curtain, the anxiety showing on her face. She had never seen the two brothers exchange such angry words, till now.

Kumbha came to a halt right in front of his brother and looking him straight in the eye, said: 'I said no such thing. I did my duty as your friend and well-wisher and told you what I think is right. Now I will do my duty as your brother and go onto the battlefield to defend your honour and kingdom.'

Ravana was confused. What was Kumbha talking about? How could he hold two diametrically opposite views on the same issue? Was it possible that the untimely awakening had left his brother in a confused state? He felt at a complete loss, and, but for the restraining and soothing touch of Mandodari's hand on his back, would have slapped his brother to bring him into full wakefulness. 'But you are all the same person!' Ravana blurted out, unable to hold back any longer.

'Yes. But my duties and responsibilities are different in different capacities. As your obedient younger brother, I will do whatever you command; I will do that to the best of my capabilities.

'I am also your greatest well-wisher. My boundless affection and regard for you and my intimate understanding of your personality—your strengths and your weaknesses—also make it incumbent upon me to tender my sincere opinion on all matters,' Kumbha recommenced his pacing. It took him a while to organize his thoughts and he began speaking slowly and clearly, his manner making it clear that he should not be interrupted.

'Bhrata, you are very strong. In fact, you are the strongest person in the world. You are also very intelligent. But this has proved to be a deadly combination and your strength has overpowered your intelligence. You have stopped applying your mind and prevail almost solely on the basis of your immense physical strength. There is no deliberate thought given to the why and wherefore of your actions. Such an approach to personal and state-related issues was bound to yield negative results sooner or later.

'Vibhee tried very hard to rectify this fault in your style of functioning. But your power-drunk self brushed his words aside as the advice of the weak. When this conflict climaxed, you reacted by throwing him out. Where could he go? Where would he go? You did not spare a thought to this aspect and Vibhee had no option but to go to your enemy. This action, mind you, is not one of treachery against you, but is one of love for Lanka. He wants to save Lanka from a ruler like you.

'There is a basic rule with regard to warfare. You were the first one to learn this when pita shree taught us, and you were the one to explain it to both Vibhee and myself. So, I can say that I learnt this lesson from you. The lesson is that one must make an objective assessment of the opponent's strength before waging war. Go on the offensive only if you are stronger. If the enemy is equal in strength and resources, it would be wise to make peace with him—work for truce. And, in the event of the enemy being superior to you in men, material and skills, then surrender is the best policy.

'Consultation with your ministers in all important matters, even when they are not strictly matters of state, is a good policy and enables the king to understand the inner workings of his ministers' minds. This enables him to distinguish between sincere advice based on the merits of the issues involved and opinions that voice what they think the king wants to hear. Advice of the second variety is not only useless, but often leads to crisis situations.'

Kumbhakarna paused for breath, breaking his step to gaze at the carpet with unseeing eyes, and Ravana stared at him in total disbelief. One part of his mind acknowledged the innate worth of his younger brother's words, but another part—the one preoccupied with the here and now of the ongoing war—rebelled against the lecture.

'Whom did you consult before you abducted and imprisoned that saadhvi, Sita, here in Lanka?' Kumbhakarna locked eyes with the king, demanding an answer.

Ravana's rage boiled over. Whatever he had expected his brother to do on being woken up midway through his sleepcycle, this definitely was not it. 'I see. I should have convened a public meeting and collected opinion as to what my response should be to the chopping off of my only sister's ears and nose! I am sorry! That is not how I react to the humiliation of any of my family members, particularly women. I believe in avenging such an insult,' Ravana breathed fire from his nostrils, even as his lips curled in a sarcastic smile.

'No! I am not suggesting that you accept humiliation; not even when its perpetrator is much stronger than you. But I do hold you responsible for the circumstances that created this situation. Had the law in Lanka permitted Surpanakha and other widowed women to remarry or cohabit with persons of their choice, you would not have had to pack our sister off to that jungle and she would not have taken a fancy to that manava. Manavas have a different set of rules and the two men Surpi approached with proposals of marriage refused to entertain her on the ground that they were already married. Our wilful sister was unable to handle the rejection and tried to kill the woman who she thought stood in the way of her getting Rama. She suffered the consequences of her aggression, and you abducted the same woman when she was alone! How was she responsible for what happened to Surpi?'

Kumbhakarna held up a hand to prevent his elder brother from interrupting him. 'Sita is in no way responsible for what happened to our sister. If you had to avenge her disfigurement, you should have taken on Rama, whose refusal to wed Surpi led to this situation, or Lakshmana, who actually cut off her ears and nose. How is our sister's honour restored with the imprisonment of that nara-kanta here?'

Kumbhakarna looked around, distracted by a sound. He noticed that Ravana, who had been standing throughout their conversation, was sitting down now; it was the thud of his dropping into the settee that had interrupted Kumbhakarna. Ravana looked lost, not knowing what to say or do.

Mandodari, who was supporting her husband, spoke for the first time. 'Kumbha, it is not my intention to discuss the merits and demerits of your bhrata's actions. My only appeal to you is that this is not the time for such assessments. There is a war happening right at Lanka's doorstep and the king has been working round the clock to protect the kingdom. There have been heavy casualties on our side and he needs your support and expertise to repel the enemy force. That is why you were woken up.'

Kumbha bowed in front of Mandodari. 'Vadina, believe me when I say that it is not my intention to hurt or humiliate bhrata, whom I hold in the highest possible regard. I see that bhrata is imagining defeat at his doorstep. I want him to understand that this will not happen while I am alive. My beloved bhrata, Dashagreeva Ravana, is the only king who can rule over Lanka. I spoke these bitter truths only because I want him to rethink his ways when he is rebuilding Lanka after this war.

'Vadina, do you know that Lakshmana, the younger of the two brothers who are trying to capture Lanka, is considered the best brother; the ideal brother. I tell you that he does not deserve this reputation. How can he, who left his brother's wife unprotected, just because she used harsh language against him, be an obedient brother? I alone qualify for that title. I would never do anything that goes against my bhrata's wishes. I promise you this—Lanka will be rid of the enemy menace by tomorrow. I may or may not be there to share that moment. That is why I wanted to spell out certain guidelines for good governance—not that bhrata does not know them, but because these have been lost under layers of exigent actions.

'Please bless me as a mother that I live up to this challenge and have the satisfaction of earning recognition as the ideal brother.' So saying, Kumbha stepped forward to touch Mandodari's feet, only to be scooped up midway and wrapped in a bearhug by his brother.

Ravana's eyes danced wildly as he chanted: 'I have my brother; I have nothing to fear…I have my brother; I have nothing to fear…'

A nudge from his wife stopped the chant. Ravana looked around in a bid to recover his balance and then he blessed his younger brother: 'Kumbha, you are the strongest person in this universe. I trust you to avenge the deaths of so many family members, friends and yodhas. I await your victorious return from the battlefield. The celebration of this victory will be such that Lanka has not seen in its entire history. Here, wear this maniharam as my blessing and good luck charm,' so saying Ravana took off a long necklace studded with precious stones and lovingly placed it around his younger brother's neck.

Ravana and Mandodari watched Kumbha stride purposefully towards the north gate where he had ordered a battalion to be ready to follow him into battle. The sight of Vajrajwala, a petite woman with a loping gait, trying to catch up with the gigantic figure of Kumbhakarna was comic, and Ravana and his wife could not help a chuckle escaping their lips as they turned to return indoors.

'Kumbha gave you quite a lesson on how to manage the affairs of state, along with his promise that Lanka would be rid of its enemies by tomorrow. Will you remember to follow his advice?' Mandodari asked gently. She held his hand lovingly in both of hers and allowed herself a tinkle of laughter to remove any hint of criticism that he might perceive in her words, but at the same suggesting that there was merit in what Kumbha had said.

Ravana was in high spirits for the first time in several days. He joined his wife in the laughter. He led her back to the settee on which they had been sitting earlier and made her sit facing him. 'I quite like taking orders from you, my darling! But this sermon for improvement from you is a joke, since you are at the root of all this trouble,' he said.

The words, though spoken in a light-hearted manner, caused a frown to appear on Mandodari's brow. 'What do you mean,"I am at the root of all this trouble"?' she demanded, stiffening her spine a little.

Ravana laughed and ran a finger across his wife's brow, pushing away a stray tendril of hair and smoothing the area between her brows. 'I am not accusing you of anything, but I do think there is a degree of truth in what I said.' He paused before continuing thoughtfully: 'You know, I feel it is possible that I might not have reacted to Surpi's complaint the way I did had you been with me. You shut me out of your life and I do not know if you can even imagine how much I have missed you and longed for you. I could not accept that you took such objection to one fling. That, I think, is why I fell in line with Surpi's proposal to kidnap Rama's wife.'

'I have missed you even more, nath! And I don't know if you will believe me, but it was not your fling with another woman that upset me. In fact, I had met some of these women and understood the depth of their commitment to you. I did not want to deprive them of your company. After all, it is the only thing they have to look forward to in life. I sympathized with their plight when you stopped seeing them after our wedding. I wanted to tell you, persuade you, to marry at least some of them. I was preparing for this when I saw you in that palace.'

Mandodari spoke haltingly, as though making a confession to herself rather than stating it to someone. Ravana leant closer to her to catch her words, his eyes widening in disbelief at what was being admitted. Mandodari continued: 'I was upset not because you went there, but because you chose to go there without telling me. I think I wanted to feel large-hearted for sharing my husband with other women. I think I wanted to feel that I had given you permission to marry other women.'

Mandodari turned and, for the first time since this conversation had begun, looked her husband straight in the eye. 'I think that is the whole truth, nath. But…I really do not know…I only know that I have ached for you every day since that fateful day.'

Ravana drew her close and held her head to his chest. There was peace and companionship between them.

They stayed that way, with no thought about the war that was raging just outside Lanka's gates. Sita was forgotten. They were only aware of each other.

A loud howling and the noisy entry of Vajrajwala shattered their dream. Vajrajwala was wailing and her clothes were bloodstained. So soaked was she in blood that she left a trail of it as she walked. It took some time for the onlookers to realize that the blood was dripping from her husband's head, which she carried in her arms. 'They have killed him...killed him...my brave and valiant husband. He gave his life to save this throne... This is all that I have of him now...his hands and legs were chopped off and he was rendered helpless before the life was taken out of him,' Vajrajwala was inconsolable.

Ravana rose like a man in a dream. He walked to the hunched figure of his brother's wife and tried to take Kumbha's head from her hands. It was a futile effort, as Vajrajwala clutched it harder to her bosom. A sound of indescribable anguish rent the air as Kumbha's brother and wife wept for the lost life.

chapter 35

*M*andodari used the edge of her sari to wipe the sweat off her brow. It was more fatigue than the presence of sweat that caused the action. She looked at her husband, rolling restlessly on the floor even in his state of unconsciousness and repeatedly mumbling the name of his dear and dead brother Kumbha. Her husband, the mighty Dashagreeva Ravana, Emperor of Lanka, so proud of his good looks and so particular about the way he dressed and everything around him, was rolling on the bloodstained carpet, muttering incoherently. He was unaware of the tears streaming down his cheeks. All her efforts to rouse him had gone in vain. The news of Kumbha's death had shattered him.

The other person who was equally devastated by the untimely, unexpected and unacceptably gory end to this unparalleled rakshasa veera was his wife, Vajrajwala. Her intense and all consuming grief came as a bit of a surprise to Mandodari, who had considered the marriage of Kumbhakarna and Vajrajwala to be more of a union of convenience rather than of love. Obviously she had been mistaken about their bonds of affection, if Vajrajwala's reaction to his death on the battlefield was any indication. She had not allowed anyone to come near her or to touch her husband's head, which she held close to her chest.

Vajrajwala, who as a mark of decorum and royal protocol, never came before Ravana and never spoke to him directly, was now only a few feet away from him on the same carpet. Her attire was in complete disarray, her top garment—her odhani—missing. And in this state, she had wrestled with her brother-in-law, refusing to let him take her husband's salvaged mortal remains. It took all of Mandodari's tact and persuasive skills, not to mention physical strength, to separate them. Vajrajwala had fallen to the floor during that tussle and there she had stayed ever since, unaware of anything around her and completely lost in grief. She was on her haunches; her husband's severed head hugged tightly to her bosom. She made peculiar sounds; sounds that made no sense whatsoever to Mandodari. However, there was a lilt and rhythm to them and Mandodari dully noticed that Vajrajwala's body also swayed to the same rhythm. She was possibly praying, Mandodari thought.

There was something about her posture, her chanting and her rocking that raised Mandodari's concern for Kumbha's widow. She tried several times to move Vajrajwala, to remove the dead man's head from her iron grip and also to get her talking, instead of this baleful chant that she kept up without any break. All to no avail! Vajrajwala did not even accept a sip of water the elder woman offered her.

No, something had changed! Mandodari was unable to identify it initially, but knew that Vajrajwala was undergoing a subtle change. And then it struck her. Vajrajwala had shrunk significantly and even the pool of blood around her had shrunk. Mandodari was dumbstruck with what was taking place in front of her eyes. Vajrajwala's chant was now barely a murmur, even as her rocking continued.

Oh! What would she not give to have her husband's comforting arm around her just then! Mandodari needed emotional and physical support to cope with this unearthly phenomenon unfolding in front of her eyes. But Ravana too was lost in his personal world of grief. He had slipped and fallen in the tussle with Vajrajwala for Kumbha's severed head. He was howling like a child and begging Vajrajwala to let him hold Kumbha. 'I have carried him as a baby...he is my brother...my Kumbha...please...please...'

As he appealed to Vajrajwala, she reached out a hand to him and he held it in both his hands. Tears flowed from their eyes and Vajrajwala, looking into Ravana's eyes as if she found a kindred spirit, began speaking haltingly. 'My husband...your brother...is a great warrior. We both love him deeply... He is a dutiful brother to you and a loving husband to me... He is great...there cannot be another Kumbhakarna in this world... He did not need the help of missiles to kill the enemy. The giant among rakshasas just needed to walk through the battlefield...he crushed scores of vanaras under his foot...he picked up many more with both his hands... and swallowed them. There was not a drop of blood on his body as he wreaked havoc in the enemy camp...but those two brothers and a few very large monkeys...attacked him together...chopped off his arms and then both his legs...made him a helpless being and then...and then...used very sharp arrows...many of them at the same time...to separate his head...' Vajrajwala paused, grief choking her next words. But she had to share her thoughts with Ravana. 'You know...they wanted to take away his head...like a war trophy...I was watching...I could not let them do that...' her eyes welled afresh when Ravana nodded his head in understanding. 'I used my powers...and brought him back... He is mine...mine alone... I take him with me... I go with him...' Her voice had trailed off.

Ravana was once again overcome with grief. He rolled on the floor beseeching Kumbha to come back. 'How can I live without you Kumbha...what an end to your glorious life...I should not have sent you into battle...' he cried and fell unconscious.

Suddenly, Mandodari realized that a fresh day had dawned. The sun was bright and quite high in the sky. It had been a long night—a night of intense grief. Mandodari noticed that Vajrajwala's mumbling chant had ceased. But where was she? The spot where she had spent the night rocking and chanting was empty! There was no trace of her and no trace of Kumbha's head. Even the pool of blood on the carpet had vanished.

Realization dawned. Vajrajwala, a being from Mahar-loka, had used her special and unearthly powers to return to whence she came. Was it possible that, in that galaxy, Vajrajwala would have the power to bring her husband back to life—just as her parents had been brought back after the birth of her twins Kumbha and Nikumbha? With great effort, Mandodari shook herself out of this surreal development to deal with the present.

Mandodari shook her husband vigorously. He must be woken up and informed of this inexplicable development. Moreover, the strategy for the day's war had to be formulated. Ravana had work to do and personal grief must take a back seat. 'Nath...nath, please wake up,' she said, shaking him by the shoulder.

Ravana opened his eyes and Mandodari felt as if there was a different person in front of her. She was so surprised by her husband's calm countenance that she had difficulty remembering what she had intended to say to him. Ravana had no such problem and his voice, when he spoke, was calm.

'I will return Sita to her husband and call off this war.'

Mandodari was not sure that she had heard right. Her disbelief showed in her eyes. 'I know what I am saying, Mandodari. This war is purposeless. I have lost both my brothers—one to the enemy and one to Yama. My mother, grandfather and sister have all gone away. So many soldiers have sacrificed their lives—for what?

'That woman...Sita...she is evil. She has brought great misfortune to Lanka.

'And Kumbha! How right he was in pointing out that a king must weigh his responsibilities before contemplating war with anyone! I will be the king that he wanted me to be!'

The words were music to Mandodari. She rushed forth to hug Ravana and tell him that a good decision, even at this late stage, was worthwhile and in the best interests of Lanka.

'Lanka has been breached...the enemy forces are inside Lanka,' declared a messenger who rushed in without waiting to be announced.

'When? How? Come on, out with all details,' Ravana's each word was like a lash.

'Prabhu, it happened in the early hours of this morning. A large army of monkeys arrived at the gates. Lakshmana, the younger of the two manava brothers, was the leader. They entered from the north gate.'

'North gate? Was Nikumbila temple their target? Where and how is Meghnaad? Had he completed his yagna?' questions rolled off Ravana's tongue as fast as his mind was racing.

'You are right about the target, Prabhu. But there is nothing to worry about! Indrajeet has successfully pushed the enemy back.'

Ravana's chest swelled with pride at the mention of Indrajeet's success and he immediately began thinking about reinforcing his depleted troops. Even so, he needed to be first reassured that the yagna, which provided invincibility to his son, had been completed.

'Tell me about the yagna. I can see the hand of that traitor Vibheeshana in this breach. Only he could have led them to the north gate. And he alone knows about the significance of Indrajeet's yagna. Tell me that my son completed the yagna and secured the celestial chariot and divine missiles,' he demanded, a sense of urgency in his tone. Completion of the yagna was vital to Indrajeet's power. It was this power that enabled him to become invisible and wage war from the skies.

The messenger hung his head low. 'Prabhu, the enemy reached the temple in relative stealth and directed a forceful attack on our defences around the temple. They made inroads through the outer wall of the first security ring. Kumbha and Nikumbha, who guard the innermost ring, put up a spirited fight and even managed to push the enemy back. But outside the gate was waiting an army of hundreds of monkeys. Kumbha and Nikumbha fought valiantly for several hours, but being hugely outnumbered, laid down their lives defending the territorial integrity of Lanka. The enemy breached the gate once again, trampling over the bodies of Kumbha and Nikumbha, and gained entry into the sanctum sanctorum of Nikumbila Maata's mandir. At that point, Indrajeet was just preparing to make his offering to the yagna-purush. Since he was not to touch his weapons till the yagna was concluded, he tried warding off the attackers by throwing things at them. He had to pick up his sword when the monkeys jumped all over the yagnashaala and doused the agni in the havan-kund.

'Indrajeet is a skilled warrior with the added advantage of great agility. He not only repelled the onslaught on the temple, but also pushed the intruders back through the same gate. Right now he is engaging the enemy in a fierce battle and ensuring that its retreat is completed and with heavy casualties.

'Prabhu, I have been told to convey to you that there is a need to augment the forces following Indrajeet and also to review the security arrangements at the four gates,' the messenger said and making a deep bow, retreated.

Ravana strode out without a backward glance, the events of the previous day clearly having been consigned to the pages of memory. His priority right now was to provide adequate cover to his son, who had been deprived of his power of subterfuge and was thus dependent solely on his skills of warfare.

He went round the boundary wall himself, checking that the security apparatus at all the four gates was adequate and functioning at its optimal efficiency. When he noticed a slide in morale among the security guards, he stopped to address them. That done, he organized a battery of messengers to bring him a continuous stream of information from the battlefield.

The news during the first half of the day was encouraging. Ravana gloated when he heard about the heavy death toll in the enemy camp. He was, however, irritated that there should be such high praise of the enemy's battle tactics.

The best moment for him was when he received news that Indrajeet, who was engaged in direct combat with Lakshmana, had felled the manava with the use of the shakti-astra gifted to him by Brahma. The shakti-astra was almost as powerful as the Brahma-astra and it was impossible for anyone to overcome and survive the missile. Ravana was tempted to count the war as won and over. For Lakshmana's death was certain, stricken as he was by Indrajeet's missile. The death of Lakshmana, in effect, meant that the enemy's backbone was broken. Rama would not be able to survive the shock of the loss of his brother and it was quite likely that he would call off his offensive against Lanka.

When he propounded this theory to Mandodari, who had come to the central control room to check on the developments on the battlefield, she was sceptical. 'What are the chances of Lakshmana recovering from the shakti-astra?' she asked, recalling the fact that he had survived the naga-pasha-astra in the past.

'That happened because Garuda was sent by Vishnu to scare off the snakes,' Ravana explained patiently.

'Is there an antidote to the shakti-astra? And if there is, then what are the chances of the enemy procuring it? she asked.

'There is an antidote to the shakti-astra, because there is no astra that cannot be countered. However, the shakti-astra is a very powerful missile that affects the victim deeply, making it almost impossible for him to recover from its effects on his own. The antidote is a herb that grows only on one particular mountain peak in the Himalayas. But this mountain peak is so far away that the life will ebb out of the victim before the herb can be fetched—and that is if anyone in the enemy camp knows about it,' he said reassuringly.

Mandodari wanted to believe her husband, but was unable to shake off a niggling doubt. She remained by her husband's side, watching him strategize, give crisp and clear orders for action that would bring victory at the soonest. She knew Ravana was doing his best, convinced that the enemy had been weakened. It was an eventful day, that stretched longer than expected.

The fighting between the two sides raged till very late that day, neither side backing down even after the sun had set and darkness had descended. Updates from the field became more and more sketchy and confusing. Reports suggesting demoralization in the enemy camp following Lakshmana's collapse gladdened Ravana. But soon enough he began wondering about the absence of reports about his son's heroic advances and victories. He allowed himself to be persuaded to think that field reports had slackened on account of the darkness on the near-moonless night.

However, at the back of his mind, Ravana knew that the war was not progressing in their favour and his worst fears were confirmed well after daybreak the next day. The delay was on account of multiple checks to confirm the news of Indrajeet's death. More time elapsed before the slain prince's body was recovered from the battlefield.

Mandodari broke down and wept bitterly when Indrajeet's lifeless body, with a thousand arrows embedded in it and the head almost severed from the body, was presented before the royal couple. 'My son...how can you die before your parents...you are a brave soldier...you are the only one who could defeat Indra... you are "Indrajeet"...Brahma himself gave you that name...he also gave you many astras and shastras...you are invincible...how could this happen to you...how am I to believe that you met your end at the hands of a mere human...my son...open your eyes and look at me...tell me that I am dreaming...this is not true...' So she wept. She ran her hands over her son's body, trying to remove the arrowheads and trying to stem the flow of blood from numerous wounds.

Ravana stood like a stone statue, his eyes seeing nothing. Then, all of a sudden, he raised his eyes—eyes that showered fire. 'How dare they do this to my son? Those two brothers do not know what they have invited upon themselves... I am alive to finish them off,' he thundered.

He turned around sharply as if he would stride straight onto the battlefield, and in so doing, the edge of his dhoti brushed against his crouching wife's head. This brush brought Mandodari back to the present. She gripped Ravana's ankle with both her hands. 'Please nath...enough is enough...stop this madness of war immediately,' she pleaded.

'No,' Ravana's voice matched the fire in his eyes. 'My son's death in the prime of his youth will not be for nothing. The perpetrators of this cruel act will not escape my wrath. Their dead bodies must be fed to the vultures before the sun sets today.'

'No, pranesha...it is your anger born out of grief that is speaking thus. Understand that we are not dealing with mere humans. They are here for a purpose and they have the support and help of cosmic powers to achieve that purpose. So give up your lust for war...return that manava-kanta to her people...let there be peace in Lanka.'

'I almost forgot about that woman. Sita...she is the root of all this trouble. You need to destroy the root to end the trouble. Yes, that is what I should do...I will kill Sita. I will give them a taste of the grief they have inflicted on me,' so saying, Ravana grabbed a sword and strode away.

Mandodari rose to her feet, depositing her son's head, which she had taken into her lap, on the ground. She ran out into the street to catch up with her husband. By the time she reached Ravana, a curious crowd of bystanders had gathered to watch the rare spectacle of the royal couple arguing on the streets, in full view of the public.

Mandodari set aside her grief in her attempt to return Lanka Naresh Ravana to sanity. It was in a persuasive voice that she appealed to him: 'Nath, you are blessed with the intelligence of a thousand seers and learned men. You are the son of sage Vishravasu Brahma, an epitome of vedic learning. You have mastered the vedas at his feet, practicing brahmacharya. Your thinking and decision-making capabilities are known the world over because you are no ordinary person, but Dashakantha Ravana. Will you stoop to kill a woman?'

Ravana glared at her, trying to shake off her hand that was gripping his wrist. Mandodari continued: 'I understand your anger and anguish. I share them in full measure with you. But direct the anger in the right direction. Shower it on Rama. Kill him, for the murder of your son. We can decide on what to do with Sita after that.'

Ravana nodded. He turned on his heel and announced: 'You are right. I will go onto the battlefield and kill Rama.'

*R*avana looked around, dazed. Why was he not on the battlefield? Why was he here in this small, cramped clearing, where his chariot barely fit? Ravana shook his head vigorously to clear his mind and understand why he was where he was now. He noticed his charioteer tending to the four horses, which were still harnessed to the chariot. Anger, which had been his predominant emotion since he had seen his only son's wounded and dead body, flared once again.

'Mahaparshva!' he roared in anger. 'Why have you driven me off the battlefield? Have you decided that I am incapable of fighting… of facing the enemy squarely and courageously? Do you think I am a coward to run away?' He paused, a sudden thought occuring to him. 'Tell me the truth…have you been bought over? Have you taken a bribe from the enemy to humiliate me?'

The charioteer did not take offence at the accusations thrown in his face. 'No, Prabhu, I am your loyal and devoted servant. I have your best interests at heart. As your charioteer, it is my responsibility to ensure your safety. I noticed that you were fatigued; your concentration was straying; your eyes were unable to focus on your target. The horses were also fatigued and not fit for battle. That is why I steered you from harm's way so that you could recover, strategize and then return to battle. The horses will also have a chance to rest. If you still think my action was unwarranted, I am open to any punishment you choose to give me, Prabhu.'

Ravana acknowledged that Mahaparshva was right. His trusted charioteer, who had been with him in almost all his battles, had done the right thing. Otherwise, he would probably be lying dead on the battlefield. He had neither eaten nor rested properly since this war had begun, and he was disturbed by his encounter with his youngest brother Vibheeshana on the battlefield. The shameless fellow had been raining arrows on him, his own elder brother who had held his finger and taught him to walk!

That Vibhee was standing next to Lakshmana had been his worst shock of the day. How did this manava recover from the lethal effect of the shakti-astra? Was it possible that he had received the juice of the divine sanjivani root? Who could have traversed the Jamboodweepa and returned with the herb in such a short while? Ravana remembered the monkey who had flown across the hundred-yojana ocean and ravaged Lanka. His questions were answered and Ravana tried to focus on repulsing Lakshmana's attack.

Ravana had been quite impressed by the puny manava's prowess with the bow. Lakshmana had shot multiple arrows simultaneously and the arrows had struck their target unfailingly. It was another matter that the arrows were ineffective in piercing Ravana's kavacha, his armour, and that Lakshmana himself was bleeding profusely from the missiles fired at him by Ravana. Vibhee had joined Lakshmana in targeting Ravana. What temerity! Ravana had not been able to stop himself from castigating his younger brother: 'Are you not ashamed of yourself, Vibheeshana? How could you contemplate such treachery against me? You have lost your sense of balance, which is why you have joined forces with my enemy. You chose to ignore the consequence of your actions. They will use you and then kill you. I cannot accept that my own younger brother does this.'

'Do not accuse me of treachery, bhrata. You know me better than that. Though born a rakshasa, I have never supported cruelty. Is that reason enough for throwing out your own younger brother?

You have strayed from dharma. I have been taught to shun people who stray from dharma and commit the cardinal sin of coveting another's wife. You are a great and learned person, born to lead. But all your good qualities have been overshadowed. You also know that you cannot avoid the consequences of your actions. My presence by your side would not have altered this, and I prefer to stand on the right side of dharma,' his younger brother had responded boldly and defiantly.

Vibheeshana's words had touched a raw nerve and Ravana's eyes had clouded with tears. He admired Vibhee who stood by his principles under the most trying situations—unlike himself, who let himself be an easy prey to temptations. Vibhee's words were echoing in his mind when he found himself in this clearing.

Ravana shook his head once again, this time to remove the memory of his interaction with his brother. He needed to focus on the task on hand. He took three deep breaths with his eyes closed and felt immediately energized. He ordered Mahaparshva to go back into battle.

Ravana was clear about his strategy. He would not waste his time killing all and sundry. He would also not attack his younger brother, except to neutralize his missiles, should he try and hurt him. He would go for the two manava brothers. He would first target the younger brother and then deal with Rama.

It was an invigorating exchange of missiles between Ravana and Lakshmana, and Ravana would have enjoyed the sparring, if the outcome were not so vital to his survival. And, he realized that he needed to conserve his energy and the sharpest weapons for the elder brother. So, he used the mahashakti missile, which was a gift from Brahma and was as good as the Brahma-astra. Ravana was surprised to note that his missile was deflected by another just a fraction of a second before it touched home. Thus, mahashakti, which was aimed at the centre of Lakshmana's brow, merely grazed his temple. Even this was sufficient to incapacitate his target. Lakshmana fell to the ground.

'Take me to Rama,' Ravana commanded, his voice upbeat with the success over Lakshmana.

Ravana was prepared for an equally matched fight with this exiled manava king. If anything, Rama's battle skills would be a shade better than those of his younger brother, he surmised as he caught sight of the confident figure of Rama, giving instructions for the safe removal of Lakshmana from the battlefield. Ravana was determined to finish the fight at the earliest, and he felt he held the advantage as he was riding a chariot and had the assistance of the skilled Mahaparshva in manoeuvring the vehicle. Rama, on the other hand, was on foot and thus had limited scope for movement.

However, it soon became clear that Rama was not handicapped by the absence of a vehicle. Ravana watched as all his missiles were effectively neutralized by his opponent. How was he able to counter the attack with such speed, Ravana wondered and felt his eyes play tricks on him. He saw Rama with four arms; what were the weapons he carried in his two extra hands? Why was he imagining a crown on Rama's head? Ravana put down his mighty bow and rubbed his eyes and shook his head vigorously to clear his vision.

It worked for a while and he was able to hit his target. While Rama bled from his various cuts and arrow wounds, he did not appear to feel any pain. And then it happened again—Ravana's mind was back to playing its tricks. Not only did his opponent appear again with four arms and a crown on his head, dressed in the finest of regal clothes, but now he was also mounted on a chariot! And it was no ordinary vehicle. It was obviously very powerful with several features of advantage built into it. How had Rama acquired this vehicle? And how had he, Ravana, missed noticing when and how it had appeared? He had not even noticed Rama getting into it. And most important and irritating was the absence of the feeling of animosity towards his enemy. How could he deliver fatal blows if he did not have an angry and hateful fire burning bright in his bosom?

Ravana told himself that there was nothing to worry about if his opponent too was mounted on a chariot. 'I just have to deal with this situation,' he thought to himself and concentrated on disabling Rama's charioteer. 'And I have to remember that I hate this fellow...I hate this fellow...I hate him and consider him to be my worst enemy. He has wiped out all my beloved family members,' he repeated to himself several times, hoping that this would improve his concentration.

Ravana laughed to himself when Rama's arrows struck home unfailingly and managed to chop of his head. 'He can go on doing this till his arms drop from fatigue. He does not know that I cannot be beheaded. A new head will appear every time my head is separated from my body. That is one of the boons I acquired after intense tapasya for long years,' he thought. At the same time, he was not so sanguine about the tricky vision he seemed to have developed. This was the first time he had come face to face with this enemy. But he seemed strangely familiar; it was as though he was a long-lost friend.

Then he saw it coming—a strange and immensely powerful missile that Rama released from his bow. Its head seemed as if it was the sun itself rushing at him. Its tail too was different from that of any arrow he had ever seen. Was it the wind propelling the sun, or was it a snake pushing the sun? Whatever it was, Ravana instinctively knew that this missile would take the life out of him.

Ravana's lips parted in a demonic grin as he suddenly recognized the missile. It was the Brahma-astra, Brahma's most potent weapon that knows no failure. The missile follows its intended target endlessly till it hits and kills. He debated with himself—should he try and duck it or face it squarely and die as a brave soldier? 'Why should I even attempt avoiding it, when I know its character,' he asked himself. In fact, being hit by this missile was his victory. It showed his opponent's admission that there was no other way of getting the better of him. And, he would go down in history as the only being on whom this magical astra had been used. The decision was made—Ravana took the full impact of the missile on his chest. The earth shook and the ocean rose as Ravana collapsed.

Ravana felt himself slipping from his seat onto the floor of his chariot, but he was unable to do anything about it. Then there was someone lifting him out of his chariot and laying him flat on a soft bed of grass, right in the middle of the battlefield. Ravana wondered who it was; it could not be Mahaparshva, as he had been burnt to death by the heat of the missile that had struck Ravana. Then he heard words and voices. They were all crying—crying that he lay there dying. He recognized the voice of Mandodari, his dear and beloved wife. He was sorry that he would be leaving her alone in this world and wanted to tell her so. But he could not utter any words. In fact, it took all his energy just to open his eyes.

Mandodari was weeping inconsolably, her words coming in a torrent on occasion and halting and mumbled at other times. 'Praneshwara, who would have imagined that you, the mighty Dashakantha Ravana, would fall to a manava! It has to be a game of death itself that played out and placed you in this situation. Death has visited you in the guise of Rama. How else can you explain how a single human being killed thousands of rakshasa veeras in one go? Did I not warn you that this was no mere human? When that monkey came and played havoc in Lanka, did we not know that there was a cosmic conspiracy to wipe you out? Would the curses of all the rishis and Brahmins who suffered at your hands be in vain? Oh nath! I was so proud—proud to be daughter to a danava king; proud to be wife to a rakshasa emperor and proud to be mother to a son who defeated the king of devas! But what is left for me now? What have I to live for? You are the strongest and bravest in the entire universe! What quirk of fate then, made you steal a woman?'

The outpouring of anguish hurt him. Hurt because he had no answer to give her. Then he heard Vibhee...his dear younger brother. It soothed his heart to hear tears in his voice. 'See, he loves me,' Ravana thought to himself with happiness. Vibhee led Mandodari away. He could hear the wailing sounds of many others—women from his harem, many of whom loved him dearly, and citizens of Lanka—'Or those that have survived this war,' Ravana thought wryly.

Then he heard an unfamiliar voice. Ravana laboured to open his eyes and identify the source of this soothing voice. It was Rama, standing near his feet. Ravana shut his eyes; he did not want to see his killer.

'Oh, noble king of rakshasas! Please do not turn away from me. Death is the end of everything, all your bonds on earth, including bonds of enmity and hatred.' Rama paused and Ravana forced his eyes open again. Rama continued: 'Ravana, you have been punished for the crimes you committed. I hold no feelings of ill will towards you now.'

Ravana smiled through half-closed eyes, the curl of his lips indicating the pain he was in. 'Such pious words come easy to the winner,' he thought to himself, and waited for Rama to continue— for, he knew that Rama was seeking something from him.

'Noble king! I have great regard for you. Your wisdom is unparalleled! I request you to share that knowledge with me now,' Rama said, his arms crossed on his chest and head slightly bent in a mark of respect and attention.

Ravana smiled. It hurt to make the effort of talking. But he would not disappoint Rama. 'Rama, you are a worthy opponent, and a noble being. I admire your ability to detach yourself from your emotions. That, believe me, is the secret to a happy life.

'I have very little time left before life leaves this body permanently. I will tell you the most important lesson I have learnt in life. Ignorance is one's worst enemy. It is the ignorant mind that is drawn towards things that cause harm. It is the ignorant mind that again makes one avoid things that are good. It is what we shy away from, what we push away, that can actually help us evolve,' Ravana signalled that he had finished speaking, and was about to close his eyes once again when Rama's voice penetrated his consciousness.

'Do you regret anything, Dashagreeva?'

'I have prided myself as being the greatest devotee of Shiva. I even managed to secure his atmalinga for myself, remember? My only regret is that I have been unable to internalize even a fraction of his detachment. I am very attached to all things worldly.

'It is the same trait I admire in you Rama—your detachment. Your self-control is exemplary. You spent the best years of your life in the forest. The forest is where no rules apply, no laws exist. But you did not allow that lawlessness to affect you in any manner. You remained disciplined. I admire that in you.

'I have lived in Lanka, where there is rule of law. I was the one who was responsible for putting most of those laws in place. Yet I never shied away from a chance to bend the rules if they came in the way of what I wanted, what I desired. I could not accept a situation wherein I could not achieve my purpose.' Ravana's voice was becoming feebler with every word he uttered.

His eyes too were drooping shut, when suddenly his body went into a convulsion. His hands and legs started twitching and his voice was barely audible when he whispered the words: 'Who are you Rama…who are you truly…' His eyes closed and he heard a voice answer his question. Ravana knew the voice was not coming from the person standing by him, yet it was definitely his voice. 'I am -ence... I am eternal... I am endless... Come to me, Jaya... Come to me... Vijaya has already returned...' Ravana's face relaxed. He had found his answer and was at peace with himself.